# The Secret Self
*A Practical Guide to Spiritual Awakening and Inner Freedom*

## Christopher J. Smith

**The Secret Self**

Christopher J. Smith

Paperback Edition First Published in Great Britain in 2016
by aSys Publishing

eBook Edition First Published in Great Britain in 2016
by aSys Publishing

Copyright © Christopher J. Smith 2016

Christopher J. Smith has asserted his rights under 'the Copyright Designs and Patents Act 1988' to be identified as the author of this work.

**All rights reserved.**
No part of this document may be reproduced or transmitted in any form or by any means, electronic, mechanical, photocopying, recording, or otherwise, without prior written permission of the Author.

Edited by John Hamer
(Author of The Falsification of History and Behind the Curtain)

ISBN: 978-1-910757-53-6
aSys Publishing 2016

# Acknowledgements and Dedication

My sincere thanks go to my friend John Hamer for his patience and efforts in the editing of this book, a topic which can be tricky to put into words, but which John has been able to do to great effect through our joint co-operation and dedication.

Thanks also to my family and friends who have supported the creation of this book through their encouragement and patience. Those friends and family members who have supported the coming-to-fruition of this book, know who they are, and I am forever grateful. If it were not for the help of these people then this book may very well have never happened, and so my love and gratitude goes out to you all. Here are a few names I should single-out for special mention...

My mother and father, my sister and family, uncle Ray, my friends, Luke Brailsford, Kelvin Rush, Nico Moscoso, Kelvin Rush, Paul Watkinson and my beautiful daughter Anyssa Coral.

Thank you for all your patience and support during both the easy and more importantly, challenging times.

This book is dedicated to all the people of the world. We all share so many more similarities than differences.

...and to those who wish to seek Inspiration, Joy and the discovery of their True Infinite Nature, the Power which comes from within...

May the whole of humanity awaken.

# Table of Contents

Acknowledgements and Dedication ................................................. iii

**Introduction**
    An Awakening ........................................................................ 1
    The Invitation ........................................................................ 5
    What You can Gain from this Book ...................................... 6
    Why Write Such a Book? ........................................................ 7

**Chapter 1: What is Inner Awakening?** ..................................... 9
    The Yearning .......................................................................... 9
    Why Seek Inner Awakening? ............................................... 10
    The End of Suffering and Ignorance ................................... 11
    Your Ultimate Reality ........................................................... 11
    The Evolutionary Shift ........................................................ 12
    What is Inner Awakening? ................................................... 14
    What is a Spiritual Path? ..................................................... 16
    Who Walks the Spiritual Path? ........................................... 18
    The Journey of the Soul ...................................................... 21
    Karma, Free Will and Predestination ................................. 24
    Use this Life Well ................................................................. 26
    The Dream of Misidentification .......................................... 26
    Ego Identity .......................................................................... 27
    You are not the Body ........................................................... 29
    You are not the Brain ........................................................... 31
    Are you the Mind? ............................................................... 32
    Ego and the False 'Self' Persona .......................................... 34
    Conditioning of the Mind ................................................... 35
    Who is behind the Mask? .................................................... 37

### Chapter 2: How to Awaken .................................................................. 39
- To Never Begin and Never End ..................................................39
- Ignorance of truth ..........................................................................40
- Stuck between Heaven and Hell .................................................40
- Going all the Way ..........................................................................41
- Commitment to the Path .............................................................41
- Power of the Earnest Prayer ........................................................42
- Three main Aspects of Inner Awakening...................................43
- Belief vs. Knowing..........................................................................47
- Observation of the Ego ................................................................49
- Traits of the Ego ............................................................................50
- Intelligence and knowledge..........................................................51
- Money and Achievements............................................................51
- Race and Religion..........................................................................53
- Complaining ..................................................................................55
- Addicted to Drama........................................................................56
- Prejudice and Judgment...............................................................57
- Personal Judgements ....................................................................58
- Television and Ego-Conditioning ..............................................60
- TV and Meditation .......................................................................63
- The Art of No Reaction................................................................64
- The Unconsciousness of the Ego ................................................65
- Conclusion .....................................................................................66
- Who are you? .................................................................................66
- Mindfulness Practice.....................................................................70
- Attention and Awareness .............................................................70
- The Body ........................................................................................71
- The Breath .....................................................................................72
- Emotions.........................................................................................76
- Thinking .........................................................................................79
- Codes of Thought and Stories ....................................................81
- Meditation Practice ......................................................................85

Just Awareness ................................................. 86
The Power of Silence ........................................... 87

**Chapter 3: Awakening to the Moment .................... 91**
No Time Other than the Present ............................ 91
Mental Time Creation ......................................... 93
Your Current Experience in the Moment ................. 94
Time, Karma and the Mind ................................... 97
Fresh Moment .................................................... 98
One with the Moment .......................................... 99
Practicing being Aware of the Moment .................... 99
The Body—a Rock in 'the Now' ........................... 101
Noticing the Now .............................................. 102
Your Royal 'Here-ness' ....................................... 102
Notice Objects in the Now .................................. 103
Stillness ........................................................... 104
Moment to Moment Noticing ............................... 106
Pay Attention ................................................... 106

**Chapter 4: Have no Fear ..................................... 108**
Fear and the Ego ............................................... 108
The Fear of Death ............................................. 111
The Fear of Other's Opinions ............................... 117
Phobic Fears .................................................... 121
Practicing 'No Fear' ........................................... 123
The Art of Dying .............................................. 124
Dying Consciously ............................................ 124
Meditation #1—Life's Passing Nature .................... 126
Meditation #2—The Death of Your Body ............... 127

## Chapter 5: Letting go of Guilt ........................................................... 130
Guilt ................................................................................................131
A Zen Story .....................................................................................133
Addictions .......................................................................................133
Why Addictions Occur ...................................................................134
Beyond Feeling Good or Bad .........................................................135
The Agitated Mind .........................................................................136
The Guilt of Addiction ...................................................................137
Self-Forgiveness ..............................................................................138

## Chapter 6: Ending Shame ................................................................. 142
Shame Creation ..............................................................................143
Worthiness ......................................................................................145

## Chapter 7: Understanding Grief and Trauma ............................... 147
Prolonged Grief and Trauma ..........................................................147
Initial Grief and Trauma ................................................................151
Relationships ..................................................................................154
Conditional Love vs. Unconditional Love ....................................157
Hate .................................................................................................161
The Power of Forgiveness ..............................................................164
Compassion ....................................................................................169

## Chapter 8: Genuine Self-Expression ............................................... 174
The Inner Conversation .................................................................176
Depression ......................................................................................177
Self-Expression through Creativity ...............................................179
Martial Arts for Self-Expression ....................................................179
Conscious Communication ...........................................................180
Conscious Listening .......................................................................181
Conscious Speech ...........................................................................183
The Unseen Power of Words .........................................................186

    The Power of Sound and Intention on Water ............................... 187
    Just be yourself in each Moment .................................................... 191
    Remain Unblemished ..................................................................... 191

**Chapter 9: From Illusion to Truth** ................................................... **194**
    We Suffer our Misperceptions ......................................................... 194
    The True Essential Reality .............................................................. 198
    Partial Truth and Total Truth .......................................................... 200
    The Truth is Now and Enlightenment ............................................ 202
    Non-judgement and Discrimination ............................................... 204
    The Habit of Thinking ................................................................... 208
    The Peaceful, Tranquil Mind .......................................................... 208
    How to practice Natural Noticing Meditation ................................ 212

**Chapter 10: Dropping all Attachments** ............................................ **216**
    The Nature of Attachment ............................................................. 216
    Happiness and Attachment ............................................................. 218
    Happiness ....................................................................................... 219
    Causeless Joy .................................................................................. 222
    Love and Attachment ..................................................................... 225
    Detachment .................................................................................... 227
    Practicing Detachment ................................................................... 228
    Intensity ......................................................................................... 231
    How Awareness Flows .................................................................... 232

**Chapter 11: The Three Guidance Systems** ...................................... **234**
    Feeling Lost and Confused ............................................................. 235
    Instinctual Guidance ...................................................................... 235
    Intellectual Guidance ..................................................................... 237
    Intuitive Guidance ......................................................................... 238
    Ego vs. Intuition ............................................................................. 240
    How to Make a Decision ................................................................ 241

Three Ways to Approach Life Situations ............................................. 243
Do not Compare Paths ........................................................................ 244
Trusting Intuition ................................................................................ 245
The Real Secret .................................................................................... 247
Relax the Need to Know ..................................................................... 249

## Chapter 12: Self Investigation and Transcending Limiting Beliefs 251

Why Self-Investigation? ...................................................................... 251
What is Self-Investigation? ................................................................. 253
The Importance of Honesty ............................................................... 253
Self-Investigation
  (from Transient Nature to the Constant Self) ............................ 254
How to 'Self-Investigate' .................................................................... 256
Preparation Meditation ....................................................................... 257
'Who am I?' (Finding the Constant Self) .......................................... 258
Am I the Body? .................................................................................... 259
Am I the Mind? ................................................................................... 262
Who is Aware of the Mind? ............................................................... 263
Where am I? ......................................................................................... 264
When am I? .......................................................................................... 265
Transcending Limiting Beliefs ........................................................... 266
Identify the Thought or Belief ........................................................... 267
Conclusion ........................................................................................... 287
The Birth of Wisdom .......................................................................... 289

## Chapter 13: Practices and Teachings for Deeper Awakening ......... 291

The Art of Letting Go ........................................................................ 293
How to 'Let Go' ................................................................................... 294
Notice the 'no–Space' ......................................................................... 296
Non-Identification .............................................................................. 296
Sensing 'I AM' Presence ..................................................................... 298
To whom is the Voice Talking? ......................................................... 298

Do not Mind..................................................................299
No Watcher, only Watching.........................................301
Drop All Future Ideas..................................................301
Foundational Meditation #3—'Pure Meditation'.......304
Meditate whilst Travelling...........................................306
Shavasana Surrender ...................................................306
Drop Your Personal Self..............................................308
It Takes Nothing to be Yourself..................................309
The Secret Self.............................................................310

## Chapter 14: Enlightenment and Liberation ............... 312

Enlightenment.............................................................312
Freedom and Liberation of the Mind........................316
The Taste and Aroma of Liberation ..........................317
Trusting Life................................................................320
The Energy of Thankfulness.......................................323
The End of the Spiritual Search.................................324
End of the Story .........................................................325
Non-dual Consciousness and Boundlessness............325
Loneliness or Aloneness?............................................326
No-one there to Attain Enlightenment ....................327
No-one there to Suffer................................................328
Surrender.....................................................................329
Total Surrender...........................................................330

## Chapter 15: Awakened Purpose ................................... 332

Who Asks the Question of Purpose?.........................332
The Philosophical Frog and the Centipede ..............333
The Primary Purpose..................................................335
To be Here, Now.........................................................336
To be the Natural Self.................................................338

| | |
|---|---|
| The Gift | 338 |
| The Secondary Purpose | 340 |
| Serving Others | 340 |
| Provide Value | 341 |
| Responsibility | 343 |
| Be an Example | 344 |
| Live this Life Joyfully | 345 |
| Sharing | 345 |
| Passion | 347 |
| Passion to Serve | 347 |
| Passion for Work | 349 |
| Passion for Life | 349 |
| Reaching our Potential | 350 |
| Help Evolve Life | 352 |
| The New Era of Humanity | 353 |
| Rebellion against the Norm | 354 |
| The Journey of the One is the Journey of the All | 356 |
| Love is the Key | 357 |
| Community Spirit | 358 |
| The Purpose of Gathering | 359 |
| Physically Together | 360 |
| Mental Gathering | 361 |
| Spiritual Gathering | 361 |
| Awakening of the Heart | 361 |
| Divine Will | 363 |
| Intention and Allowance | 364 |
| Our Job is Simple | 365 |

# Introduction
## An Awakening

A number of years ago at the age of 21, after a whole range of internal and external challenges, I fell ill with salmonella, which is an extreme and potentially life-threatening form of food poisoning. This food poisoning was enough to bring me to my knees and leave me in hospital for several weeks and months of recovery. Whilst ill, I was unable to eat or drink, I became dehydrated and lost over sixty pounds in weight. I felt as though my entire life force had been sucked from me, and because I prided myself at the time on my physique and masculinity, it humbled me greatly. As time went on, I was unable to drink and eat normally, my only sustenance was via the drip-feed attached to my arm and I felt as though I was becoming weaker and that I would not recover. Each day I would feel more tired and my body would ache more intensely. My body seemed to be incapable of taking nourishment as I immediately 'passed' anything I ate or drank. It was as though my whole body was going through some extreme detoxification, both physically and energetically. The doctors were not aware at this time that it was salmonella poisoning, and so they were confused as to why I was not recovering. One night, I remember just lying there in bed, it was extremely quiet and dark, and it felt such a cold and lonely place.

> *As I lay there I began to contemplate the possibility of not recovering. What if I never got any better but continued to deteriorate, what if I was to die right here in the hospital? Many thoughts ran through my mind, thoughts of the past. But what did it all mean, what had I been doing in my life up to this point? Did it mean anything at all? What about my family and friends, what if I was to leave them behind, how would it feel, how would they feel? I felt as though I had so much that I had not achieved or seen, and so as I lay there contemplating all the things that I may lose, I began to surrender to the inevitable. But as I*

*gave up the struggle, I began to relax deeply, so deeply that a beautiful sense of peace enveloped me. I felt in that moment that whatever happened would be fine and that I could let go of my life if I had to. I felt so much peace, so much space—and so much freedom.*

*At the time I had not realised what had taken place, I knew that some subtle shift had happened within me, but I had no reference point, nothing to compare it with, and so it was only later that I discovered more of what had tantalisingly revealed a small part of itself to me.*

*Shortly after my recovery, I felt somehow drawn to the practice of meditation, primarily silent meditation, and so I began to investigate its mysteries further. I felt a strong pull towards particular books and practices, and to study the teachings, quotes and texts of ancient and more modern 'mystics,' finding myself compelled to use these quotes as 'mini-meditations' or contemplations, as I noticed they were having a profound effect on changing my perception of the world and 'self' in some inexplicable way.*

One bright, still day, I was sat on a bench in a churchyard in a quiet area next to a beautiful dam near my home, in deep introspection whilst reading to myself a powerful quote I had discovered.

The quote was...

*'As you look at a tree, see the tree and not the thoughts about the tree. When you look at it observe the shape, colour and presence of it without thinking about the shape, colour and presence of it. Just look quietly and then you will see the reality of this thing called the tree, as you will see the reality of any object'*

As I deeply contemplated this profound insight, something equally profound happened to me. I suddenly and unexpectedly experienced a shift in my perception whereby I actually 'saw' this thing which we call a 'tree' for the first time. I saw the presence of it as opposed to my thoughts and own personal interpretation of it, almost like seeing beyond an obscuring layer or veil that was preventing me from seeing the truth. The experience was incredible, almost psychedelic in nature and my consciousness somehow became more expansive for a moment, more clear and lucid. I formed a deep impression that this object named 'tree' was somehow connected with me, almost as though there was no distance between us. Was I the tree, was the tree, me? That was the impression I had, it all seemed so obvious to me in that moment.

As I slowly looked around in amazement I experienced an intense feeling of swimming in an ocean, but I also realised that the ocean was life itself, the tree, grass, the bench and the very 'empty' space that seemed to separate us all. It felt just as though there was no space or distance between anything and that I was absolutely in the centre of everything, surrounded in an extremely pleasant way. Then from nowhere, I received the affirmation in my mind . . . *'I AM connected to everything.'*

> *As this realisation grew, I began to relax and accept it more and more. It was so absolutely, incredibly beautiful, beyond description by mere words and only the actual experience could ever 'do it justice.' These poor words on this page cannot even come close to conveying my experience and perception at that moment.*
>
> *I just sat there mesmerised, in the midst of all this, feeling completely connected and boundless. I watched-on transfixed as thoughts drifted-by and somehow, some way, I could 'see' these thoughts clearer than I ever had before. It soon became apparent to me, that these thoughts were now within my range of vision and so were literally before me, which begs the question that if my thoughts really are in front of me, then where am 'I?'*

As I turned my attention towards discovering where 'I' was, I saw that I was 'behind' the thoughts, 'behind' the mind and suddenly with this realisation, I was hit with a wave of blissfulness that was so intense, so vivid, that it was overwhelming all my senses.

Then there was an intense sound of silence; I could hear all of the sounds around me so clearly, the birds tweeting, the wind blowing, even the sound of my own breathing and heartbeat. As I slowly looked around I noticed the colours of the grass and trees began to stand out in a rich and vivid way, I'd never seen trees and grass so green before.

My sense of smell became extremely heightened; I could very distinctly smell the aroma of a meal being cooked in a house nearby and my mouth began to salivate, which brought me a complete awareness of every taste and texture within my mouth. For the first time, I felt my entire body as one pleasurable sensation, leaving me completely grounded and immovable.

My range of vision shifted to an almost panoramic view of everything around me, no longer in a tunnel-vision-like state. In some strange way it seemed that I had moved 'back' as if I was standing further back from an object to see more of the view around it, while actually not moving my body at all. The only way I can describe it is that everything seemed to appear in a kind of 'three dimensional state,' whereby objects seemed entirely distinct from their background.

…Then the laughter came, joyful belly laughter so loud and intense, I was behaving like a man 'possessed,' a man possessed by himself. This laughter just continued and continued, where was it all coming from? Then it dawned upon me and all felt so obvious and familiar, 'I' was found!

> *I closed my eyes and became aware of myself in the pitch-blackness of my mind, completely fixated on my consciousness. With my eyes still closed and completely relaxed, I could feel every cell, every fibre of my being pulsating with pleasure. Suddenly 'I' was hurled back within myself, it seemed to be one hundred times the strength of the stomach 'butterflies' experienced on a theme park rollercoaster.*
>
> *What was this bliss, love and connection I was feeling so intensely, this massive injection of 'alive-ness' coursing through my whole body?*
>
> *Then almost as abruptly as it had begun, eventually the feeling subsided and I was just left with a complete sense of peacefulness, totally undisturbed by anything inside or outside of me, if there was indeed such a distinction between 'inside' and 'outside' anymore.*
>
> *Very slowly, I began to contemplate what had just taken place. What exactly had happened to me?*

As I mulled-over the myriad of thoughts drifting through my mind, two words sprung forth as they crossed the path of my awareness like a conveyer belt of thoughts passing through my mind. In trying to soundlessly describe the nature of what was being experienced at the very core of me, the words *'Silent Truth'* came to mind. What could it mean?

I realised that the place 'within,' which lies beyond all our thoughts contains an intense silence. It is a quiet, tranquil place, deafening in its noiselessness and from this still, quiet place, self-truths may become evident which provide answers to everything without actually answering anything at all.

And so while limited words cannot truly explain the deeper nature of all that is and is within, *'Silent Truth'* seems a good place to begin.

Humanity for so long has somehow been blocked from its true nature, to access our immense power and potential within, I feel this ancient story describes our plight well . . .

> *There was a lion in search of its prey. This mighty, powerful beast came upon a flock of sheep and to his amazement he found another lion amongst this flock of sheep. It was a lion who had been brought up by the sheep ever since he was a cub. It was bleating like a sheep and running around like a sheep.*
>
> *The lion went straight for him. The poor sheep-lion stood in front of the powerful lion. He trembled in every limb. The lion roared at him, "What are you doing among the sheep?" The sheep-lion bleated, "Oh, oh I'm sorry, I am a sheep." The lion said, "Oh no you're not. You're coming with me." So he took the sheep-lion to a pool of water and said, "Look!" When the sheep-lion looked at his reflection, he couldn't believe it; he looked back at the mighty lion, then back at his reflection and let out an almighty roar. And in that moment he was transformed and was never the same again."*

Much like the 'sheep-lion,' once I had experienced my 'inner-self,' I too was transformed.

## The Invitation

The invitation of this book is to you, the reader, an invitation to discover your ultimate true nature and the power within.

This book and its practices will remove all the barriers to inner awakening if you allow it to do so. This book is not a philosophy, it is about you and discovering the **Secret Self** that resides within you, yet remains hidden to most people on the planet. This book is here to remind you and summon-up the power of who you really are.

Christopher J. Smith

It has been carefully written in the correct order for spiritual awakening, and will provide all of the tools and understanding necessary for your own self-realisation ... if that is what you truly want?

## What You can Gain from this Book

The role of this book is to spark your spiritual awakening, not by actually giving you anything tangible in the areas of information or knowledge, but by removing all the obstacles which obscure what is already there, inherent within you, that is your true awakened nature. The best way to work with this book is to allow it to peel away the layers of misperception and obscurity so that your pure self shines through.

I may speak affirmatively and repeat certain statements many times, but please know that this is for the purpose of allowing what is being said in the book to be absorbed at the deepest level, by repetition. The book is structured in a format that will provide you with the maximum possible opportunity of spiritual awakening and enlightenment. If you wish to benefit from this book then you will need to commit to work with the practices and allow the book to do its work. All that is needed from you is your contemplation, introspection, practice, patience and persistence. You may find that you return to this book many times, and as your consciousness becomes more expansive and awakened, may also find that it all makes gradually more sense than previous readings. Our consciousness is such that we can only perceive the level of consciousness at which we are currently, so as your consciousness grows your understanding will grow also. The practices, meditations and methods are laid-out in this book in an order that will assist you in the absorption of its contents and will help you work with each practice step-by-step until it becomes a natural part of you. Whilst this book will inform you of the practicalities of awakening, please understand that through the book there are many opportunities to instantly realise your true nature, so please remain open-minded and ready to accept whatever realisations may be initiated within you.

Whether we call this a spiritual path or not, does not really matter. Simply understand that the spiritual path is nothing more than your essential reality, and you are not being asked to believe or accept anything. Indeed, this book is not about belief but is about the experiential knowing that comes through one's own direct experience of the truth, a truth that is accessible to us all. And if you contemplate what is within these pages and let it bypass the mind and trickle-down into the heart, then you will understand that the contents of this book are what you already know to be true within the core of your nature. This book is just a simple invitation and reminder of the truths that you already *know* in the depths of your inner being.

## Why Write Such a Book?

When you discover something so truly powerful and beautiful, how could I not wish to share it? It is our nature to share, and so I would point you towards your own paradise within . . . the heaven that is your own true nature.

Sometimes life is bursting at the seams so much that it cannot be contained and must be shared, and the contents of this book are being shared from the deepest sources of existence through a vessel known as your humble author. In truth the book seemed to almost write itself and was seeking to find and connect with those whose energy and consciousness was ready to receive, and could resonate with what is being spelled-out within its pages. As you are reading this book then it is highly likely that you are one of those who is ready to be 'reminded' of what you already know, by its contents.

The book is intended as an internal guide towards inner truth and a way of bringing some value to whoever is willing and able to accept it. Words cannot describe how our inner reality can shift so profoundly and dramatically into a new perception, or way of being, experiencing and living in the world. But the words of this book are there merely as pointers towards all those possibilities and that potential. It is with the deepest respect and gratitude that this book is presented for the enjoyment of all who gravitate towards it.

Only with your curiosity, commitment and persistence will your awakening unfold and blossom like a beautiful flower.

Please consider the words upon these pages with an open heart and an investigative mind, in order to examine and look deeply into their meaning, and engage in the meditations, contemplations and practices with your full attention and commitment.

It requires no belief on your part, as what we are ultimately speaking of is beyond belief, but requires instead, only the willingness to experience what is offered.

The pages you are about to read contain spaces to allow for your reflection on the questions, exercises and information being conveyed.

You will read many different words when referring to our true natures. No words can ultimately describe what we are, but they can act as pointers to the truth. Here are some of the words of which will become aware throughout the book, all pointing towards the same inner truth.

Awareness, pure consciousness, observer, secret self, silent truth, watcher, witness, looker, perceiver, seer, nothingness, ultimate nature, pure nature, pure self, emptiness, awakened one, nobody, true self, natural self, true nature and being-ness are the terms used in this book all corresponding to the same Self.

In summary, this book is a profoundly simple, yet powerful guidance tool which will eventually lead you, the reader, in the direction of your own true nature and destiny. Its purpose is to allow you to discover your own 'Secret Self' beyond the limitations of the body and mind, and explore the 'Silent Truth' at the core of your own being whilst also enabling you to seek-out your true purpose in this world.

This book can be carried with you wherever you go, whether in meditation, at work or travelling. Continue to read this book repeatedly as and when you feel it necessary in order to extract every drop of wisdom and insight possible, to use every pointer and practice for the crystallisation of your consciousness. You may find yourself returning to the book as certain situations and experiences arise, so do this as often it feels necessary. Just simply to hold the book without reading it, may bring you great peace, as you may feel it's 'aliveness' in the palm of your hand.

This book can be your own spiritual life-guide, a reminder of who you are, wherever your travels may take you. YOUR own journey of self-discovery begins here . . .

Enjoy the exploration and enjoy the ride.

*With my deep gratitude and joy*
*Christopher J. Smith, February 2016*

# Chapter 1
## What is Inner Awakening?

*"Whom have I in heaven but you? And besides you, I desire nothing on Earth." Psalms 73:25*

## The Yearning

If you are reading this book, it is likely you are here because you consciously have a deep yearning for the truth. We all have a deep yearning for something more, it is just that most people are unsure and confused about what exactly it is they are yearning for. It is often that we just cannot quite put our finger on what it is, but nevertheless we do strive for it. Sometimes we may forget it whilst lost in all of our other activities, but when we are alone and the dust has settled, the restless yearning often lingers.

This is why so many things have been created externally in the world, because we wish for more, and we think this 'more' will come when everything externally has been explored and created. Yet what if the yearning and pull we feel to become more, is actually the yearning to become more of ourselves.

What if our belief that the answer to becoming more of ourselves is actually in doing, creating and exploring more externally, when in actual fact, the very thing we are looking for is the one who is looking?

What if the journey to become more of ourselves resides not in outer exploration... but in inner exploration?

All of us in life eventually ask certain questions such as, *'who am I?'* and *'what am I doing here?'* and *'what is my purpose?'* and when the desire for these questions to be answered becomes a strong force within us, we are then ready for our journey towards our realisation and fulfilment.

Christopher J. Smith

# Why Seek Inner Awakening?

*"Seek ye the kingdom of heaven and all will be added unto you" Jesus*

**Treasure story**

There was once a beggar who lived under a huge banyan tree.

> *Yes, the tree was his home and begging was his means of making a living. For over 40 years he changed neither. He would go from one village to another every day and beg for alms. Whatever he got which were mostly leftovers and crumbs, he would consume by splitting it as 3 meals a day. As the days and years passed by, the man got weaker and weaker. His frugal meals couldn't sustain him any longer and one day he succumbed to hunger.*
>
> *The villagers found his body and decided to bury him right under the tree where he had lived all his life. So the men began to dig. They had barely dug 6 inches deep when their spade hit on a metal box...*
>
> *They carefully lifted the box and opened it only to find gold, diamonds and precious stones; it was a treasure chest! The beggar was sitting on a treasure chest merely 6 inches deep which could have rendered him rich had he made the effort to explore his own living space...*

This story is a metaphor of what resides within us but goes unexplored for the majority of humanity. Within are all the treasures and beauty we could ever want, yet no attention is paid to it. We have been taught to look outside ourselves for the treasure and answers, when all along the bounty and true knowledge to all the important questions are located within us. Inner awakening is a movement to discover the richness of our own true nature and to explore and answer all of the most burning questions of life.

The power and usefulness of inner awakening is for these main reasons:

- To end Suffering
- To discover Inner Truth & your Ultimate Reality
- The Evolution of Consciousness & Humanity

## The End of Suffering and Ignorance

There is and has been so much suffering in the world and this suffering that we see in the world first began as suffering and ignorance within humanity's individual and collective consciousness. All of the mayhem, mischief, conflict and suffering are a direct result of the ignorance of our true nature and our own inner suffering projected out onto the world.

When we do not know the true nature of ourselves and others, this can result in our doing horrendous things to each other and ourselves through this ignorance. We only have to look at history to see this. This unawareness of our real self also limits and binds us to certain ways of perceiving and experiencing. It is the discovery of our ultimate nature that holds the key to ending this suffering and limitation and the suffering will end only when ignorance of who we are ends.

Inner awakening is the beginning of inner truth and freedom and therefore the end of suffering and ignorance. The light that is revealed through inner awakening will chase away the darkness of ignorance and put an end to any inner turmoil we may have. As we awaken to more levels of inner truth, joy and true lasting happiness begins to flower within our hearts and radiates outwards to those around us.

Through the realisation of our Ultimate Reality, our whole experience of life becomes enhanced, and a whole new world emerges for us.

## Your Ultimate Reality

If you look closely you will see that your whole life experience is occurring within you... within your consciousness. Everything you see, hear, smell, taste and touch is experienced within you and so if you awaken to the part of yourself within which, everything in your world is experienced, then the richness and experience of your life will be magnified and enhanced greatly, because without the fullness of 'you' there can be no true and real experience of the world. As your consciousness expands, your experience of life expands also.

This inner shift is the last frontier in humanity's exploration of the world. We have seen and experienced countless things in the external world, many natural and scientific discoveries have been made, but humanity as a whole is yet to explore the most mysterious discovery of all . . . the inner world of pure consciousness. It is the inner reality from which everything in creation sprang forth and is experienced in, and it is within, you and every one of us. It is the findings of this Ultimate Reality that will help to move humanity to a level of intelligence where all of the world issues can be solved. To be able to explore within, we must be like an inner scientist, we have sciences with which to explore the outer world, and now we have the subtle scientific tools of inner awakening to look within.

Through the discovery of the 'secret self,' our Ultimate Reality, an evolutionary shift will take place.

## The Evolutionary Shift

*"At this time humanity is evolving to a higher level of intelligence, this intelligence is pure awakened consciousness"*

To understand what inner awakening really is, it is extremely helpful to see humanity's evolutionary context and journey, up to this point in time.

There was a time thousands of years ago, spoken about in ancient cultures and religions that has mostly been regarded as myth by traditional society, and that is a time that was often referred to as the 'Golden Age,' a time when humans lived on the earth in natural peace and harmony with each other and their surroundings and when stability and prosperity prevailed. The intellectual thinking mind did not seem to be something that existed much, if at all, at that time and people lived more intuitively within the moment and in perfect alignment with themselves and nature. It seemed that a more dominant feminine energy was present, nurturing and caring for them.

Then something occurred which has often been referred to as the 'fall of Man' or the descent, as humanity seemed to fall out of harmony and oneness with the creation around them and began to separate, and of course the result was wars, conflict and unhappiness as mankind moved into a more extreme, dominant masculine energy of war, power and aggression. This fall of Man occurred around the same time as the rise of the intellectual mind and thought process appearing within humanity. No doubt people wondered in amazement at all the talking taking place in the mind and then suddenly they began to listen to what was being said and to act upon it. Some even believed that these voices in the head were from a god or spirits of a higher power, and so what the mind said, most followed.

Now we are entering a new era, an era where we have an opportunity to return to the harmony and oneness of the feminine energy, but with a difference. We will return to it with the masculine energy of the intellect also, so that there is a full balance, a harmony, a oneness with understanding and knowledge. The glue that makes this true merging of masculine and feminine possible, is genderless, that which came before all gender and quality of energies, the 'secret self,' the source of all existence, the spiritual self beyond the physical body and mind which gives the body and mind it's true animation. We have an opportunity to move to a new golden age of mind, body and spirit in harmony and alignment together, like never before.

We have the possibility to take a giant leap in human consciousness. It's time has come, and we are in that age now. You may have felt it, you may already be changing because of it, but to reach the peak and to help the entirety of humanity soar to the heights of its potential and understanding, we must first discover the true nature of our 'secret self.' Only then will the true alignment of mind, body and spirit, or masculine, feminine and the pure self all come together to reach the peak of understanding and experience.

This will then move us into a golden age of science and spirituality, an age where those aspects merge together in balance for the wellbeing of the whole human race. When this happens, we will see humanity evolve light years ahead in intelligence and understanding, working in alignment with nature and the planet with systems and methods that takes little from the planet but gives more back and that does not take from humanity but instead shares all. At this time war, conflict, borders, laws, injustice and inequality will all be things of the past, and we will reach a time when maybe we will look back and wonder how we ever did the things we did, and lived the way we did.

This book is here to be a step in that direction, to guide you towards your true awakened nature and evolution.

Christopher J. Smith

# What is Inner Awakening?

*"When one realises one is asleep, at that moment one is already half-awake."*
*Pyotr Uspensky*

Have you ever been asleep at night in the midst of an intense dream, and suddenly realised that you are dreaming? And then maybe found that you have actually woken up whilst still within the dream itself? As you realise you are dreaming you may have become aware of yourself as the dreamer and see that the things you are experiencing are but an illusion of your own mind being projected inside of you.

Now being awake, with this realisation that you are simply dreaming, you can suddenly have more control, you can fly or change parts of the dream that you don't want to experience for ones that you do wish to experience. Until that moment, the content of the dream seemed to be outside your control, whereas now you are creating the dream yourself from the dreamer-state and not from the belief you are the dream itself.

In truth, the above scenario is an analogy for life itself. *'Row, row, row your boat, gently down the stream. Merrily, merrily, merrily, merrily, life is but a dream.'*

Most of us are dreaming, which is to say that we are unconsciously participating in our own lives. In other words we are not fully aware of everything we are doing. We all use a certain term; 'day-dreaming,' and day-dreaming simply means that we somehow get lost in thought codes and imaginational projections and so lose touch with 'reality' at any given moment. In other words, we are not fully conscious of our external surroundings for a great deal of the time. As we day-dream, lost within illusions of our mind, we are actually living in 'autopilot' mode, where we are never really in the 'driver's' seat of our own life experiences and direction, never really in full control of our own reactions and state of being.

These illusions of the mind take us away from true reality, as we cannot focus our complete attention on what is happening around us in actual reality if part of our attention is lost in constant thoughts and imaginings. These thought codes and imaginings are often memories of our yesterdays and assumptions about our tomorrows and this tends to propel us on a journey out of the '**now**' moment and into the hazy areas of the mind ... worrying about the future, and experiencing guilty memories of the past.

When we closely examine the constant barrage of subconscious thinking taking place within our minds, we will realise that around 95% of our thought processes are about the past and the future and so these persistent thought codes prevent us from being conscious of our present reality, which can only be right here and right now.

Our definition of being unconscious then is when we are not being fully aware and alert in the here and now, and when we are not making conscious choices.

This story of the day-dreaming priest clearly illustrates the point ...

Many years ago there lived a priest who was both lazy and poor. He did not want to work hard for a living but nevertheless used to dream of becoming rich one day. He lived from day to day by begging for alms and one particular morning someone kindly gave him a pot of milk.

He was delighted at this and took home the pot of milk. He boiled the milk, drank some of it and left the remains in the pot. Afterwards, he added a few curds to the pot to encourage the milk to curdle and then lay down to rest.

Soon he began day-dreaming about the pot of curds and also day-dreamed that if he could somehow become rich, all his worries and misery would be gone forever. His day-dream continued ...

> *"By morning the pot of milk will set and it will be converted into curd. I will churn the curd and make butter from it. I will then heat the butter and make ghee out of it and take it to the market and sell that ghee and make some money. With that money I will buy a hen and the hen will lay many eggs which will hatch and there will be many chickens. These chickens in turn will lay hundreds of eggs and I will soon have a poultry farm of my own. Then I will sell all of my hens and buy some cows and open a milk dairy and all the townsfolk will buy their milk from me. I will soon be very rich and buy expensive jewels and the king will buy all my jewels from me. I will be so rich that I will be able to marry an exceptionally beautiful girl from a rich family and we will have a handsome son. But if he misbehaves I will be very angry and to teach him a lesson, I will hit him with a big stick."*

Suddenly, he involuntarily picked up the stick next to his bed and believing that he was beating his son, hit the pot which of course broke and suddenly roused him from his vivid day-dream.

This story demonstrates that when we are lost in our own thoughts and imaginings we tend to become completely unaware of our surroundings and often make mistakes. We become ungrounded in actual reality and may lose ourselves in a world of fantasy. 'We' can never be found in fantasy, only in reality.

You see, imagination is a beautiful thing and if used purposefully and in a conscious way, it can allow creativity to flow through us, but when used without control in an unconscious way, it can bring us suffering, unhappiness and lead to serious mistakes and we can lose touch with ourselves and the actual reality of existence. When we allow our day dreams to take us over, we disconnect and lose touch with real life.

We can also become lost in worrying fantasies of the future and guilty memories of the past, which removes us from the magical reality of ourselves in the NOW moment.

This constant pondering on our yesterdays and tomorrows often has negative consequences on how we feel and how we respond to life situations. It usually consists of worries about the future and of guilt, shame and regrets of the past, the majority of which is ultimately an illusion we self-create through conditioned interpretations. (We will cover the nature of time in chapter 3) And so as most of our imaginings are based upon an illusionary past and future negativity, they will often leave us feeling drained and in a heavy contracted state of being, which ultimately leads to inner suffering and unhappiness. And so the most powerful way we can awaken to our true nature and rise beyond suffering is to walk a 'spiritual path.'

## What is a Spiritual Path?

*"Don't make goals out of the spiritual path. A goal implies time, working towards the future. But the spiritual path is about discovering what you already are. You are the goal. Now come to understand what that means and live it."*

In today's modern world there has been a resurgence of many ancient forms of spirituality and ancient practices. This is most commonly called the 'new age.' To understand the spiritual path we must first understand what it is not. Under this name of the 'new age' many of the ancient systems that are practiced and commercialised have been blanketed under the category of 'spiritual' or 'spirituality,' but it is extremely important here to make a distinction of that which is spiritual and what is not. This is not for some kind of petty arguments sake, this is for clarity of mind for those who really wish to seek and know true spirituality.

Let's first understand what the word *'spiritual'* really means, it consists of two parts—*spirit*—and—*ual*. *Spirit* means *pure spirit,* the pure source of all existence with which you are one and which is the true self and true essence of all life. The second part—*ual*—means *'pertaining to.'* So the word *'spiritual'* means *'pertaining to spirit,'* and therefore if someone is spiritual or on a spiritual path, it means they are seeking their ultimate nature within; they are seeking the spiritual essence within that which is the true essence of life itself. In other words, the spiritual path is the way to seek out the spirit, to come closer to it and discover it, and it can only be discovered and awakened within.

So if you are working with practices and methods that are not directly concerned with connecting to the spirit within you and the source of all existence, then you are not on a spiritual path.

So for instance, if you are a practicing medium and are channelling other entities, that in and of itself is not spiritual or being on a true spiritual path, and if you are a psychic and tell people their 'fortunes,' that in and of itself is not spiritual. If you practice reiki or massage, that in and of itself does not make you spiritual. If you read tarot or do fortune-telling astrology for yourself and other people, that does not mean you are on a spiritual path and if you do personal development work, that is not itself a spiritual path either.

All these practices and tools are adequate for the functions they perform, and good for helping people with certain related issues, but they have very little to do with walking a true spiritual path. The people that do these things and believe that they are on a spiritual path are not doing themselves any favours if they wish to really discover who they are. Instead they will be doing nothing but walking around in circles and will remain lost in the very thing that those who are walking a true spiritual path are becoming free from.

Now is it possible to work with these practices and also to walk a spiritual path, absolutely, but for that to be the case you must work with proper and sufficient methods that will awaken you spiritually. It is important that we get this clear in our minds so that we can make the right decisions and work with the right methods for true spiritual awakening, if that is what they choose to do. Otherwise lifetimes may be spent to no good effect, and the 'proof is in the pudding,' as they say. It is the efficiency of the correct methods that will demonstrate the results to those who walk a true spiritual path. When you are approaching closer to who you really are and awakening your true nature beyond the limitations of the physical, then you know what you are doing is efficient.

## Who Walks the Spiritual Path?

There are three main reasons why people choose, or feel drawn towards, Spirituality. One is through curiosity, another is because someone is trying to become a 'better' person and seeking self-realisation. And lastly, the one that is generally most common, is in order to end suffering. Maybe you fall into one of these categories?

But let us first look at the latter reason. The question is, have you suffered enough...?

Generally, people seek Spirituality because they see it as a potential way to end the suffering or turmoil they are going through in their life. They may seek it because they sense and recognise one thing, and that is, that suffering is largely self-created. This is a powerful realisation, because when we truly understand that we are causing our own inner suffering, we then have the responsibility to do something about it, once we recognise that it is in our own hands to change it.

Those that are not ready for the path generally have not yet reached this conclusion. They still believe on some level that outside circumstances and other people, create their suffering; they are not ready for spirituality yet because they are handing over responsibility to someone or something else. Only when we have suffered enough or have enough consciousness to recognise the truth, will we make the decision to do what it takes to be rid of the suffering and limitations, and realise that only one thing can end human suffering...full awakening and liberation.

So why does everyone not seek to end suffering?

Most people are unaware they are suffering. They are so unconsciously taken-over by the mind that the suffering they feel on a daily basis begins to feel normal; the way it has always been and the way it will always be. If you asked a large section of people if they have been suffering they would more than likely say 'no,' because in their mind suffering is just 'another day at the office,' but being ignorant of one's suffering is not the best way to live. Ignorance is not bliss and it is far better to be aware of it so that we can address the problem. It is similar to the alcoholic that is unaware of their problem. Just because they are unaware, does not mean that they do not have a problem and that it is not doing them damage and that not-knowing it is the most convenient position in which to be. The best option is to first become aware of the issue, and then attempt to remedy it.

People need their minds liberating whether they are aware of this fact or not. To the already-awakened this is all too clear and the odd thing regarding different states of consciousness and awakening is that only after we awaken and reach the new level of consciousness, can we see the stark contrast. In other words, when we are in a more contracted state of consciousness, we cannot see that it is contracted until we move to a more expansive state of consciousness, and then it becomes blatantly obvious, with hindsight. We will notice the dramatic difference in how we feel and of how much more we are now aware. If we awaken very rapidly, then the contrast will be greater than if we awaken slowly, when only a very subtle difference may be discerned.

Psychedelic plants and substances can be useful in this respect, as they usher-in a greater contrast in reality. But whilst they can be worthwhile experiences, it must be noted that these substances cannot ultimately bring us full enlightenment, because after the experience we will revert once more to our previous state of consciousness, albeit maybe with some slight differences and alterations. However, these substances can certainly bring some deep insights and allow us to purge the mind and body. The 'real work' to bring enlightenment though, must take place without reliance on any substance. This will be primarily achieved through meditation and self-investigation; these are the two most direct routes to ending suffering and discovering our pure nature.

Now let us look at curiosity...

Another common reason why we seek Spirituality, is because of general curiosity. Often those who have no previous knowledge or experience with spirituality are interested to investigate what it is all about. Maybe they have a friend or family member that attends spiritual group meeting or sessions of some kind, or maybe they know someone who has read some spiritual books and has had a conversation with them about it? Either way, their curiosity is awakened and they decide to see what it is all about. This path is usually the least likely to succeed in an ultimate inner awakening. This does not mean necessarily that it cannot happen, just that there is no strong motivation towards enlightenment at this time... or at least not consciously. Because the mind is not sure exactly for what it is searching, it follows therefore there can be no guarantee that they will enter into it fully, or whether they will simply 'fall by the wayside' and drift off towards some other goal. In the beginning, intention is everything, as we will discuss next...

> The third and most powerful motivation for us to seek the spiritual path, is the desire to become a 'better' person through the pursuit of enlightenment and self-realisation. With the previous reasons for the search for self-enlightenment, the intention is either to end suffering, or there is no real intention at all. And so this last driver is the most potent of the three because it aims directly at the goal and emanates from a clear intention to reach our potential. When we really wish to become more of who we are and to become better, then this is the most powerful intention because we are firing our aim at the ultimate target. This is the reason that this motivation is often viewed as the 'ultimate,' by many ancient spiritual systems.

Whatever brings us to the spiritual path is fine, as we all may awaken in different ways, but if we can align our body and minds with the clarity of the last-named option, it will certainly move us along the enlightened path more quickly.

# The Journey of the Soul

Who we essentially are has been called and referred to by many different names; higher-self, spirit, soul and many more. The names themselves are not really important because what we actually 'are,' can never be understood or experienced simply through a word or label, but for the sake of description we will refer to what we 'are' as the spirit with a soul, energy body.

We will discuss what the journey of our soul really is, in order to bring a wider context to why we are on the spiritual path. This may well cover issues that are mostly outside your experience, so I ask you not to believe or disbelieve what is said in this section, but to simply check whether or not it resonates with you on a deeper level and makes sense in the context of the spiritual path.

There are many different ancient schools of thought that cover the 'path of the soul,' but they all tend to have in common, enlightenment, liberation and salvation as their ultimate purpose.

It has been said that from the pure spirit and source of creation that individual souls were formed to come down to lower planes of existence in order to experience a process of re-remembering who they are, and the ecstasy, appreciation and joy it brings. In other words, an exploration of different worlds, dimensions and experiences, with the purpose of arriving 'back home' at their true infinite nature as pure divine spirit or pure consciousness. Pure consciousness will achieve this by way of a contrast, heightening our appreciation of the difference between what we are now and what we once were. Spirit needs to explore itself and experience the bliss and ecstasy of its return home. As an example, if someone is very wealthy and has everything they want whenever they want it, then their spirit will never grow or learn how to resolve the problems that poverty brings and they may even become less appreciative of what they have and become desensitised to the beauty that is all around them. But instead, should that person find himself in the slums of a poor neighbourhood with no money, daily challenges and a constant battle to survive; how much will that person now grow, learn, expand and appreciate to what they will soon return? What a thrill and joy it would be, to return home! What an experience for the pure spirit to discover if it can be fully consciousness in the most challenging of times and in the densest of realities. That is an analogy of how the spirit through the individual soul comes to know itself once again through the contrast of worldly existence.

As part of this exploration, we have the ability to assume certain roles and identities, and some souls become confused and attached to their roles, experiences and identities, they began to suffer in them and so the soul became affected in some way. This led to what has been called 'samsara,' in Buddhism, which means to be trapped in the cycle of life death and rebirth, and which the Hindu culture referred to as 'maya' or becoming trapped in the world of illusion. This ties into what has been called 'karma.' The root of karma is not the, 'cause and effect' aspect which is a natural function of reality, a law of existence. For example, you could say, 'if I touch a hot stove, then the hot stove is the cause and being burnt and experiencing pain is the effect,' but when speaking of karma itself, it is referring to something even closer to home than outside causes and effects, it is referring to the mind, memory, identity and intention, it is referring to the karma that is stored and imprinted at the soul and subconscious mind level.

Many of the serious modern and ancient yogis of the Himalayas refer to karma as originating in the mind. Karma is the mind and memory, and the continued cycle of karma is contained within intentions made from a mind-identified state. When we are identified as the mind and body we create either good karma or bad karma, do not think of this as being about the outside, it is what happens inside firstly, that is important. Our state of mind, memory, identity and intention then usually decide the actions we take and it is only then that the natural flow of consequences via cause and effect takes place. In other words, our internal state of consciousness and intentions are like the seeds of karma and then the actions we subsequently take begin to create certain consequences, and become stored as memory at the subconscious soul level.

For example, if we have criminal tendencies stored at a memory level of the soul (karma) and are then identified with those tendencies and memory as who we are, we will likely act them out at some point in time. Our karma is the internal state of identity we experience and we may take certain actions which of course will have consequences in the external world. If, for example, the soul in a previous incarnation became lost in the identity of a master criminal, and these imprints of identities were stored as memory (karma) of the soul, then it is highly likely that when that soul incarnates into another body, they will still possess all these same attributes and tendencies within them. This is how souls are forever destined to play out their karmic imprints from one incarnation to another until all karma has been resolved and purified. Or, there is another possibility...

When we awaken beyond the mind identity, we become enlightened and transcend all karma. All karmic effects no longer have any effect. Why is this? Because we will have risen beyond the identity of the mind, its memory and its content, and will have freed ourselves from the limited identity where all karma is stored and has effect. The inside affect may still continue within the mind, but there is no personal identity there any longer to be affected or latched-onto by us. We are beyond the effects of the karmic mind and we will be unaffected and undisturbed by whatever karma persists within the mind, and eventually, if we remain as the true self, the karma begins to completely dissolve and burn itself out.

You may then say, 'but what about external affects? Does karma not still occur in the sense of cause and effect?' Please see the section on 'Karma, free will and predestination.'

Many of the ancient cultures felt that the soul is often affected by the experiences and possible traumas of this world, and that this creates a karmic residue on the soul, in which we would need to have the soul cleansed in order to break free from the cycles of rebirth and return to higher dimensions of existence and the pure source of all existence itself... spirit. In other words, the soul becomes lost and disconnected from its source and becomes lost in the lower identities of existence, attaching to the lower dimensions and losing itself in the world, thus having to rebirth time and time again to give itself another opportunity to become liberated from its self-imposed chains (karma) and in order to move into higher planes of existence and therefore its true nature.

The whole of existence is like a paint stroke. If we take a paint brush and move it a long distance on a piece of paper or wall, it begins thickly yet becomes thinner as the paint on it is used up. This is akin to existence. There are dimensions layered upon each other occupying the same space, but they move from dense to light and into lighter and more subtle states of existence. When this pure cleansing happens it is referred to as liberation, enlightenment or self-realisation and it would be the end of suffering and the beginning of freedom, and a step into full consciousness and free will. At this time we would then be sufficiently cleansed and a 'match' for the higher and supreme energies of existence. From there, without karma, we have the full choice of experiencing all realities.

The whole of existence is one of pure energy and resonance, and so when we are trapped in a lower resonance it becomes impossible for us at that moment to move to the higher planes of existence or back to the source. We then have more limited choices. We may either remain in lower planes of existence or undergo rebirth for an opportunity to resolve karmic imprints and awaken so as to move on to higher levels. Karma is not a punishment or reward system, it is just simply a consequence of intention and action and what is being held and identified within the mind as memory (karma). For example, there are many souls that have become trapped in 'limbo' states of existence. No-one is actually trapping these poor tormented souls, or holding them hostage, apart from themselves, and this is exactly the same as in this reality; suffering is self-created, and this is indeed mirrored in all of existence. We have complete and utter freewill over ourselves, but only when we become fully conscious.

## Karma, Free Will and Predestination

So the more conscious and awake we become, the more free will and conscious choice we have. So one may ask the question, 'how does predestination interact with free-will and karma, as often things seem to happen to people when they have not chosen them?'

In order to understand karma, firstly we must understand that freewill and predestination in its entirety is quite complex... but luckily the solution is not. The solution is actually very simple, and this book provides the ultimate solution.

Free-will and choice is the ultimate reality for us all. However, what may appear to be predestined may actually be something that was first decided through choice, and so what we are experiencing are the consequences, internally and externally, of what was already chosen by us. For example, imagine a car travelling along a road at one hundred miles per hour. This represents our karma and our previous choices, that is, the choice to travel in a certain direction at a certain speed. But when the brakes are suddenly applied, the car will not stop instantly because there is so much momentum behind it. This is how our karma and consequences can work both internally and externally. When we have created this karma and then suddenly stop and disengage from it, there will still be a great momentum afterwards which represents certain life experiences and certain thoughts and tendencies continuing to run in the mind. What appears to be predestined, therefore, is just previously-created karma.

So then the question may arise, 'but why would we choose things that we do not want?' The reason is that we either chose it unconsciously, or that we chose it before this incarnation consciously, because we knew that it was something that was needed for our own personal growth and possible liberation, even if we are unable to recognise this from our current vantage point.

The content of our life and mind ultimately derives from unconscious choice and intention or conscious choice and intention. Unconsciousness means that we are not yet fully awake and aware of the choices we are making, whereas a fully conscious being who has awakened to their true nature beyond the body/mind identity, has the ability to make conscious free-will choices. Their destiny is now in their hands.

So most of us, throughout existence, from one incarnation to the next have been largely making unconscious decisions based upon limited knowledge, fear or conditioning, and so for the most part have not been exercising conscious free will, but instead the will of others, society or through the conditioned mind/ego. This unconscious choice creates a certain type of karma within us and it imprints itself at the individual soul level, thus persisting at the time of leaving the body into other planes of lower existence, or possibly through the reincarnation process into another physical incarnation. And so, if we do not liberate ourselves, we will be limited in our choices within this life and when we leave the body. At some time, whether it is in this life, the next life or in some other lower dimension, all karma must be cleansed through the awakening process.

The soul's journey is all about awakening to full choice through full consciousness, and returning back to the pure spirit of all existence, while enjoying and evolving through all the many experiences to be had along the way. Only certain awakened beings throughout history and in modern times have broken this cycle and cleansed the soul to connect with the higher dimensions and spiritual source of all existence.

Everyone has this potential to awaken at any moment, will you be one of them?

## Use this Life Well

Do not waste time, use this life well to awaken to your true nature and enjoy all experiences. Sometimes we believe that awakening in this life is 'not for us.' I say that is complete nonsense; it is available to us all right now, if only we may come to know ourselves more deeply. Why wait? It is the ego that is the culprit for this, as the ego fears its end and being out of control. What we must all comprehend is that the mind will often generate many excuses as to why we cannot awaken or do not 'have time' to awaken, or that we are too old and it is too late to awaken. The mind will often provide plenty of reasons not to, but we must remain committed, persistent and commit ourselves fully to the process. Also it should be pointed-out that awakening can happen in an instant, or it can happen in one single flash of realisation, and so it need not take a whole lifetime to realise the self... we are here, now, if only we could recognise this.

## The Dream of Misidentification

So to get to the real 'heart' of this chapter, essentially, 'Inner Awakening' occurs when we wake-up from the hazy dream that the conditioned, thinking mind creates, the dream that clouds our perception, and we realise our 'true awakened' nature, beyond the limitations of body and mind identity. It is when we become conscious of ourselves in the reality of the 'here and now' and perceive things clearly, without mental illusions and false perceptions, that we become fully awake... aware and alive.

Here are the basic themes and teachings of this book. They will provide you with a fundamental understanding of the book's message, throughout. This framework is known as the 'Seven Silent Truths.' You may return to this framework at any time.

1. *Your True nature is not that of thought, Ego mind or the physical body*
2. *When you believe/identify yourself with thought, body and mind a sense of separation is born, Self limitation, suffering & inner turmoil is then created.*
3. *The here & now is the only solid availability and true reality*
4. *The only Inner truth of this life is to see 'what is' all else is perspective*
5. *Greater depth of Inner Awakening depends on Allowance and cooperation with 'what is'. This takes us deeper into the flow of Truth.*
6. *Life is a constant fluctuation, a sense of Self & Happiness cannot remain stable in it*
7. *Letting go of mental clinging and attachment leads to Total Inner Freedom. In this there is nothing for the mind to grasp or be limited by. This awakens the sense of Boundlessness*

The embodiment and continued depth through the above Teachings opens a dimensional doorway to Inner Truth, Self Realization & Spiritual sovereignty.

So, what exactly and precisely are these illusions and false perceptions that prevent us from being fully awake, aware and alive in the 'now' moment?

It is the total identification with the body and mind which is ego, and it is the conditioned false personas we hide behind.

# Ego Identity

*"Ego is just like a dust in the eyes. Without clearing the dust you can't see anything clearly. So clear the ego and see the world"*

When most people in modern western society think of 'ego,' they usually think of someone who is overly confident, cocky and full of themselves. People may say that, 'he or she has a big ego,' but spiritual speaking, the word 'ego' is used in a much different context.

The word 'ego' is a Latin word that means 'I', and this 'I' is the false mental identity that most people believe themselves to be. The ego is a term that is used to refer to identification with the body and mind. In other words, when a being or pure soul identifies itself as being the physical body and mind organism, the ego is born. This ego is an individualised personal sense of self, and mental and physical sense of self. The ego believes that it is a separate entity from the rest of creation, and so it believes in doing what is ultimately best for it, in other words, what is best for the 'personal self.'

All inner suffering and conflict is created because of the ego identity and personalised sense of self. As soon as we believe we are the 'person' we take everything 'personally,' and so by taking everything personally we tend to suffer and tend to become defensive. We always defend who we think we are. When there is a personal sense of self, everything that happens in our life experience is then 'reported back' to the 'person,' and then the person creates mental stories and dialogues about whatever may occur. It is through these inner mental conversations that a personal relationship with the mind is created, and so people have conversations with themselves because they have created 'two' within, where in fact, there is only 'one.' In other words, identification with the body and thought has created the illusion of an internal split, whereby we unconsciously believe that there are two entities within. This is why we often seem to speak to ourselves, but have you ever asked the question, 'who exactly is the chatter in my head talking to?' Is there a singular existence within you or a dual existence?

It is this creation of the personal dual existence, the personal relationship with self, which creates all of the inner turmoil we experience. It takes two to have a conversation and to create a conflict, and when we identify with the thinking audio of the mind, and believe it to be who we are, we will always suffer, because whatever the thinking mind tells us about itself, we believe it and then suffer it, because we believe it is us saying it. When someone is unpleasant to us, the mind takes it personally and becomes defensive. Then, through the mind, an inner mental conversation is formulated about it, and if we believe what the mind is saying to be true and we believe that the mind is 'us,' then the result is suffering. Another way of expressing this could be . . . 'no mind, no problem . . . no person, no issue.' Whenever a sense of 'person' is present, there will be a problem, because the mind, which takes things personally, will always report to 'you' with a problem. But when there is no mental sense of self, there is no problem, because there is no-one for the mind to now complain. There is no longer anything 'there' to now take anything personally.

The thinking mind is just like an overlay, but as long as 'you' believe yourself to be the mind and its every thought, you will be lost in the ego self and will suffer.

The key to awakening is to first recognise and understand what you are not.

## You are not the Body

As we begin to move more into our Inner Awakening, it rapidly begins to become obvious that we are not the body. As we become more established in the unchanging observer-consciousness within, we also begin to become highly aware of the constant changing of the body and begin to recognise that this deeper 'you' as pure awareness is an unchanging reality and that everything apart from it changes and 'comes and goes' while ourselves as pure awareness, remain the same.

We can experience the reality of our unchanging awareness simply by reflection; think back to when you were a child, who was it in **you** that were having that experience then? Were you aware? Please look...

> *Now try to recall the time when you were a teenager; who was it in you that were having that experience then? Were you aware then also? Please look...*

And so who is it that is having **this** experience right now? Are **you** aware right now? Please look...

> *You see, there always has been an element constantly within you that has remained static while all other things on the surface have changed. Your thoughts and beliefs have changed over time, your body has changed over time, yet the 'experiencer' within has always been there, through all your life's ups and downs and changes.*
>
> *Can you be aware of this 'experiencer' that has always been present? Please look now...*

Your body is an accumulation of matter from the earth gathered over a long period of time, can you see? The matter that you eat and drink is digested by the body and then becomes a part of the body itself, this matter we ingest indeed becomes the matter which makes-up the body. Most of us will have heard the expression 'you are what you eat,' and that is certainly true, except for the fact that **you** are not the body itself. Whatever you accumulate cannot be you, it can only be yours.

Even if say, you buy a car, a house and many other material possessions, they are **yours**, you have gathered them to you, but they can never be **you**. Please look closely...

> We even use the phrase 'I have a body,' whatever we have is ours but is not us, please look...

If you look closely at the language and phrases we use every day you will see some clarity in this, for example, when we say 'I am large or small... or I am rich or poor' we have the '**I**' that is originally who we are, and then we have that which we attach and identify the '**I**' to or with, which in the above examples is large, small, rich and poor, which is not who we are but instead something that we '**have**' or are experiencing. So in a statement like 'I am the body' there is the '**I**' as who we are and then there is the body as something that we '**have**' and we are experiencing, but which is not us. The same way that the items being carried in a bag are not the bag itself, please contemplate this...

Do you exist right at this moment? Did you exist five years ago? Are you the body? Most people would answer 'yes' to these questions, but if you believe that you are your body and that you exist now and also did so seven years ago, then you have a problem.

The body that you had and that you believed was you, seven years ago, does not exist anymore. In the space of those seven years the molecules and atoms that made-up your body at that time have been completely changed for brand new matter and not one single particle or atom remains present in your body that was there seven years ago. It is not that the body you had still exists and has just changed somewhat, oh no, the body you had is now completely gone, so how can you possibly have ever been that body if you still exist and it does not? Please contemplate this...

## The Secret Self

Studies done at the Oak Ridge Atomic Research Centre have shown that about 98% of all the atoms in the human body are replaced every year. You get a new liver every six weeks, a new suit of skin every month and a new stomach lining every five days. Even your bones are not the solid, stable, concrete-like things that you may have thought they were. The bones you have today are different from the bones you had a year ago. Experts in this area of research have concluded that there is a complete, 100% replacement of all the atoms in the body at least every seven years.

So once again the question arises; if you are your body, then which seven-year version are you? If you say you are this body now, then in seven years **you** should be completely gone and a totally new model will be in place. Please contemplate this deeply...

When you look at an old picture of yourself from seven to ten years ago, please be aware that that old body does not exist any longer. Yet **you** still exist, you are not gone. So who is it in **you** that are still there, remaining constant throughout the complete replacement of each successive body? Who is it that has witnessed all of this change while itself remaining the same? Please look...

## You are not the Brain

Most people believe they are that brain floating around in their skull, but regarding the rapid replacement of molecular particles that make up brain cells, Paul Weiss wrote...

> "Recent studies on the turnover of the molecular population within a given nerve [brain] cell have indicated that...their macromolecular contingent is renewed about ten thousand times in a lifetime."
> Paul Weiss, *The Living System: Determinism Stratified*, in Arthur Koestler and J.R Smythies eds, *Beyond Reductionism* (London: Hutchinson, 1969) p. 13

So your brain is a completely new model at least once every week, with an even more rapid turnover than the body. You see, you the 'true self, observer self' is the one that is using and experiencing the body and the brain and not the other way around.

It is similar to stepping out of one car and getting into another. Those vehicles are the different bodies, whilst you are the driver of the bodies and not the bodies themselves. Please observe this ...

## Are you the Mind?

When we speak of the mind here, we are referring to the thought process that is constantly chattering away in your head, the inner voice in other words. The fluent dialogue of thinking, analysing and judging that constantly occurs within the mind, the voice that is always interpreting every situation and experience. You know what I mean I presume. It is probably taking place in your mind right now, sifting, analysing and judging every word being read. Can you be aware and observe this chatter right now? Please observe ...

I would like you to do something right now, for me. Try to completely put a stop to this constant chattering in the mind for one minute. Do that now please; stop the mental chatter completely right now ...

> So, were you successful in completely stopping the background noise in the mind, just for one short minute?

More than likely you found it pretty difficult or even impossible to do this and it is probable that you were still bombarded with many different messages whilst trying to stop them altogether. Often, people are so closely identified with their 'thinking mind,' that they are not even aware that there is a constant stream of random and unruly chatter taking place. In other words, they may have been trying to find the 'thinking mind' with the very thinking mind itself, which cannot be done.

It is like trying to see the whole of a wood whilst standing in the middle of it. The only way to achieve that view is by climbing to higher ground in order to see the full picture, otherwise you quite literally, 'cannot see the wood for the trees.'

So the attempt to control the mind, and being unable to do so, clearly illustrates the fact that the mind is not the 'true self.' It is an extremely common occurrence that many people, before going to sleep, cannot switch off the background noise in their mind and often this can lead to a sleepless night. You really just want to stop thinking but yet the uncontrollable torrent of thoughts just keeps spilling out into your mind. Have you ever had this experience before? Or maybe you have had the experience of wanting to stop thinking about a particular situation or person, yet no matter how hard you try, the thoughts just keep on coming? Or maybe sometimes you have been trying to concentrate on something in particular but yet you keep getting distracted with all manner of different, conflicting thoughts that seem to take your attention away from the task at hand?

This shows us clearly and logically that we are not the mind itself and that the mind has a life of its own, regardless of what we want, or our trying to control it. The mind just continues to spin along like a bicycle wheel that has been spun whilst the bike is turned upside down, all that needs to be done for the wheel to slow down, is to stop spinning it. There is no need to try and stop it, but instead to simply disengage from spinning it any further, stand back and allow the wheel to keep spinning on and eventually the wheel just like the mind will begin to slow down, because you are no longer doing anything with it. You see, it's our awareness and identity with the mind that gives it the energy to keep-on going round and round. Our awareness and attention is like fuel for the mechanism that is the thinking mind and so if we starve it of that fuel, eventually its power over us will diminish. The thinking mind is a mechanism for us as awareness to use when we wish to use it, but for nearly every person this mechanism has taken over their awareness and instead uses them, hence the compulsion of continuous thinking. For most the mechanism of the mind has become the master and their awareness the servant, Inner awakening is all about making you as awareness the master and you're body and mind as the servant, this is the right relationship for self and life mastery.

So where does all of this thinking come? Studies now tell us that the average person has anywhere from thirty to sixty thousand thoughts every day, and that 98% of this thinking is negative, repetitive codes of thought that constantly play back and forth in the mind like a nagging audio tape, forever stuck on 'repeat.'

From where do all these thoughts emanate and why do they create such suffering and disturbance in our life? They come from conditioning wrapped up as the false persona...

Christopher J. Smith
# Ego and the False 'Self' Persona

*"When does total awareness occur? When the ego departs... When is the true self known? When you see beyond the persona"*

After the ego identity is born, the ego begins to accumulate and pick up many forms of conditioning and other identities. All of these identities become added on top of the basic sense of ego self and formulate what is known as the personality or persona...

## You are not the personality.

The word 'personality' derives from the Latin word 'persona,' meaning 'mask.' The study of personality may therefore be understood as the study of the 'masks' that people wear.

When you stop acting the way you have been taught, who remains and what action comes from that? Please look...

When you remove the mask of the personality, who is there? Please observe...

The mask or personality, is the conditioned-self that most people believe themselves to be. It is a limited identity that is bound by 'conditions' and which therefore limits our reality, decision-making and interactions with others and in confronting life's rich experiences. It is your identifying with the false persona that is causing you all the problems in your life and you end up at war with yourself and others because the conditioned-self has been taught to be more focussed on self-preservation and survival than anything else. Which would be to ask, how can 'I' benefit from each situation as opposed to 'we' all benefiting from each situation?

This conditioned false persona is often very self-centred in its perception and approach to life and it is the clash of personas in the world that causes all of the differences that separate us and creates all of the constant human conflicts and wars that we see. So in other words, it is the misidentification with being the false persona wrapped up in the ego that causes all the suffering in the world.

This false persona that most people identify with themselves is formed by what we refer to as 'learned behaviour' or conditioning.

## Conditioning of the Mind

The following example illustrates the nature of conditioning...

In India young elephants are trained in obedience in order to stop them from escaping by tying them to a huge immovable object, such as a tree, when they are very young. The tree is so large that no matter how hard the baby elephant pulls and tugs at it, it cannot break free. This develops what is known as 'learned helplessness' in the creature and after trying so hard and for so long to break the hold, only to be thwarted time and again, it eventually comes to believe that no matter what it does, it cannot escape. And so ultimately, as a fully-grown adult weighing several tonnes, it can actually be tied to the smallest, flimsy twig and it will not escape; in fact it won't even try to escape.

So conditioning is repetitive learned behaviour which binds us to limitations, limitations of how we act in accordance with people and in certain situations and limitations of how we see and experience ourselves. It is what we believe about ourselves, others and life that binds us to predictable, repetitive and limited ways of responding to life's situations.

We become predictable, almost machine-like and cold in our behaviours, never really operating as consciously as we should, reacting with conditioned responses to situations, in auto-pilot mode so to speak.

Our conditioning mainly derives from one source, our culture. That is from our upbringing, education, media and society overall. Another form of conditioning happens through the mental interpretations of our life experiences, for example, if we experience unsuccessful business after unsuccessful business many times, we may come to believe that we are hopeless at business and not built for it, that business just isn't for us. This type of belief may have formed because we already had a conditioned belief passed on from the first source that said 'if a business doesn't work then you're a failure'. So we have two main types of conditioning, those that were directly given to us and those that developed through other beliefs already in place in response to certain life experiences.

Our identity with this conditioning is often referred to as the 'ego,' which is identification with the chatter in the mind (that voice in your head) and the conditioned codes of thought that constantly play around the mind like a stuck needle on a vinyl record. In eastern spiritual systems it is known as the 'monkey mind' as this thinking part of the mind constantly jumps from one thought to another, just like a monkey swinging on branches through the trees in the jungle.

From the minute a baby is born, limitations and a sense of separation is immediately created. We label the baby with a name, the actual name does not matter, it is just a label but as soon as something or someone acquires a label of any kind, it distinguishes it from the rest of reality. Having a name in and of itself is not the issue, the issue arises when we are taught to identify ourselves as that name and we then start to believe, 'I am John / Chris / Jane or Jill.' In other words, I am this limited identity of thoughts, conditioned reactions and a body.

Then 'John' begins to be conditioned and moulded by various influences. His parents will have been brought-up in their own particular ways with certain perceptions about the world and will mould John whether consciously or unconsciously according to that specific set of perceptions. An example of this is when the parents may say to John, '...*money doesn't come easily you know.*' That is a belief that they have now passed onto John and if they say it often enough, he will likely believe that to be true and grow up with it implanted in his mind. Another example may be that not brushing your teeth twice a day is wrong or that you always must keep everything clean and tidy all of the time. I personally know of people who have really strong compulsions to be meticulously clean at all times because they had it instilled into them from a young age to be that way and if they do not constantly keep themselves and their possessions clean, then they tend to become very agitated. They will have been constantly pestered by their own minds to clean this and that until they eventually surrender to their own compulsive thoughts and conditioning.

These conditioned beliefs are formed in every area of our lives, from how we have been taught to deal with certain situations, to religious and economic conditioning, to relationship and societal conditioning. As we grow-up and mature, we begin to take on these conditionings and they are then stored at a subconscious level. 'Sub' means 'below' and therefore subconscious means below the threshold of the mind. In other words, most of this conditioning we acquire becomes completely imperceptible to us, yet still strongly influences how we see ourselves, the world and the quality of the decisions we make.

Inner-awakening into full 'Self Realization' only occurs when all mental conditioning, self-identity with the body and thought ceases, and as it ends our true awareness and natural state of being begins to shine through in all of its power and beauty.

## Who is behind the Mask?

*"Realisation is not an acquisition of anything new nor is it a new faculty. It is only the removal of all camouflage."* Ramana Maharshi

Only true 'seeing' creates an inner knowing within you, and so whatever words are used to direct you, towards who you are, please do not concentrate on the words themselves. The words are simply pointing towards that which cannot be described but only experienced and seen.

> *"Don't think, experience. It's like a finger pointing at the moon. Do not concentrate on the finger or you will miss all of the heavenly glory."*
> Bruce Lee

Please bear in mind the above quote as we continue through the ensuing chapters on how to awaken and the using of practices and introspections.

One of the greatest ways to discover who we are, is to first understand what we are not, as we looked at earlier. Simply by using the power of logic alone we can discern what we **are not**, but to ground ourselves more deeply in what we **are**, requires us to throw away all logic in that final step.

In the ancient yogic systems, the final step after an initial inner awakening is often referred-to as 'liberation,' to be unchained from illusions and attachments of the mind. The mind and body can take us part-way there, like an instrument to the divine, but at the last moment, the instrument or methodology must also be abandoned in order to experience the final liberation. Liberation in this case means freedom from limitations and therefore a union with the unlimited universal force.

The word 'Zen' is derived from the Chinese word 'chán' and the Sanskrit word 'dhyana,' which means 'meditation.' In Sanskrit, the root meaning is 'to see, to observe, to look.'

The following short story on the nature of Zen Illustrates this point.

> *Nan-in, a Japanese master during the Meiji era (1868-1912), received a university professor who had come to inquire about Zen. Nan-in served tea. He poured his visitor's cup full, and then kept on pouring. The professor watched the overflow until he no longer could restrain himself. "It is overfull. No more will go in!" "Like this cup," Nan-in said, "you are full of your own opinions and speculations. How can I show you Zen unless you first empty your cup?"*

So now you have a clear understanding of what you **are not**, it opens the door to discovering what you actually **are.**

Let us now continue to explore and discover the next steps down the road towards your inner awakening and liberation...

# Chapter 2
## How to Awaken

*"Enlightenment is not about becoming something different, it's simply about recognising what is already within."*

It is very easy, in spirituality or the awakening process, to assume that awakening happens through change and becoming something different, but in essence, awakening is a disengagement and disentanglement of that which is ultimately not you.

Awakening is not about changing or transforming one's self into something greater, it is the realisation of the greatness already contained within, and about discovering who we already are behind the facade of the ego identity and who is behind the mind. All that is needed is the intention, curiosity and willingness to see who we really are, and a commitment to discovering that ultimate truth within.

There are certain methods, practices and pointers that will assist with this inner awakening all throughout this book, but a certain foundation of these means must be put in place within our everyday life in order to nurture and ripen our opening into our Ultimate nature. In other words, the practices, methods and pointers within this book have been placed in the most efficient order and type to assist you step by step, and at the appropriate time, through the awakening process. Allow the book to do its work in assisting in your awakening and deepening of awakening.

The first step is to begin the discovery...

## To Never Begin and Never End

*"There are only two mistakes one can make along the road to truth; not going all the way, and not starting" Buddha*

In relation to the spiritual path there are three main types of people, the ones that walk the path and continue all the way to full awakening, those that that never begin, and those that start the journey but do not complete it.

## Ignorance of truth

Ignorance may sound insulting, but ignorance simply means being unaware of something, so the majority of beings in the world are ignorant of who and what they really are and are therefore ignorant of all ultimate truth. These beings may never start on the path, they may live their whole life completely unaware of the tremendous treasure and beauty that lies within, unaware of what truths they can discover about themselves and the world, and how good they can feel. For these beings there may be a hope, the type of hope that may force them to look within, and this is the catalyst of suffering. The interesting thing is, is that most people suffer all the time, but because they become used to it over time and is not usually too intense, it never quite sends them 'over the edge' into an inner awakening or makes them feel drawn towards the spiritual path. Until, maybe one day, if it becomes bad enough, they will awaken to their true nature.

## Stuck between Heaven and Hell

Being stuck between heaven and hell occurs when someone begins the spiritual path and awakens to taste the freedom, truth and bliss it can bring, but then fails to continue all the way. This path is like a path of limbo, where we may seem to remain suspended in 'no man's land,' or where we never quite make it to the 'promised land.' This place is the worse to be of all the three points of the path. Why? Because before starting our journey along the path, we were in ignorance and didn't know any different. We had nothing else with which to compare our regular life experience, no basis for comparison, and so we become lost in unconsciousness, none the wiser.

However, upon experiencing our initial awakening, where we taste the sweetness of pure consciousness, meditation and bliss, it will then seem like a huge backward step to revert back into the unconsciousness of the mind. We may now feel the great contrast and differential like never before, our bliss and consciousness heightened, but then suddenly depression and suffering taking over and breaking the spell. This is known as the 'pendulum effect,' high one minute, low the next, moments of extreme bliss and moments of extreme suffering, times of feeling expansive and times of compression. This 'up and down' effect occurs because we are constantly moving between being in and then out, of the mind identity, and it is because we have not finished the spiritual path and have not achieved full awakening yet. So, what is across that 'finishing line?' ... Liberation of the mind.

# Going all the Way

The end of the path is where the inner treasure resides, here is where the searcher becomes found, where the seeker is revealed and where the full truth is uncovered. In this place no ignorance of self exists, and there is no one in limbo. There is no falling-down and standing-up again, as both the falling and rising are recognised by that which is awake. Here the bliss and suffering are both viewed and treated in just the same way and is where we go beyond any sense of 'path,' and have in fact reached the end of our journey. When the mind is unravelled we feel liberated, when the self is recognised, we are realised and when both occur we are enlightened. Continue all the way and what will remain is the ecstasy of existence itself.

You must dissolve fully, the tablet will only be potent and of any real use when it's dissolving is complete.

# Commitment to the Path

It is very important that we develop clarity of mind about what we truly want. If we wish to be free of suffering and discover our ultimate nature, then this requires a commitment, which is very important, because this will focus all of your energies on the task in hand. When we are unsure of our goals, then our actions and mind will waver. A lack of real commitment will cause great uncertainty.

The spiritual path and discovering our ultimate nature must be a priority, it must be our greatest intention and desire. This does not necessarily mean that all else in life should be neglected, but we must honour what is most important to us, and if we wish to truly discover our ultimate nature, this should become our priority. There is every possibility that in the beginning it will require all of our effort and commitment to begin the process, to establish a foundational practice of meditation and daily practices, and to use subtle efforts to become more introspective and investigative. We must want it more than anything else, to regain our 'true selves,' must be our only true intention, and this reminds me of the story of the man who wanted to know God...

> *A hermit was meditating by a river when a young man interrupted him. "Master, I wish to become your disciple," said the man.*
>
> *"Why?" replied the hermit.*
>
> *The young man thought for a moment.*
>
> *"Because I want to find God." The master jumped up, grabbed him by the scruff of his neck, dragged him into the river, and plunged his head under water. After holding him there for a minute, with him kicking and struggling to free himself, the master finally pulled him up out of the river. The young man coughed up water and gasped to get his breath. When he eventually quieted down, the master spoke...*
>
> *"Tell me, what you wanted most of all when you were under water." "Air!" answered the man.*
>
> *"Very well," said the master. "Go home and come back to me when you want God as much as you just wanted air."*

When the desire to know our ultimate nature becomes a strong enough force within us... that is when the spiritual path will really begin and inner awakening will 'come knocking.'

## Power of the Earnest Prayer

One of the intentions to which I made a commitment, was to say a heartfelt, earnest prayer. The earnest prayer is mentioned in the Bible, and it refers to a declaration that is to be put into action 'earnestly.' This prayer is a declaration of your intentions, and how keen and committed you are to usher-in its occurrence.

The earnest prayer is not complicated, it is very simple, but we must say it, and mean it, from the heart. In other words, we must really mean what we say.

The prayer may go something like this...

> *"I ask the universe (or god, higher self, existence. Whatever means most to you) to bring me awakening by whatever means is best and whatever means is quickest, I wish to awaken at all costs. I surrender to awakening."*

Say it with a true heartfelt intention and then surrender it to the universe, and then continue with your practices and introspection. Go about your business and grace will provide the rest. You can say it as many times as you wish, but one heartfelt time with a true, sincere intention is enough for it to be ushered in earnestly.

## Three main Aspects of Inner Awakening

There are three main aspects to inner awakening and connecting to our true nature beyond the body and mind, and these can be remembered as the three 'P's... Perspective, Perception and Practice.

Contemplate and reflect on all these things...

### #1 *True Perspective*

*"As soon as you look at the world through an ideology you are finished. No reality fits an ideology. Life is beyond that. That is why people are always searching for a meaning to life... Meaning is only found when you go beyond meaning. Life only makes sense when you perceive it as mystery and it makes no sense to the conceptualizing mind."* Anthony de Mello

True perspective is the power of understanding and seeing things as they are and not as the mind interprets them to be; it is our false perspectives (beliefs) about ourselves, others and life's situations that keeps our awareness in a limited inaccessible state. Our awareness becomes funnelled into narrow bands of perception (belief structures) that limit and block our inner sense of awareness, wakefulness and freewill choice-making ability. Many of us often hold particular beliefs that harm us and damage our connections with others and these beliefs create a distortion in our experience of reality.

Imagine a dirty mirror that once cleaned gives a true, faithful reflection. The dirt creating the distortion on the mirror is similar to our conditioned belief systems but when we wipe the mind clean, (ridding ourselves of conditioning) just as with the mirror, we gain an accurate, honest perspective of life—just like seeing the clear reflection in the mirror.

As an example; one might believe that people are not to be trusted, therefore creating a state of constant anxiety or fear of sharing information or creating bonds with others. In other words, existing in a constant 'defensive mode,' when in reality one may only be seeing their own beliefs projected onto other people. The likelihood is that most people we encounter are trustworthy but one's *own* belief makes it seem as though people are something they are not...almost like wearing rose-tinted glasses and seeing red everywhere we look. Please contemplate this...

Someone may believe themselves to have no value or self-worth, thereby believing that they do not deserve an intimate relationship or that they do not deserve to get that promotion they were promised, at work. Or, they may attend a job interview and the interviewer picks up on their lack of confidence and as a result they do not get the job they wanted.

Most of you will have heard of the 'glass half-empty and glass half-full' analogy, however I would take this one step further by saying that we can also just see the glass with water in it, neither seeing it half empty or half full but seeing each situation in a neutral way. In life there are three ways of looking at things; the first one being the negative viewpoint (which is to say, seeing the glass as half-empty). Our 'conditioned' perceptions are most often formed of negativity, and it sees the lack in everything that happens in life.

However viewing events in a positive light (which is to say, seeing the glass as half-full), regarding events as opportunities and 'clouds' as having a 'silver lining,' is a very good and healthy way of living—but true, honest perception derives from the third perspective...

The perspective from which we see the glass simply containing liquid and neither half-empty or half-full is the only sure way of seeing life just 'as it is' and without any thought-based interpretation overlying it. To regard something as 'negative' or 'positive' ascribes meaning to something from the mind, yet not allocating an interpretation or meaning to it, is viewing life exactly as it really is. Not pre-judging anything will result in a totally different personal experience and state of consciousness in oneself. It will remove all the distortions of perception, both good and bad. Thus, when we simply observe the world in its reality, it may be regarded as the viewpoint of the heart and not the mind... almost like peering-in at life directly, from the spirit.

This short story demonstrates the benefits of neutrality, as opposed to making a 'black or white' decision in each set of circumstances.

> *"Once upon the time there was an old farmer who had worked his crops for many years. One day his horse ran away. Upon hearing the news, his neighbours came to visit. 'Such bad luck,' they said sympathetically.*
>
> *'Perhaps,' the farmer replied.*
>
> *The next morning the horse returned, bringing with it three other wild horses. 'What great luck!' the neighbours exclaimed.*
>
> *'Perhaps,' replied the old man.*
>
> *The following day, his son tried to ride one of the untamed horses, but was thrown and broke his leg. The neighbours again came to offer their sympathy on his misfortune, 'how terrible,' they all said.*
>
> *'Perhaps,' answered the farmer.*
>
> *The day after that, military officials came to the village to draft young men into the army. Seeing that the son's leg was broken, they passed him by. The neighbours congratulated the farmer on how well things had turned out.*
>
> *'Perhaps,' said the farmer...*

This story illustrates the impossibility of understanding the 'bigger picture' surrounding any event. Something that may seem terrible at first glance may result directly in the avoidance of a much more extreme situation with far greater negative consequences. Life is a tapestry of different events that makes-up the whole and which inevitably leads to unknown future consequences. It would be foolish in the extreme to label any event as 'good' or 'bad' when we cannot possibly know its true meaning or consequences and how that may fit-in with the ongoing evolution of existence and ourselves?

Each interpretation made by the mind is an honest lie at best; they are all different, yet limited views of the same event. It is similar to watching a football game in a huge stadium. Everyone is watching the same game, but yet everyone will see it from a different angle, a different perspective. Each individual judgement and mental viewpoint is like a watching the same game from a different seat, but yet if we can refrain our opinion or judgement, suddenly we arrive at the neutral position of just seeing the game 'as it really is.' After all, it is only a game of football with people kicking a ball around whilst themselves moving backwards and forwards on the pitch. In other words, we are simply watching what is actually there, not a mental dialogue or opinion of what is there.

*At this point please try this brief exercise, 'Relaxing concepts':*

Whether you are indoors or outside, firstly, find an object such as a tree or flower, or a vase or ornament. As you observe the object, your mind is 'labelling' it or forming some concept of it.

Now try this... Look carefully at this object and by relaxing, just allow all your concepts of it to slowly, completely dissipate. In other words, just view the object as if you do not know what it is and as though seeing it for the very first time. Do that now as you release all mental preconceptions of it.

What often can happen when we perform this exercise, is that we begin to see the object as being more vibrant and alive, emphasising and making more vivid its colours and shape. You see, when we become fixated on the 'labels' of things, 'cup,' 'tree' or 'car,' etc. rather than the actual object itself, we tend to focus our attention solely on its name, believing falsely that we already know what it is. When we already believe we know what it is, we see our minds ideas about it and therefore overlook its true nature.

So as regards to our 'inner awakening,' true understanding can only be achieved by looking at life stripped-bare of all our mental notions and filters. Once this happens, our awareness begins to awaken and blossom as the old conditioned-programming that was acting as a filter begins to dissolve, leaving only the absolute, undiluted truth of 'life' and 'self.'

This also applies to how we see ourselves; so many people have very limiting ideas about themselves and believe these ideas to be the 'complete truth' of who they really are. However, by looking within ourselves, without those conditioned filters or ideas, only then may we begin to see ourselves 'naturally' or as we REALLY are.

We often develop our ideas about ourselves through what other people tell us and also by how we believe we should relate to 'society.' We may believe for instance that, 'I'm a sporty-type,' a 'business-type' or 'a working-class or blue-collar person.' And we often also believe the same with regards to our personalities. We may say for example, 'I'm an introvert,' 'I'm an extrovert' or even more damaging things such as, 'I'm a naturally lazy person,' or 'a pessimistic person.' When we are fixated on the level of the 'monkey mind,' then whatever we believe about ourselves completely limits us and prevents us from reaching our limitless potential. Believing negatives about ourselves is very harmful indeed to our self-esteem.

In order to assist and develop the awakening process, I would strongly recommend that you divest yourself of all your inherent beliefs about yourself, good or bad, as they will all erect barriers to the pure, unbounded awareness within. Once you are established as the 'true self' beyond the mind and you are coming from inner neutrality, then you can build upon that with positivity, as true positivity comes from first seeing the truth of reality and self. Once you are able to truly discern clearly what you are not, then all obstacles will be removed, enabling you to both 'see' and experience your core 'essence.'

## Belief vs. Knowing

*"Just because you believe, does not mean you know."*

In our search for truth it is very important to establish the difference between a belief and knowing.

Let me ask you a question. Do you believe that gas exists?

Most people would say that they do not simply 'believe' that gas exists, they 'know' it exists, because they have experienced it, smelt it and are aware that it powers many things. A belief is always about something that we do not ultimately know. When someone says that they 'believe' something, they are saying that they think it is true, hope it is true or even assume it to be true, but ultimately they cannot say for certain that it is true.

'Knowing' however, is being aware that something is definitely true because you have had direct experience of it and have seen much factual evidence of it. For example, we would not say that we 'believe' in oxygen, as we 'know' it exists because we are aware of it and we see its by-product, carbon dioxide, exiting our mouths on a frosty day. There is no doubt that it exists, so no need to believe whether it exists or not... we just know it does. That is the truth and for this reason, there is no lasting benefit to a belief system. Maybe positive beliefs can serve to transport us to a certain point in life, but every belief system has its limits, so to achieve our unlimited nature and potential we must go beyond all belief systems, and instead arrive at a place of 'knowing.' How do we do that? We do it by exploring and by searching within our own experience and exploring life.

You see, beliefs can become a barrier to experiencing something and knowing something, because if we are content to hold a belief about something that we do not know for sure, then we may never seek for the real truth. And so, in this sense, holding beliefs will lead to ignorance of self and life. For instance, if we believe in a god and that god is a certain thing that looks a particular way, then you will never actually have a direct experience of God because you will never search any further for the truth, because you believe that you already know it. This leads to actual ignorance of what God truly is, which can only be experienced and observed within us. A 'belief' is always about something we do not know, and of that which we are not sure, whereas 'knowing' always concerns something that we have experienced and can state with certainty.

Instead of simply saying that we 'believe' something, it would be more intelligent and honest just to admit that we do not know, and then this will drive us to become a seeker of the truth. And then as we search for the truth, we will experience things that will create a level of knowing in us from direct experience and we will become beings of truth and knowing instead of merely 'believers.' When we become real seekers of truth we will move into our true perspectives.

## #2 Direct Perception of the True Self

*"What is behind your eyes holds more power than what is in front of them"*
Gary Zukav

Direct perception of the True Self comes from our awakening to what is beyond thought. It is a glimpse or recognition of our self, beyond the constant chatter of the mind mechanism. What we must first understand about direct perception is that it is not something far away and out of reach; in fact what we seek is the entity within, the one doing the actual seeking. In other words, we are looking for ourselves with the very eyes of ourselves. To put it yet another way, the one within us who is looking to find the observer, is the very same observer itself for which it is searching.

> *"The eye with which I see God, is the same eye in which God sees me."*
> Meister Eckhart

So to have direct perception of ourselves, we must first understand what we are not and only then delve within to see what we really are. We must use the art of introspection or self-investigation as a way to observe and watch what we are not and in doing so stumble upon what we are...

# Observation of the Ego

*"Starve the ego. Feed the soul."*

When the ego goes unobserved, it carries on regardless and runs amok. To awaken out of the ego identity requires observation of its nature and movements, the ego relies upon us being unaware and being lost in thinking and operates at its best and is most powerful when it stealthily 'flies under the radar.' It also relies on a personal relationship with the thinking voice in the mind, the more you interact with it the more it comes to life and the stronger it appears to become. It is similar to expecting a raging fire to cool down by throwing more coals on it. Stop putting coals on the fire and it will cool down of its own accord. Similarly the ego and our relationship with it, works in the same way, and so what needs to be done is to cease feeding it, and the way to starve it of fuel is through the observation of it and its ways. In observing it, we automatically move to a position of consciousness that is beyond it and prior to it. When we are not observing the mind we become lost in it, but as soon as it is observed, we immediately detach from it and its activity.

Awareness and observation is the key to inner awakening, watch the mind and in an instant you are in the awakened state, by watching the mind you move from the unconsciousness of the mind and thought to the consciousness of observation. It is that simple, see if you can observe the mind and its activity right this instant...

The more specific we are in recognising how to detect the ego in ourselves and others, the less power it will have over us and the more we can begin to rapidly break free from it. For the mind-identified person, engaging in certain mind activity and particular formations of thought has become such a habit that only intense observation and present moment awareness will begin to break that habit, to break our thought-based association.

To assist in this specific identification of the ego and how it operates, here are some of the most prevalent and common traits of the ego. Can you recognise any of these traits within yourself or others at any time previously?

# Traits of the Ego

*"The ultimate aim of ego is not to see something, but to be something"*

So, let us now examine certain traits of the ego we may see in ourselves and others, and then by identifying how the ego operates, we can then disassociate ourselves from these behaviours and instead become a silent watcher of such traits. This is the way by which we transcend the ego.

The whole issue has always been that we have become lost in the ego mind and its traits, not realising that it is not us. By being aware of the ego, we are able to stand back and disengage from its activity and the more we do this, the less power the ego mind will have over us, until eventually it is dissolved like salt in warm water.

## Intelligence and knowledge

The basis of what the ego thrives off of is power and control. Sometimes the ego can pride itself on intelligence and knowledge, on being 'smart.' It becomes another form of identity for the ego to cling to. It may say 'I am more intelligent than most people,' and take much pride in that or it may downplay others that it perceives not to be as intelligent as it is. Some people spend much time trying to increase their intelligence with conceptual knowledge, and the ego does this to inflate its identity, and to demonstrate 'how intelligent and powerful I am.' The ego often can become very arrogant, due to its belief in its own intelligence, and believe that it 'knows best' because of it. To disassociate from this form of ego, just simply appreciate the intelligence that is there and use it as and when needed, but do not attempt to gain a sense of self from it. Recognise that which stands prior to intellectual and conceptual intelligence.

## Money and Achievements

The ego can often identify with money and achievements. It assumes many conditionings and one of the greatest conditionings we have, states that success is usually measured by how much money or material possessions we may have gathered. So the ego often latches onto this idea and develops a sense of self and pride in it.

Sometimes people may boast about how much money they make, or how much money they have in the bank, they may display and/or show-off their wealth to others, to try and impress them. They may drive around in expensive sports cars or wear expensive clothes as a sign to everyone of how much money they have or how successful they are. The ego feeds off the responses of others, and so usually does those things to elicit a response. Good attention is always preferred, but a negative response is often acceptable too, as any attention is better than no attention to the ego. It prefers any kind of response to no response at all. Sometimes, when the ego receives no response it may say indignantly, 'do you not know who I am!' This is because its identity has been hurt in some way as maybe it is used to people always responding in a certain fashion. We can sometimes observe this with certain celebrities or wealthy people. They become so used to having their egos boosted all of the time by others, that when someone fails to praise them, it is possible to see the ego's reaction. It may think, 'how dare they, I am used to better treatment than this.' The ego wants what it wants, and when it does not get it, it becomes upset, and will often foist the blame upon the world and other people. This type of blaming action can happen the same in an individual, family, community or nation. It is apparent in all the conflicts we see within the world, both large and small.

The ego may also look to show off its achievements, and through this an enlarged sense of ego may arise, as the ego will often regard itself as better than others or others in its field of achievement, as the ego is always comparing itself to others. It may say to others, 'look what I have achieved in the world, no-one else has achieved what I have.' It is not that money and achievements should not be enjoyed in the world, they should, and they should be enjoyed consciously. The only difference between the ego and the conscious self in this regard, is that the ego has its identity embedded within it, whilst the conscious self, realises that what it has or what it does is unimportant, and so remains unidentified whilst at the same time fully enjoying those experiences. In that sense, it is completely free.

The ego may even be present in the good things that we do for others. For example, once again we may often see so-called 'celebrities,' who will donate money or do good things for charity, but often do it in a very public way so that everyone will see what they have done and then praise or think highly of them. This is another way by which the ego boosts its personal sense of identity and feel-good factor of itself and also to gain other peoples appreciation in the process. When an act of kindness is performed in this way, it is not from selflessness or altruism, it is done in order that the ego self can derive something from it for itself. Anyone who truly wishes to make a difference for others will not seek praise, indeed they will not expect anything in return at all and to them, the satisfaction of helping people is reward enough. There are some celebrities who work in this way, but we never hear about them because their deeds have not been made public. They do not do it for attention or praise, they do it simply because it is was the 'right thing to do,' and many of the great, historical Saints behaved in this selfless way too.

The ego tends to cling to its past achievements and boast about them, constantly living in the past, yet looking towards the future for happiness. The purpose of this boasting about past achievements is that the ego is ultimately trying to impress other people and each time it does this it gains a little more energy with which to enlarge itself further. Every good impression made is like more money in the 'ego bank.' The ego wants to be special, it wants to show its uniqueness, to show that it is better than others and every time it has an opportunity to show this, it will.

Another tactic that the ego uses to boost itself, is 'name-dropping,' the mentioning of famous people with whom it may have interacted or even—what is somewhat more popular these days, the showing of 'selfies,' photographs taken with someone who is considered important. Associating itself with someone that people will be in awe of, so that others may see them as more important is a way for the psychological ego self to identify and distinguish itself in the eyes of others because if it is seen with important people, then by association it will be regarded as important too. We have all met people who cannot resist telling you which celebrities they have met, telling the story as if they are an actual friend of this person.

One of the jobs I used to do, was working in security as a doorman on pub and nightclub doors, and it was quite common that people denied entry would try to convince me to let them in. Often they would begin to 'name-drop,' naming someone who was considered a local celebrity in the hope of associating themselves with this person, presumably so that I would say, 'oh sorry, why didn't you say that before?' and let them in. This is another sneaky tactic of the ego, used not just in those situations, but in everyday situations in order to impress people and to create a greater sense of self-importance.

## Race and Religion

A very powerful type of ego identity that traps many people is identifying themselves with a particular race or religion. When a person describes themselves as for example, 'black,' 'white,' 'Spanish' or 'Asian,' it is because they are fixated upon identification with the external body. Race and ethnicity is a very bodily-superficial thing. In relation to the true self which ultimately stands beyond the body and mind, a certain body or racial type is no different than what one brand of car is to another. Most people know not to identify with their vehicles (although some may do,) because they see that it is superficial to them, as is the body to the pure conscious self. It sees that the body is no more than a temporary package that will soon expire and be left behind, so identifying with it restricts us to the level of the body, and when trapped on this level suffering will be inevitable, as whatever happens to the body and is said about the body will bring inner suffering.

When the ego identifies itself as being of one specific race, it automatically creates a barrier between it and other races, and is one of the many ways that wars and conflicts are generated. The ideal way, is to put culture and race second and humanity first and to put individual family second and the human family first. One day it may be that humanity will have to be second also, and a 'universal family first,' but let us firstly achieve the former before concerning about that.

The ego will also often cling to a particular belief system or religion. Mind often identifies itself with its own beliefs, and when assuming this identity, it develops a sense of pride in it, a sense of right and wrong that its beliefs and religion are right, and yours are wrong. Through the ego, many people are trying to 'find themselves,' and they often come to believe that this 'self' which they believe they are, is contained within a belief system and that we must 'believe in something.' But a belief is not truth and never can be truth, (see the section on belief vs. knowing), and so the ego will attach itself to a belief system to give its sense of identity something more substantial on which to hold. The ego ultimately holds onto so many things in the world of form, and has so many identities and the reason it does this is because of its fear of extinction. The ego fears death and loss of identity more than anything, and so the only way it thinks it can hold onto its identity, is to identify with as many things as possible, to cling to as many things as possible. It feels less fear when it does this, but the identity and clinging comes at a price, and that is the price of those identities being threatened or lost, and that is why the ego will always fight to protect what it believes it is and in what it believes. This defensiveness is the ultimate cause of all conflicts we see, race against race, religion against religion, partner against partner and ultimately, one belief system against another.

# Complaining

Have you ever noticed in yourself or others the tendency to complain? That is the ego in action. Here in England we have a reputation for complaining about things as a nation, and most people almost have a sense of pride in it, yet complaints are made but very little is done to remedy them. This is a classic trait of what is known as 'victim identity.' When we complain, and continue to complain constantly, it arises from a sense of victimhood and powerlessness and may also at times be through jealousy or maybe even just through unhappiness. So much time and energy is spent on complaining, it can be exhausting, but yet many people constantly complain, sometimes regarding the smallest things.

When complaining arises from a sense of victimhood, it is because we feel powerless to do anything about that which we are complaining and so we may vent our frustration to other people. This also acts as an encouragement to others to agree with us, in order to validate our opinions and affirm them as correct. There are regular comedy shows on TV that satirise news and political issues and we love to watch those shows because it provides us with a way of 'laughing-off' our frustrations. However, we may indeed laugh, but then we often do nothing about it, and simply forget it all afterwards. Nevertheless, in an ideal world, complaining is not a positive course of action. Acceptance of the situation, followed by an attempt to deal with it without frustration, is the way of the truly awakened. This derives from the acceptance of what life has brought us right now in the present moment, to accept what the 'grand intelligence' has bestowed upon us and then to address any issues in the best way we can.

When we struggle against the moment we lose the energy to make a real change. When we respect what the moment has brought us, we will have lots of energy and an alignment with life enabling us to do all we can to change it.

Another common reason for constant complaint is jealousy. Sometimes when others are doing well, or possess something that we wish that we had, the mind compares itself to that person and is reminded that it is inferior in some way and so we become upset and find fault or complain about the one whom we believe is in a 'better' position than ourselves. Maybe you have done it yourself or have been around others that have spoken negatively about a person who is not there and complain about them or what they are doing, when instead they could use all that energy taken-up in focusing on someone else, to actually improve their own life situation, or to discover themselves more deeply. 'Where attention goes, energy flows,' as they say.

The most basic foundation of all complaint derives from unhappiness. When we are unhappy or feel uneasy within our bodies, we tend to take our 'revenge' on the external world and the ego will always apportion the blame outside of itself and towards others. For example, you may have noticed in yourself or in observing others that when we are unhappy, it just takes the slightest negative incident for us to snap and lose our temper, but conversely, when we are feeling happy or when others around us are happy, it needs something much more extreme to break us from that sense of happiness. So, when things are not going the ego's way, it tends to become unhappy, and when it is unhappy, it complains more. Try to be aware of this in a non-judgmental way, in both yourself and in others. The True Self minds neither, its happiness does not depend on what happens outside of it, nor does it become unhappy by what happens outside of it, but treats both the same, and it itself remains the same, because it is the unaffected silent watcher.

## Addicted to Drama

One of the most destructive traits of the ego that is often dismissed as harmless, is the addiction to negativity and drama. This addiction is like a drip-feed of energy for the ego, and this energy seems to be accumulated in the body at an emotional level.

Maybe you have noticed within your own experience or through witnessing others that some people seem to get a thrill out of drama, conflict and negativity? It seems to be feeding them in some way and sometimes the ego becomes addicted to this negative energy. You may know someone who has this ego trait. It seems as though they have to have their 'daily fix' of drama, and are constantly searching for negativity in order that they may thrive upon it in some way. This is why the tabloid press, certain TV programmes and 'celebrity' magazines are so popular, because they constantly feed the ego with tales of the extreme drama, albeit often untrue, in other people's lives. But this power-boost for the ego comes at a price for the body and our consciousness. As the ego grows stronger, our intelligence decreases and the body suffers energetically, because real intelligence comes from our level of awareness and our health derives from the quality of the energy it contains. Awareness grows in direct proportion to any decrease in the ego. Just like clouds blocking the sun, when the clouds dissolve, the pure light of awareness shines through brightly and strongly and the more the ego disperses, the more that awareness thrives and this feeds the body with higher vibrational, nourishing energy.

As a practice, try to become aware of this need for drama and conflict arising in yourself or in others. Do not judge yourself or others personally, do not judge it to be right or wrong, just notice and be aware of this behaviour, much like a scientist observing an experiment in a laboratory. If this urge arises within yourself, notice how the body feels as it builds, notice how your body and mind is being boosted in anticipation of receiving the energy of drama. Does it feel pleasant or does it have a more dense and anxious quality to it? Notice in other people how an energetic 'switch' occurs when their ego senses drama. You may also notice their body language become more pronounced when they are speaking negatively about others. Once again, make no judgement as to the rights or wrongs of this behaviour, as that would mean that your ego has also become active, just pure neutral and curious observation of the phenomena is all that is required. Become a master of detecting the ego in yourself and others. The more you observe, the more conscious you will become.

## Prejudice and Judgment

Prejudice means 'pre-judgment,' or forming an opinion before becoming aware of the relevant facts of a case and this is a powerful trait of the conditioned ego. Maybe you have noticed this in your own mind, or in witnessing others, that often, people will judge without knowing the full facts. This is often apparent in the media. Public figures or celebrities will immediately be judged by the media and therefore the majority of the public, but yet in reality none of us were actually there to know whether what is being said is actually true or not and the mind then bases its judgement on hearsay and assumptions. Yet these supposed truths are planted in people's minds and often an opinion is formed without knowledge of the full facts. This is a good example of the irrationality and illogicality of the mind, deciding something based on no direct experience of it and very little, if any, facts.

This happens in everyday life too. We may find ourselves with a group of friends or family members, and they may be speaking about someone, speaking about what this person is supposed to have done, and they may end up judging, criticising and forming opinions of them without any real evidence of anything, only hearsay and gossip. The ego mind loves to judge because it loves drama, it loves to denigrate others to boost itself and this is one of the reasons that the media is so popular. The mind loves gossip, it loves to be involved in other people's business and pick it apart, like a vulture picking at its dead prey. There is some kind of guilty pleasure behind this need to judge and criticise others, and it is an addictive kind of energy that feeds the ego. This is the reason why TV dramas are so popular. It is an interesting phenomenon that certain people who for example, avidly watch TV 'soap operas' and the like, actually send hate mail, death threats and sometimes even physically confront the actors. They seem to have an inability to separate fiction from reality. People will also become angry, judgmental and take part in heated conversations about fictional TV characters as though they are real people doing real things. This is a result of the extreme 'craziness' of the ego. It sees what is not there, believes what is untrue and severely criticises and chastises others, in order to make itself feel better.

## Personal Judgements

But, what of a judgement of something about which we have the true facts? The ego mind is judgemental to a personal degree, but the true self is much more discerning and not 'personal' at all. For example, if we were to order food in a restaurant, and it is in some way unsatisfactory, the ego mind will immediately take the opportunity to complain, and not necessarily simply about the food, it may often make the complaint personal, directing its anger towards the individual who served them. The ego always makes things personal because it is itself a personal identity, a personal sense of self, and so it views everything on a 'personal' level, as if the order was wrong on purpose. The ego may say, 'why have they done this to me?' Or 'how dare they do this to me?' In other words, the ego reacts and takes offense because it takes everything personally.

But just as the ego always makes things personal, the true conscious self has no personal identity, it is just pure life itself, and so the true self may react completely differently or even not react at all. It still recognises that the order is wrong, but will approach the staff calmly and ask for them to correct it without taking offence or viewing it at a personal level. This is the conscious way. Indeed, why complain and get upset at all? The restaurant staff did not mean to upset us personally, it was just an accident, so why make an issue out of it, and why cause ourselves unnecessary stress or anger? It makes no sense at all to do so, it would be best to simply ask them to correct the order. And then, if we do this in a calm and reasonable manner, we may notice that something interesting happens, and that is that they will be more than willing to help us and may apologise.

Often, when we take things personally and try to blame someone, we only serve to cause a reaction in their own ego, which results in resistance, and this may escalate into conflict, one ego versus another. So the lesson is that it would be best just stick to the facts without making anything too personal. Here are the two possible reactions to the above situation. Decide which one you feel is most appropriate...

> *"Oh great! They have messed my order up again! Now I will have to take it back, what an inconvenience, I've not got the time for this! I bet they did this on purpose. I'm going to give them a piece of my mind!"*
>
> Or...
>
> *"Oh dear, they have given me the wrong meal. Someone must have made a mistake so I had better send it back and ask them to change it."*

I am sure you agree that the second option above is likely to be much more effective in our objective of having them replace our incorrect order and in addition will cause much less, or even no conflict at all. The first example is an unconscious way of responding to a situation and the second is a conscious one. The more we act consciously in all of life's situations, and refrain from making them personal, the more conscious, peaceful and awake we will become, and we may even notice that life becomes much less tense, once we drop the ego. Try to reflect upon the many situations in which the ego mind may judge certain people or incidents personally.

## Television and Ego-Conditioning

One form of conditioning that adds more complexities to the ego, comes from an invasive box that sits in the corner of most people's rooms, the TV. For sure, the TV is one of the most polarised devices in the world. It has connected the majority of the world, providing the ability to communicate with millions worldwide, to keep people informed of world events of which they would probably be otherwise unaware. It has given people access to more information and knowledge, but the TV also has a potential dark side, a side that manifests itself either intentionally or unintentionally, and that is the conditioning of nations and individuals.

What we must first understand is how TV affects most people's minds, whether they are aware of it or not. The brain operates in several different ways using, gamma, beta, alpha, theta and delta waves and these brain states are activated for different functions. For example, delta is active when we are in deep sleep and alpha opens up the subconscious mind. In alpha state we become very relaxed and we become more accepting of what we see, hear and experience. The TV has been proven to induce an alpha state of mind after about ten minutes of watching, for most people. What this means is that when we watch TV, without knowing it, we are absorbing what we see and hear and are influenced by the beliefs and opinions being expressed, without questioning them. When in the alpha state, the mind takes information and filters it straight through to the subconscious mind, which means that the paradigm of the world being portrayed is more likely to be accepted as real and true. So, what is the issue with this exactly? Well, I am not sure if you have watched any TV lately, but it is filled with some very extreme material; wars, violence, murders, rapes, and people being abused, physically and mentally, lied to and cheated and all forms of suffering, terrorism and conflict on the news programmes, twenty four hours a day. There are also films containing extreme and traumatic violence and revenge, horror movies with blood guts and extreme fear and whether we realise it or not, all of these things are influencing our minds in some way, some more obviously than others. TV also renders the subconscious mind more receptive to any other opinions, ideas and beliefs being portrayed, which means that many of the beliefs and ideas in our minds are not original, but have been taken on by us.

When we see violence and conflict every day, we begin to believe it is normal and then slowly but surely we may even begin to exhibit some of these behaviours ourselves without realising, or become less willing to do anything about the injustices we see in the world, as a result. There are many young women and teenage girls out there, that emulate certain celebrities that take-off their clothes in an attempt to become famous, and many young men that want to be the macho-man in the films that gets all the girls and that attacks all his rivals to do so. It may initially sound a little farfetched to say this, but if we look closely we see that so many people are influenced without being fully aware of it and are mimicking others they have seen, or are adopting particular beliefs that the TV promotes. For example, it is common knowledge that many years ago there were huge, expensive ad campaigns promoting smoking to be cool, sexy and the thing to do, and so many people began to smoke because of it. They were influenced by the idea and so changed themselves, their beliefs and actions, purely based on what the media and advertising told them. Today, we are bombarded with so many advertisements and messages in our media, from so many sources, that it is an absolute 'mine-field,' for the mind to negotiate. These advertisers and media companies are masters of influencing the human psyche, to sell an idea or product and huge budgets are available for discovering the best ways to sell products or ideas to the masses. We must stay vigilant if we are to remain uninfluenced by all this. As we become more awake and conscious, it becomes impossible for us to be swayed by an outside influence, should we choose not to be.

There are many psychological experts that now recognise that the TV and media can have a massive influence on affecting what we believe and what we do. As we develop with this massive influence of conditioning from the TV and media, it adds into the 'shopping basket' of the ego identity and only serves to confuse us further, restricting us even more from accessing the true, conscious self, as it constantly dictates what to believe and not believe about the world and ourselves. All of this conditioning only serves to confuse and prevents the true self within from being realised. So one of the best pieces of advice I could give to someone who wants to break free from the ego and conditioning to realise themselves, is to turn off the TV. It can create a strong gravitational pull towards it, and can become very addictive. Have you felt and/or been aware of this?

So, the message is... spend less time focused on the TV and turn your attention towards yourself. Become curious of who is there, who is behind your mind, who it is within 'you,' having your experiences and who you really are. And can you then locate and rest within that one?

Spend time in silence with yourself, in yourself... in order to know yourself.

The TV portrays a particular, pre-determined and engineered paradigm of the world and most people, whether consciously or unconsciously believe and absorb the majority of what is shown to them on TV. What most of us have forgotten, is that ultimately TV is entertainment, and TV is a business and all business needs profit. So the truth is that all TV programmes need good ratings and audience retention to keep making money. Most of us maybe forget this, and do not realise the implications of this, or that what we are watching on TV is not reality, but a kind of manufactured and exaggerated idea of reality.

This even applies to news programmes. In the UK, most news programmes begin with a loud introduction, such as a bong or gong sound. This immediately draws our attention and psychologically tells us that what we are about to see is extremely serious. In fact almost 100% of news stories are very negative, all 'doom and gloom,' and as we watch this day after day, we subconsciously or consciously generate a belief that the world is a dark and terrible place and that life is one endless round of negativity and suffering. This feeds into the ego mind and often either hardens the ego to become less empathetic or drives the ego into more of a softened, victim state, where we feel powerless and fearful of the world. Spend time in silence, and in nature, and we will naturally become more introspective and connected. Once we become more aware, we could sit in a room with one hundred TVs and not be affected or influenced by it. But it helps in the beginning to distance ourselves from it and thereby re-establish a more conscious state of being. However, if you are unable to drag yourself away from the TV, then there is still something you can do in order to expand awareness...

## TV and Meditation

So you may wish to be rid of the TV and watch it less, but have a family or live with house mates who watch it constantly.

But what if you could use the TV to serve you in awakening...?

There are two ways that this can be done, and both are fun and expansive. Firstly we can use the TV to explore how the ego operates in other people. For example, when watching a documentary, news or live entertainment programme, observe people's behaviours and reactions, and notice any ego traits they may exhibit, based on what they say and how they react to things. For example, do they take things personally, become angry, brag about themselves or take sides against another? As you observe their behaviour, remember to not judge them personally as individuals, instead just watch them in the same detached way that a doctor would examine a patient, impartially and non-judgementally. You can also do this in your everyday life of course; observe your own mind and its reactions and to watch other people's reactions. This is a great way to watch the TV as you will be more conscious and vigilant and will therefore not be unconsciously influenced by it.

The second way to use TV for awakening, is to meditate upon it. Yes, really! What you must first understand is that there are two main types of meditation that most refer to, one is non-directive meditation (this is pure meditation), and the other is directive meditation, this means to place your attention on one or a number of things in particular.

So we can use directive meditation upon anything, including the TV and here is what we should do. Firstly, close your eyes and be comfortable...

Now, as you sit there with the TV on and your eyes closed, just allow yourself to completely relax... relax all of your body...

Let go of all tension... And allow your eyes to retreat comfortably into the blackness of your mind...

Now, very subtly begin to become aware of the noise the TV is making. As you listen to the noise, begin to tune-in to what is being said or what sounds are playing. Just listen... do not judge or think about it, just simply listen and try to follow the sounds that emanate from it.

Listen to the TV in the same way that you would listen to a piece of music. Really tune-in and listen...

You should not think about or judge what you hear...you are not concerned with the information or content being heard...just pay attention to that sound, the sound of every word spoken, the sound of every note of music being played and the sound of every noise heard...

Stay relaxed, meditating on the sound of the TV for however long it feels comfortable...

I used to love and enjoy this so much. I would relax, meditating upon the TV and melt away into the depths of my being and feel so very refreshed and relaxed when I opened my eyes. It is a great way to generate more meditation time, time that you would not usually have spare. Use all these moments of waiting and doing nothing as an opportunity to enjoy meditation, eyes closed inside your own Self, being aware of your own body and paying attention to all the sounds around, with your eyes closed. If you use your time wisely, you can make much progress in a very short period of time, but you must love it, and you must reach a point where you cannot wait to connect with yourself even more deeply. The deeper you go inside yourself the more quickly you will awake.

## The Art of No Reaction

The ego mind is a very reactive entity and it has several in-built responses and reactions. We have all on many different levels been conditioned to react to particular situations in a certain way. For example, when we play a game and lose or our goals are not met, many people react with disappointment or may even get angry. These responses may originate from being taught as a young child that getting what you want means you are a better person, in other words, that winning is good and losing is bad. These are just simply ideas that have been instilled into us. Getting what we want or not is neither good nor bad, it is just purely what it is, nothing more, and nothing less. It is only the mind that will label it as good or bad, or right or wrong, but yet the ego mind reacts in one of the above ways. However, the true self just sees 'what is,' and is neutral and truthful, and offers no mental interpretation of an event. So, in this sense your true nature is non-reactive, it does not judge or attach a meaning to what has happened, it just remains a silent neutral watcher to 'what is.'

So a beautiful art we can learn is the practice of 'non-reaction.' When we do not react to life's events, we remain peaceful and untouched, but when we react to those events we will become lost in unconsciousness and become unhappy. It disturbs the natural, inner-peace that stands in the place of fully awakened neutrality, so the test is, that when confronted with all potentially reactive situations, see if you can remain a neutral observer of what is taking place. If you lose a game of chess, observe how the mind reacts... and just remain as an observer, do not react to it. What this practice teaches us, is to curb and tame the reactive forces within us that causes us pain and our natural peace to be disturbed.

The more we do not react but instead watch all reactions that manifest in the mind and body, the more conscious and peaceful we will become, until eventually we will realise that we remain peaceful in all situations—even the most challenging ones.

## The Unconsciousness of the Ego

The ego is unconscious because it is asleep to itself. Conditioning is lost in conditioning and ego is lost in ego and is a law unto itself when it is not being observed. However, the very act of observation instantaneously renders it accountable, because observing it makes what was unconscious, fully conscious. Most people are lost in a personal identity, believing that *they* are the thought formations in the mind, and it is this identity of being thought itself, that forces the conscious self to go around in circles, unable to see consciously and clearly. The mind is like the middle of a vast, deep, dark forest, whereas the conscious self is perched upon the hill and able to see the bright sky above. When we are in the dark, we fumble around, tripping over ourselves and this is the mind's unconsciousness. To be unconscious, literally means we are not fully aware of what we are doing. For example, have you ever had the experience of rushing out to work say, and then suddenly wondered with dread, if you left the gas on at home, or if you left the lights on, or that you forgot something that you needed to take with you?

This usually happens because we are experiencing moments of unconsciousness. What tends to happen, is that we are busy 'thinking' about where we need to be and what we have to do when we get there, that we give very little attention to what we are doing before we leave. In other words, what we are doing in the present moment. When we become lost in thought, thinking about the future or reflecting on the past, we cease to pay full attention to this moment and to our true self in that moment. This is when mistakes and accidents happen; this is when we become unhappy and restless, because our attention is elsewhere other than right here and now.

To wake-up is to be conscious in each moment, to be ever-conscious in all situations and experiences, and if this sounds a difficult task to the mind, if the mind says, 'how can I be conscious all of the time, It sounds like a lot of work,' the good news is that we only ever have to be fully conscious, one moment at a time, as life does not throw moments at you in bunches, they only come one at a time. And all that is needed is to be conscious in one moment at a time, starting from now.

## Conclusion

When we are aware of these ego traits in ourselves and others, without personal judgement or a judgement of right or wrong, we can be aware of them as they occur and practice refraining from these traits, as a type of spiritual practice. Each time we are aware and disengage from those various functionings of the ego and watch how they manifest, they become a little weaker and our power of observation becomes stronger as we become more conscious. Eventually, the ego will wilt and wither under the intensity of our awareness, it will progressively die and what will be left is the freedom of a more expansive and spacious awareness. We will become free of ego, and less ego means less suffering and more peace, joy and truth.

## Who are you?

*"My true self is free. It cannot be contained." Marcus Aurelius*

## The Secret Self

As previously mentioned, who you 'are' cannot ultimately be explained by words, but words can certainly act as guides towards that which is wordless. You are not your body, brain, personality or the mind (thought processes), so what is your essential nature?

The following story illustrates the point...

> *"The king, interested in the teachings of Zen, approached a renowned master and said 'I want you to tell me the nature of Zen in one sentence.' The master calmly replied 'I can tell you in one word' the king said with interest, 'yes please do tell me.'*
>
> *So the Zen master wrote it on a piece of paper upon which he had written 'awareness' and then passed it to the king. Slightly puzzled, the king asked, 'Can you please elaborate?' So the Zen master took back the piece of paper and wrote, 'awareness awareness' and then passed it back to the king.*
>
> *The king looked at the piece of paper again and said in bewilderment 'Yes, but what does awareness, awareness mean?' So the master took back the piece of paper and wrote 'awareness, awareness means AWARENESS.'*

The closest we can come to explain the nature of who we are, is to use the word 'awareness.'

Are you aware right now?

Before your mind responds 'yes,' please take the time to check that you are truly aware, just for these exercises, as the mind has a tendency to bypass things without paying full attention to them. So please do that now, see if you are aware right now...

> *Now take the time to see if you can discover whom it is that is aware that you are aware...*
>
> *Allow me to ask you another question; are you having an experience right now? Please take the time to check...*
>
> *Try to be aware of who is having the experience. Who is the experiencer...?*

So there is intelligence present and this intelligence within you is aware and it is also aware that it is experiencing its own existence. I feel that the one certain thing that we can say about our own life experience is, 'I exist.' The deeper we delve into it, the more we realise that everything else is debateable.

We will explore these questions later in more depth in chapter 12 on Self Investigation & Transcending Limiting Beliefs.

So we can say that our nature is one of awareness and awareness just is a forever present reality, but do not allow your mind to hold this word 'awareness' and believe that it fully comprehends what it is, that it somehow explains what you are. That can only be known through the actual seeing and experiencing of it, the experience of you, and so the foundational key of moving deeper and deeper in to our true nature of awareness, is to become more and more self-aware in each moment until all unconsciousness is gone and only awareness remains. In this way you will become more and more established in the observer consciousness that you are, fully aware of each breath, of each passing thought, of each current experience and moment and each action and movement we make, so that the whole of our life becomes one continuing conscious experience filled with joy, love and laughter.

Awareness is synonymous with 'observer.' There is an observer within each one of us that is able to watch thoughts, emotions and sensations without being lost or fully engaged in those thoughts feeling and sensations. This is our true self and the more it observes the thought process in the mind, the more connected with your awareness you will become. With time, this awareness in you will become more expansive, the mind will become quieter and thoughts will take second place to the silent awareness that you are, whilst thoughts will become a faint noise in the background.

As the thought process quietens, you will find yourself ever more conscious of the present moment; your mind will be much clearer and more focussed and as a direct result of the volume of the thinking mind being reduced, more pleasant feelings and a sense of grounded-ness will pervade your being. You will then become more 'alive' because your attention will be shared more evenly throughout your body, as opposed to being simply concentrated on constant thinking. In fact, 'joy' will become your default nature.

At the very least, 'peace' will always be your natural state of being, no matter with what life circumstances you may be confronted. So be aware and every aspect of our creative endeavours will then be performed with care, intensity and to the benefit of all concerned, with our full potential being fulfilled, squeezing the last, small drop out of every life experience. You will feel as alive as it is possible to feel, in the here and now.

With each passing moment as we become self-aware, it is as though we are teasing open the gates of the infinite intelligence, in order that we might feel more at home within. Our inner sight and self-observation propels us and merges us more deeply within ourselves.

So go now and chase away the night and shadows of the mind so that only light may be seen and felt, so, as each moment of self-awareness happens, another small cloud in the sky dissolves and the light of the sun little by little, shines through more brightly, casting aside the darkness.

Awareness, awareness, awareness, now, now and now.

## #3 Practice being aware

*"Spiritual practice involves being constantly aware"* Shri Radhe Maa

I already sense the question ... *'How can I practice being aware if you say that we are always already aware?'*

Good question! Maybe the answer is to practice being conscious that you are aware. Please try this exercise right now. Try as hard as you can to not be aware of anything.

*Did you succeed in not being aware?*

No, I am sure you did not succeed. It is nigh on impossible to not be aware because we are always aware of something, be it thoughts, feelings or situations. But are you aware that you are aware? Very few people can manage to do this without practice. It is, put simply, turning your awareness in on itself, in other words being completely self-aware.

You see, you are always aware, it's just that your awareness seems to get lost in the masses of 'traffic' constantly passing through the mind, in memories and imaginings. It is just as though your awareness is being 'dragged along for the ride' in your constant pondering of all the possible things that may happen tomorrow, next week or even next year. There is also a tendency for the mind to drift away into memories of previous experiences, of things people said or did to you, or of certain events that happened. Your mind does this because it has become an unconscious habit to do so, in autopilot mode as it were and so you must maintain control by remaining conscious of this possibility at all times. Indeed in order to change this unconscious habit of compulsive thinking, we must become more and more self-aware.

A good way to achieve this is by becoming more aware of the body and mind; what the Buddhist tradition refers to as 'mindfulness,' or 'mindful awareness.'

## Mindfulness Practice

*'When walking walk, when eating eat.' Zen proverb*

Mindfulness practice is not just about being aware of the body, it's also about being aware of the breath and emotions, and being aware of the thoughts that flit through your mind. It is really all about being totally aware of yourself in the 'here and now' and when you are fully consciousness of yourself in the moment, you are practicing mindfulness.

## Attention and Awareness

*"Mindfulness means paying attention in a particular way: on purpose, in the present moment, non-judgementally"- Jon Kabat-Zinn*

What is the difference between attention and awareness?

Attention is simply the concentration and focus of your awareness into a certain direction. Attention requires some effort as it is an initiated action.

Awareness is different, it is a subtle effortless noticing, and we will speak more about awareness towards the end of this chapter.

When most people start-out on the spiritual path or the path of awakening, much attention and effort is required to break the habit and the heavy 'pull' of the mind into constant thinking. Sometimes the mind has such a huge 'pull' and is so busy that it requires some training of the mind and lessening of its load to create enough space to allow the subtly of awareness to shine through. When engaging in mindfulness practice as laid out below, it is important to start with close attention to each practice, not excessive effort, but enough effort to purposely draw our attention in a particular direction. The mind needs to be trained to resist the old reactive forces and habits and to cultivate our attention to focus on mindfulness in the present moment.

Imagine that the mind is a small baby. When the baby is laid on its back being changed, she will tend to move one way and then another and will not sit still and simply allow us to do whatever is necessary, and so we must gently re-position her. She may then do this again and again and so we must patiently bring her back until we succeed. Eventually, after much practice, the baby will learn to stay put and not move around and the mind, when trained, is very much the same. Most people's minds have been allowed to become unruly and to wander wherever and whenever they want. So much so, that the mind has become the master and we, its servant, but through training we will 'tame' the mind and bring back order to chaos, as we re-assume the position of the master with the mind as our servant. Through the use of attention we apply a gentle force to bring the mind back onside. This makes it easier to move to the next stage of effortless meditation and living.

## The Body

Let us firstly talk more about the practice of being aware of the body. By becoming more aware of our body, an immediate shift can take place. This shift moves our attention from being lost in thinking and concentrates it more into our bodies. If you fully concentrate on your foot or both feet for instance, it is almost impossible to have full attention of your feet whilst at the same time being aware of your thoughts. If for example, you focus one hundred percent of your attention on one of your feet and the sensations therein, notice how the mind seems to subside. Please try that now...

In order to make induce consciousness of any part of the body, we must first focus our attention upon it, much like shining a flashlight into a dark recess. We may do this with all parts of the body, but try beginning with those places that are most sensitive, such as the feet and hands or the lips and tongue. Simply bring your full attention to these areas without judgement or mental self-comment or any mental dialogue such as, 'oh my lips are itching, I wish they would stop itching, this is so annoying etc.'

If you become entangled in this type of mental 'tennis' whilst concentrating on any particular area of the body, then this means that you have lapsed back into the thought processes of the mind and therefore are not being mindful. Instead you must remain in pure, silent awareness, lost within the feeling or sensation. To help with this, you could repeat to yourselves 'lips...lips...lips...' whilst you observe and feel the lips completely.

## The Breath

*"Feelings come and go like clouds in a windy sky. Conscious breathing is my anchor." Thich Nhat Hanh*

Let us now discuss being mindful of our breathing. If there is one thing we can rely upon to always be there whilst we are in this body, it is the constant movement caused by our breathing reflex. The breath is the very thing that ties us to the body itself, as without it we would immediately leave the body. The inhalation and exhalation of breath also connects us to all other beings and all other lifeforms. Just pause and contemplate for a few seconds on the fact that we are all sharing this resource—the air we all breathe—and every single one of us not only shares but totally depends on this gift of breath on our planet.

So, because the activity of the breath is always present, we can very easily use it as a point of focus for meditation and mindfulness. The very second we start to become aware of the breath and its movement, we start to become more aware and mindful. The very essence of mindful awareness is to be conscious of ourselves in the moment but for the majority of people, breathing is a totally unconscious process. Most people breathe in a very shallow way because they hardly ever pay any attention at all to their breathing and often tend to take the breath for granted, immediately relegating it to autopilot mode. The price of the breath becoming unconscious is that we often breathe incorrectly, which in-turn affects our health, our nervous system and our brain-functions. However, when we breathe correctly, we oxygenate our blood and therefore send more oxygen to the brain and this extra oxygen in the brain helps to bring about a greater clarity of mind and focus. This then helps relax our nervous system and the body, because our brain is connected to the entire nervous system via the spinal cord. These are just some of the physical benefits of correct breathing but there are several spiritual benefits too.

One spiritual benefit is the ability to be more 'grounded' in the present moment whilst remaining in-touch with the body. In the yogic traditions, the breath moving through the body is known as 'prana,' which is life-force energy and in some Chinese traditions it is known by the different name of 'chi.' This life-force energy can be directed and has been used traditionally for healing purposes and to detoxify the body and mind. So, if you had to choose one element only in order to become more healthy and mindful of yourself in the moment, then mindfulness of the breath and the movement of the breath would be that one aspect. As soon as we become fully conscious of the breath and its activity, we are immediately transported into the 'now' moment.

Please try this breathing practice...

> *Ideally find somewhere to sit comfortably. Sit with your back straight and feet planted firmly on the floor at a 90 degree angle (you can also sit in the upright cross legged position.) Close your eyes and begin to pay attention to the breath. Are you breathing? The mind will say 'yes of course I am' and so often dismiss the question but please take the time to become aware of the actual experience of breathing. Do that now please, become aware of the breathing taking place...*
>
> *Notice how your chest rises and falls with each inhalation and exhalation of the breath...*
>
> *Do not try to force the breath, instead just allow it to happen naturally whilst you pay attention to it...*
>
> *Be aware of the air as it passes in through your nostrils on the in-breath and how the air passes your lips or nostrils on the out-breath...*
>
> *Each time you breathe out, allow your body to relax more and more. Allow yourself to watch and feel the breath for a couple of minutes or so...*

Christopher J. Smith

# The Five Senses

*'Lose your mind and come to your senses'*

We have five senses of the body, smell, taste, touch, sight and hearing and when we pay full attention to our senses, our awareness becomes greatly magnified. Imagine that you had a volume control for each of the five senses, like those on a radio or CD player, what would happen if you could crank-up those controls on each of the senses, to its greatest level? Your whole life-experience would be enriched to the peak of its capabilities. For example, your taste buds would be enhanced to such a point whereby each mouthful of food and drink with all of its exquisite flavours and textures, would be experienced to the full.

The sense of smell would be heightened to the point where we could enjoy to the maximum, a multiplicity of fragrant aromas of food and beautiful perfumes, flowers and freshly cut grass in the summer. Our ears would be attuned to appreciate each individual element of the various sounds created by all the individual instruments in any piece of music, especially that piece of music you love so dearly. All the sounds of nature, birdsong, the wind blowing and the sound of waves as they crash onto the beach or up against rocks, would literally become 'music to our ears.'

Imagine your sense of sight being so greatly enhanced that when you look at objects and wildlife it is as though you are seeing them for the first time with their individual colourings, so bright and vivid. You would maybe also notice for the first time, all the fine details of everything and even the spaces between them would appear beautiful. Appreciating the beauty of shapes, objects, people and nature would be a given.

And lastly, you would be able to experience in all its beauty, the gift of touch and feeling; being able to feel the ultimate sensitivity of your body and others' bodies during intimacy. You would be totally aware of the wind that blows on your face and through your hair and the feel of the grass or sand on bare feet. Imagine every single one of your senses being fully enhanced to the extent that your perception of life is completely changed and taken to another, far higher, level of experience.

Most people do not even experience as much as thirty-percent of their senses' capabilities. Why is this? Because, it requires our full attention to be absolutely aware of our senses and most people's attention-span is small and is usually tied-up in 'thinking' and paying attention to our own ''mind-chatter.' In fact their minds never stop chattering and because they identify with their mind as to who they believe 'they are,' they pay far more attention to it than is justified. More attention to the mind means less attention for the body and the five senses. 'Where attention goes, energy flows,' so the more someone continues to pay attention to the mind and its constant background babble, the more the 'mental noise' takes over their consciousness. Conversely, if they were to pay more attention to the body and the five senses, then their experience of life would become energised and so grow stronger and more magnified.

So a great way to become more mindful and divert attention away from thinking, is to become extremely aware of your senses. Start to pay more attention to the various sounds in your room, like the clock ticking or the car passing-by, outside. Or simply go and listen to the sounds of nature; listen to the wind blowing through the leaves and the birds singing. 'True' listening means just simply to listen, without thought or judgement about what it is that you are listening to. If thought and judgement is applied whilst listening to something, it means that the intellect is at work and therefore you will never really experience the sound in its purity as the layer of mental chatter will distort it. Have you ever been in a conversation with a person and they are speaking to you but you are not fully listening or focussing on what they say because you are already formulating the next thing that YOU want to say? The amazing truth is that most people do not *really* listen to each other when they are communicating, they usually only hear their mind's interpretation of what the other person is saying, hence people's true intentions will often be misconstrued.

Often, people pay very little notice to the taste of whatever they are eating. Instead they may 'drift-off' into other thoughts, in memories of the past or an imagination of tomorrow. Does this sound familiar? As a result of this, they never really experience the 'true,' full taste of their food. The harsh reality is that due to this preponderance of thinking, they are left in a kind of unreal, daydream, make-believe world and this means that they never really experience all that life truly has to offer. Hypnotised by the mind and its conditioned programs that command most of their attention, they do not realise that they are missing-out on so many pleasurable sensations in the 'real' world.

Please now try these actions...

> *As you are reading this book, become aware of how the book feels in your hands, how it feels upon your skin. Try to avoid the tendency to mentally describe it but instead, just feel it.*
>
> *Next time you sit down to eat, try to make yourself extremely mindful of each mouthful of food you chew. See if you can eat more slowly and savour each bite, whilst enjoying all of the flavours and textures of each mouthful. Be aware of and guard against the compulsion to eat too quickly and to let your mind wander as you are eating. Should you become aware that this is happening, revert back to eating more slowly and focus all of your attention upon the act of eating and the multitude of tastes and textures of your food.*

When we try to live more through our senses as opposed to living constantly through the intellect, we will soon find ourselves more 'grounded' and 'present' in the moment and as we become more established within that moment, through our senses we will rediscover our capacity to experience life in a wholly new, different way, making us feel more alive and awake than ever before. What an absolute joy it is to live and experience life through our senses and as you will discover for yourself, it is nothing short of amazing!

The lesson here is that you should practice becoming a 'walking, talking sensory organ,' experiencing life in every moment through your senses and not through the mind. Opening-up and becoming mindful of the senses is a large part of the process of Inner Awakening.

# Emotions

*'The basis of emotional stability and peace, is not to allow the outside to disturb your peace'*

Emotion is energy in motion, *E-motion*. Most people will often say that their emotions seem to emanate from nowhere and easily overwhelm them, almost as though the emotion comes upon them too quickly for them to control, such as a fast-as-lightening response to some outside stimuli or other. But actually there is an internal trigger for all our emotions and they are definitely not caused by outside stimuli as most people would tend to assume. (I will speak about this in more detail in chapter 13—Practices & Teachings for Deeper Awakening)

The reason that our emotions seem to occur so quickly and overwhelm us, is that we tend to believe that we are the emotion ourselves, but in truth, this emotion is just a response engendered by our bodies in response to a mental stimulus. Your emotions are created directly by your thoughts and these thoughts come from beliefs and conditioned thought-codes stored within the mind. Emotions can also be stimulated by specific memories of previous experiences and of course, memories are also simply thoughts. These memories may often be stored at the subconscious level which is why it is important to clear out the subconscious mind with the power of self-awareness, otherwise, there may be stored memories that will 'rear their ugly heads' when a similar situation arises.

For example, let us assume that when you were a child you had a bad experience with a roller-coaster ride. You may have been terrified by the height it attained or may have become sick with all of the sudden and rapid motion. Whatever the issue, your mind would have recorded this experience with all of its associated emotions and stored it as a 'bad' memory. Then, from that point on, every time you encounter a roller coaster or even simply think about one, you may now once again, feel the fear and nervousness associated with that memory as the emotions you felt at that time are remembered and begin to manifest themselves again. You may believe that it is the roller coaster itself causing the fear and nervousness, but in reality it is just your memory causing the uncomfortable feelings that you are now experiencing. This is just one of countless potential stored memories that we all retain within our sub-conscience throughout our lives.

This principle also applies to those who have unfortunately experienced all kinds of abuse, grief, phobias and indeed any traumas, which of course is all of us. There may also be more subtle triggers such as a song or a movie that you dislike, simply because of the bad or traumatic memories with which you associate it. It may be that you dislike a certain person because of a bad experience or relationship you had with them, but the point is that we often look at things in the 'here and now' through the lenses of the past and this creates a 'distortion' in the present moment.

So, emotions seem to overwhelm us quickly because our mind has become accustomed to responding to events and situations in a reactive and judgemental way. But as soon as we can become more mindful and aware of our emotions and our thought processes, we can then begin to gain more control and not be taken-over completely by them.

Please try this exercise...

> *Firstly, think of a situation in which you often become emotional. For example, maybe for instance a situation which always angers or frustrates. Try to remember your usual feelings at this moment in time.*
>
> *Now, try to imagine yourself dealing with and reacting to that situation in a different way. Can you see that it is possible to act differently in those instances? Your mind may resist and say that it is the only way to respond but if so, please give it a chance and try once again to imagine yourself dealing with it differently.*
>
> *Imagine dealing with it in a calmer way, being totally relaxed about the situation. How does it feel to be calm and relaxed in that situation? Please notice and remember how that feels.*

Would you prefer to be calmer and more relaxed in these situations? Of course you would. Only an insane person would choose not to be.

You see, we all have a choice as to how we react and respond to situations, but choice only comes through consciousness, by being aware. When you do things automatically through the subconscious mind, then it is not 'you,' it is your instinctive conditioned reactions controlling it and it is how you have been taught to respond. If you wish to exercise both choice and control in your actions and over the body's various functions, then you must become conscious of all these processes, which requires you to pay attention. There will be another exercise to help you become more aware of your emotions later in this chapter, in the daily practices section.

# Thinking

*'Awaken. Be the witness of your thought.' Siddhartha Gautama, the 'Buddha'*

As we touched-upon earlier, true Inner Awakening only takes place when we see beyond thinking and the thought processes of the mind. Once we are able to observe the thought process more detachedly, we then wake-up to a level of reality within ourselves that is vast, open, expansive and free. This then creates an inner reality that is free from the knots and tangles of compulsive thinking and we become unbound from the limitations of the body and mind whilst transcending to a different state of consciousness. We move from a contracted state of awareness to a vast, open one and then become aware of all of the blocks that we experience before our inner awakening and realise that all of the internal suffering we experience comes from what we 'believe' and pay attention to within the mind. Once we step-out of the thought processes and establish ourselves as the watcher of our thoughts, we are freed in that instant.

However, a quite common experience is that following this 'awakening,' a slipping-back into the identity of thoughts may then occur which triggers a yearning to return to the previous state of 'no-mind,' and a 'back and forth' process of switching between the two states often ensues. This place of 'no-mind' is our true home and it is a free and joyful place and so many people that glimpse it, however briefly, strive to get back there. This process is often normal in the early stages of our inner awakening and this is why it is often essential to practice being aware of thinking. The moment that you practice being aware of thoughts, you automatically shift to the stance of the observer-consciousness that you are and as you shift to this observer-consciousness and become aware of the coming and going of the different thoughts in the mind, you then move more into a state of inner-stillness and calm. The basis of all mindfulness practice is this stillness.

Please imagine now in your mind's eye if you would, a vast lake. When it is raining the lake begins to fill with tiny ripples from the millions of droplets falling from the clouds and these circular ripples expand far and wide across the lake. Once the rain stops, then so do the ripples and their gradual cessation and the return to calmness of the lake's surface are a parallel to the stillness of mind as you quieten-down your conscious thought-processes. Your thinking processes are an interesting phenomenon because the moment you begin to try to closely observe them, they begin to disappear. It is similar to clouds evaporating under the heat of a blisteringly hot sun on a summer's day. Clouds cannot survive in the intense heat, leaving the sky clear and blue.

Try this exercise now please ...

Ask yourself, *'what thoughts are occupying my mind right now?'*

Allow this question to draw your attention towards what is happening in your mind right now and simply observe whatever thoughts or images are present at this moment. Do not judge or indulge in a mental debate about what is there. Just simply observe detachedly as though you are watching the mind from a distance. Continue to do that for a while.

The more that you practice this exercise at intervals throughout the day and even when you are sat at home or lying in your bed, you will gradually begin to experience a greater capacity to disengage from the mind. The more you are able to disengage from the mind, the more peace, joy and inner freedom you will feel. The trick here is to not allow the mind to pull you back into thinking when you are observing the thoughts in the mind, but in the beginning you may find that this does happen from time to time. Nevertheless, please stay with it as the more you do so, the more that you will find that you can 'watch' the mind for longer and longer periods without falling back into the 'thinking trap.' The real key here is to not allow yourself to become enmeshed in a struggle with your mind. Should you become enveloped in a tussle it unfortunately means that you have fallen back into the ways of the mind once again, totally defeating the object of the exercise. The best way to approach the busy, 'thinking' mind is illustrated by this story.

> *One time, Buddha was walking from one town to another town with a few of his followers and while they were travelling, they happened to pass a lake. They stopped there and Buddha asked one of his disciples, "I am thirsty. Please fetch me some water from that lake there."*

*The disciple walked up to the lake but when he reached it, he noticed that right at that moment, a bullock cart started crossing through the lake and as a result, the water became very muddy, very turbid. The disciple thought, "How can I give this muddy water to Buddha to drink!?"*

*So he returned and told Buddha, "The water in there is very muddy. I don't think it is fit to drink." After about half an hour, again Buddha asked the same disciple to go back to the lake and get him some water to drink. The disciple obediently went back to the lake.*

*This time too he found that the lake was still muddy and so he returned and informed Buddha again. After some time, again Buddha asked the same disciple to go back. The disciple reached the lake to find the lake absolutely clean and clear with pure water in it. The mud had settled down and the water above it looked fit to drink and so he collected some water in a pot and brought it to Buddha.*

*Buddha looked at the water, and then he looked up at the disciple and said, "see what you did to make the water clean. You let it be and the mud settled down on its own—and you got clear water. Your mind is also like that. When it is disturbed, just let it be. Give it a little time and it will settle down on its own. You don't have to put in any effort to calm it down. It will happen. It is effortless."*

So be effortless in you observations and do not allow a battle to develop whereby you are trying to somehow 'force' the mind to quieten. Instead, just relax and watch closely but in a more casual way and always bear in mind that the aim is not really to silence the mind, the aim is just to observe and you should then find, by default, that the mind's activity becomes significantly reduced.

## Codes of Thought and Stories

As you begin to observe the mind, you will undoubtedly come across the various conditioned codes of thoughts that play through it, over and over again. It may be a repeating thought that says '*nothing ever goes right for me,*' or maybe it is a thought along the lines of, '*I'm not lovable; nobody wants to be with me.*' Most people have particular codes of thoughts that repeat much of the time or that play in response to certain situations or occurrences such as for example the arrival of a bill in the post or when travelling in heavy traffic on the way to work. Most people are unaware of these thoughts as they are taking place below the threshold of the mind in the subconscious regions and it is only when we begin to observe the mind (hence, look under the rock) that all of this negative activity becomes visible and apparent. This is a very large step towards becoming more conscious, and towards our inner awakening and improving every area of your life, because only when you are able to recognise these patterns do you have any chance of changing them and learning how to disengage from them. It is these thousands of negative thoughts that are creating suffering and both inner and outer conflict in our lives.

All the many thoughts and beliefs that are being held in your subconscious mind are also affecting your health and state of vibration. We all have energy that we emanate and which has been scientifically measured as the aura and life-force energies. When our thoughts and beliefs are negative and limiting, this will negatively impact upon our mental and physical health and severely restrict our ability to be a positive influence in the world.

Do you ever wonder why you or others find it hard to break out of old habits? It is because the subconscious has been programmed a certain way and unconscious, compulsive behaviour ensues. One of the most common and most energy-sapping compulsions in which most people engage, is the compulsion to speak badly about others. You are no doubt aware of how tempting it is to speak negatively of others or a particular person and if you have experienced it yourself or witnessed it in others, you will know that most people just cannot seem to control themselves, almost like an indulgence in the guilty pleasures of the mind. This need to 'gossip' about others can really drain our energy and if you have experienced it for yourself you will know that you can often walk away from these situations and conversations feeling tired and sapped of all energy. If you wish for inner awakening or even just to live a more energetic, happy and productive life, you must cease this destructive, compulsive behaviour. We have a limited supply only of energy at any given time and if we waste it on idle gossip, you will just be inhibiting yourself and severely limiting your own state of consciousness.

What we often do not realise is that our actions and words are a direct reflection of our state of being at that time. If, for example, we are speaking ill of others, then it demonstrates a weakness within us that must be remedied if we wish to elevate our life and life experiences to a higher level. It is a fact that those people that are joyful beings and the financially successful in the world, are usually people that do not waste their precious energies speaking badly of others. Conversely, it seems that those who do not seem to fare that well in life, those who are unhappy and/or lack financial resources, tend to be 'complainers,' moaners and doubters of themselves and others. They limit their own potentials with their negative words and so never seem to fulfil their own potential. We can so easily become encumbered and restricted by our habits, often unconscious, programmed habits that have been inherited unknowingly from our parents, community or society in general. But we must strive to 'rise above' these and take back our self-control in order to become joyful and achieve whatever we wish to achieve in this world.

Now, please try this powerful, little exercise...

> *Upon a piece of paper, write down at least one negative recurring thought code that pops into your mind from time to time. Maybe it only appears in a particular situation, such as when you are on the way to work or when dealing with a certain family situation. Contemplate and write down at least one thought, but the more you can recall, the better.*
>
> *Did you do it? OK, good.*
>
> *The purpose of this exercise is to become aware of this particular recurring thought so that next time it pops into the mind, you will recognise it and realise it is not who you are, but just a conditioned replaying thought code. The more you develop the ability to recognise it and intercept it as it comes to mind, the easier you will be able to distance yourself from this thought and eventually it will disappear altogether as you are not empowering it with your belief anymore. The more mind-patterns like this that you can find, the more you will clear your*

*mind of negative 'clutter' and the damaging, repeating thoughts that inhibit you.*

Another major negative activity to be aware of in the mind is the 'soap-opera complex.' The mind tends to create stories around things in life, in certain situations or often just in general. As explained earlier, the mind largely exists in a reality of memory and imagination, and so most people live their lives through their own mental life-story. We often hear the phrase *'the past shapes us into who we are.'* This is far from ideal if we have had traumatic events in our pasts. Fortunately as explained in chapter 1, What is Inner Awakening?, we are not our past. Why is this? Because there is no past, there is just 'now' and so we are 'now.' Also see chapter 3, Awakening to the moment.

Our previous life experiences can affect our body, but can never truly affect the core essence of that which we are. Only the surface level changes, whilst the core remains the same. So, our misperception that we are an accumulation of the past is what actually creates the fundamental basis for a life story that is formed in the mind. When we relinquish the past, then we simultaneously drop our own 'mental story.' So, for our Inner Awakening to occur, we must drop our personal mental story as this blocks the way to the 'truth' of our current experience in the moment.

Given that the vast majority of mental conditioning that people experience is highly negative, it is no wonder that most people's mental 'life-stories' are negative too. For example, do these thoughts seem at all familiar . . .? *'All my relationships fail, I will never find the right one. I'm just unlucky in love I suppose'* or *'I'm a failure'* or *'I'm a shy person'* or *'I can't do that.'* These are all self-imposed limitations created in the mind and to persist with these illusions, for such they are, simply turns them into self-fulfilling prophecies.

But, what if we were to have a totally positive story constantly playing through the mind? If that is what you would choose, then fine, but firstly it is best to 'clean out' the mind through inner awakening anyway. Of course it is much more difficult to change the mind from negative to positive but once we have first stepped-out of the mind itself, then if one chooses positive thought and imagination, it is effortless to do so. To truly transform the body and mind, we must transpose our outlooks into another dimension of awareness and only then will we metamorphise from caterpillars into beautiful butterflies.

Please try this exercise...

> *On a piece of paper, write down a negative story that you have been holding onto. For example, a traumatic experience or a past failure or a relationship failure or bankruptcy. Whatever it is, write it down...*
>
> *Notice how this negative story still affects you in some way? Maybe you find yourself nervous or anxious just thinking about it or when faced with the possibility of it recurring?*
>
> *Once again this exercise is designed to make you aware of the negative story as it arises in the mind. So that when it repeats itself, you can 'catch it' before it takes you over. When it arises once again, try to distance your association with the story. If it is a negative story that no longer serves you, see if you can let go of it and see that it is no longer relevant NOW.*

The more you are able to 'drop' these old, unnecessary stories, the more you will be able to step into the moment.

# Meditation Practice

*"The thing with meditation is; you become more and more you." David Lynch*

In the beginning stages of our Inner Awakening, meditation is an essential key as it allows us to become familiar and confident with our own awareness. But, which meditation practices should we choose; there are so many out there?

In fact, there are so many different meditation techniques that rely upon mind activity, such as visualisation meditation for example. However, there is a meditation that can take us beyond the mind and hence into inner awakening. There are three main types of meditation that will best serve our purpose and they all have one thing in common... absolute silence and total awareness. These three meditations are the foundation of true awakening, and are designed to take us beyond the body and mind identity. Each practice, if done in the correct order builds upon the next, strengthening and familiarising us with pure, watching awareness.

At the present time, most people's ultimate nature has become entangled with the body/mind functioning, and so the pure consciousness that they are, has become a cocktail of body/mind identity and conditioning, where no differences may be seen.

Our intention with these practices is to create a significant enough *'gap'* between *'you'* as the ultimate watching awareness, and the body/mind functioning. When a large enough gap has been created, it will be very easy to step out of the body/mind identity at any time and will enable the depth of inner awakening to become a total liberation of the mind.

By just simply stepping out of the body and mind, the body and mind can begin to realign itself functionally. In other words, the body and mind then has the potential to become a complement to our ultimate nature, so that mind, body and spirit are together in harmony.

# Just Awareness

*"Meditation is not concentration, it is not attention. Meditation is awareness"* Osho

Awareness just is, it need not be forced or cultivated, and it just is what it is ... always present ... never disappearing or appearing ... it is always there and remains there even when the disappearing and appearing is witnessed by it.

Awareness is always there just as the stars are always there whether it is night or day. So when we speak of being aware, you should know that you are always aware. If you were not aware, you would not be able to read these words or experience anything of any kind.

*Can you at this moment be aware of who it is that is being aware? Please try that now ...*

So when we speak of becoming more aware, we should not try to become more aware, you are always aware. Just simply notice this. Be aware that you are aware ...

It is a case of consistently recognising awareness ...

Try this, try to not be aware right now ...

Turn awareness on itself...

Become aware of awareness itself...

Most people become so lost in the busy mind and the external world that they simply forget awareness, or they 'think' they are aware and take this for granted and so never turn awareness on itself. In other words, they overlook awareness. It becomes like a precious object that is locked away in a box and forgotten. In other words, it is not appreciated or noticed and the consequence of this is that what we ignore, diminishes in our experience. When awareness goes unnoticed, its expansiveness in terms of how it is experienced, depletes greatly.

This is what true meditation is, simply being aware... just noticing... without any thought or judgement.

# The Power of Silence

*"Silence is a great source of strength." Lao Tzu*

Our minds tend to dislike and reject silence. Have you ever heard someone say *'I just want some peace and quiet'* and then they go off and do some activity like reading a book, doing a crossword puzzle or watching the TV? This is not *true* quietness or silence at all; this is the mind using its own time to undergo different forms of mental activity. The mind loves information input and mental stimuli and likes whenever possible to keep thinking and moving (the monkey mind), and so in actuality, it hates true silence. Most people have never really experienced true silence because even whilst they are in quiet surroundings, their minds are never still and therefore they can never get in touch with the true power of silence.

But what is this mysterious power that silence brings? Have you ever been in the countryside in the middle of nowhere at night and heard the deafening silence there? It is sometimes so silent that you can almost 'hear' the lack of sound of any kind.

This deafening silence reverberates at a frequency of 432 HZ and in the mystical traditions there is what is known as the 'crown chakra,' which is a portal to the divine source of pure consciousness within. Each of the chakras of the human energy body resonates at a particular frequency, the crown chakras (the top of the head) frequency is 432

HZ and so for us to be able to align and connect ourselves with the source consciousness through the crown chakra, the frequency of 432 HZ must be attained. Listening and being enveloped in silence then allows us to connect to our true higher selves.

Silence therefore is an integral part of moving towards the silent, joyful observer consciousness within, the consciousness that extends beyond the limitations of the body and mind so that as Jesus said, we can be '*in the world but not of the world.*' In other words we become free from the bondages of the limited unconscious identity and merge with the liberated supreme source of pure consciousness within and all around.

The more time we spend in silence, the closer the gap will become between the limited and unlimited identity, until they become as one.

Here is the first practice to work with to establish the right foundation...

## Meditation #1: I watch the mind ... I watch the body

> *So find a quiet place where you will be more than likely undisturbed. Sit in an upright position with your back straight and head looking forward at a 45 degree angle from the floor and choose a comfortable, upright position such as the cross-legged sitting position on a cushion or sat in a chair with your feet planted firmly on the ground and your knees at a 90 degree angle...*
>
> *You can either place your hands one palm on top of the other on your lap, or you can turn the palms of your hands upwards and place them on your knees, whatever feels most comfortable...*
>
> *Now close your eyes...*
>
> *As you close your eyes, look towards where the tip of the nose would be if you had your eyes open and allow your gaze to focus on the blackness of the mind...*
>
> *Now when you are ready, take three medium length breaths in through the nose and out through the nose...*
>
> *Once you have inhaled and exhaled three times, repeat this internal mantra with the breath...*

## The Secret Self

*Say, 'I watch the mind' on the inhale...*

*And 'I watch the body' on the exhale...*

*As you breathe in gently, say to yourself 'I watch the mind'*

*As you breathe out gently, say to yourself 'I watch the body'*

*Make sure to take a pause for a few seconds in between the inhale and exhale of the breath, and allow the mantras to turn your awareness towards watching the body and mind.*

*As you say the mantra, allow it to gently direct your awareness towards both the body and mind as you breathe. Silently watch whatever takes place in the body and mind without judgement. Repeat each mantra at the same time as the inhalation and exhalation of the breath...*

*If you find that you have become distracted by external noise, then just simply become aware and acknowledge whatever the distraction was and gently return to the inhaling and exhaling of the breath with each internal mantra...*

*If you find that you becoming lost in thinking or distracted by bodily sensations, then simply acknowledge what you became lost in... Let it go... and return awareness back to the breath and mantras whilst watching the body and mind activity once again.*

*Each time you become unaware, make a conscious note of it but do not judge yourself or become angry. Simply return to the mantras and breathing...*

*Allow the practice to turn you into a silent watcher of the body and minds activities, watching and noticing the different movements of thoughts and the different sensations that arise in the body, watch them impartially without judgement.*

*Continue with this practice for 15 to 30 minutes each day, build it up over a period of weeks from 15 minutes to 30 minutes, for at least a period of forty days to see powerful results. See if you can get to a point with the practice where you can say the mantras less and breath less and just sit there as a silent watcher of the body and mind, if you sit there for some time and things begin to distract you, then return to the mantras and breathing more often until you can once again let the mantras and breath become less.*

*Once forty days of this practice is done consistently, you may come to find the practice very easy and effortless. Once this is the case and it becomes very natural to slip into this meditation easily, then you may continue on to the next meditation practice called 'Labelling' (chapter 9).*

*Remember that with all practices and methods, patience and persistence is the key to success...*

# Chapter 3
## Awakening to the Moment

*"The present moment is the only moment available to us, and it is the door to all moments"* Thich Nhat Hanh

When we awaken to the moment, we awaken to the true reality of life, and we awaken to the reality of ourselves as we can only be discovered in the here and now. The present moment is the door to life and when present moment awakening occurs, it elevates us to a level of consciousness and dimension of reality beyond the mind. Access to the present moment is the end of fear, worry, stress and unconsciousness. By knocking at the door of the present moment, only clarity and truth will be found, and all unconsciousness will be left outside the door.

I remember as the realisation came, *'there is only this moment now, I am always in my current experience,'* laughter and tears of joy came so hard. 'Where had I been all this time?' I thought...

## No Time Other than the Present

Most people, through the 'thinking identity,' live in a mental invention called 'time.' This invention has been created and based upon the idea that we move forwards from past, through the present and into the future. In fact, most people's minds are structured and operate in this way as does the whole of our so-called 'society.' However, if we peer deeply into the nature of this elusive thing called 'time,' we will see that it is a mere mirage and misperception of the mind. Only 'now' is the true nature of life and our experience of life.

What we often tend to forget is that the idea of time has been constructed by the intellect of the mind in an attempt to understand through dissection, the nature of change, movement and impermanence. What we have been calling 'time' is nothing more than the observation of movement and impermanence via our tools of measurement; calendars and clocks. Seconds, minutes, hours, days and years are a totally artificial constructs that in effect, can enslave us.

For example, when the earth travels around the sun we say it takes 365 days to do so, however the '365 days' is a metric that the human mind has created in order to attempt to understand and measure this motion. This focus on the measurement as being a form of reality, creates the illusion of time, when in actuality there is only motion that can be seen. When a rabbit scurries across an open field from one end to the other, all we are witnessing is simply, pure movement, but then if we happened to have a stop watch and timed that motion, we would say it took 'so and so' many seconds, but clocks, hours, minutes and seconds are nothing more than a human creation and having nothing to do with actual nature itself.

In other words, time is but a creation of the human mind and is not built-into the nature of existence itself. What *is* built into nature and often misperceived as time is 'change' and change can give the appearance that time is passing if the human mind is mentally recording a previous event and then holds onto that memory as if it is still in existence. This constant 'holding-on' and referencing of previous experiences is what keeps the illusion of time and of yesterday alive and the tendency to imagine what may be in the next moment is what gives life to the idea of the morrow, both of which only appearing to be real by their constant acknowledgement.

What we often refer to as time, is nothing more than seeing different vantage points within the present moment. As we go from A to B, our mind often records each experience along the way and then we perceive that as time, as now I am here instead of there, but all places and people are always within the present moment, just being viewed from different vantage points within it. In other words, we are all just 'moving through' the present moment. Another way to express it, could be that life is just always 'here' and we are moving through it. Life is always now and everything is contained within the now. Please look.

Even if time travel was possible, we would still be in the 'now.' No-one has ever seen the future or the past, but even if we could time-travel, it would still be just the 'now' moment for us. All realities exist simultaneously in the present moment and if time travel was possible then only through parallel universes would it be possible, and even then, all realities would be coexisting side by side, in the present moment. All life is now, and there can be nothing else.

So, knowing this, should we destroy all clocks and live without them? Was the invention of clock-time a big mistake leaving us all entrapped in the clutches of a grand illusion? Certainly not. Clocks are marvellous inventions that can be used in a whole manner of useful ways, especially in today's highly structured and scheduled society. Clocks give us the ability to arrange meetings with others and to structure our lives so that we can be more effective with our endeavours. Clock-time is not the problem. The problem is our creation of mental-time that traps us into the bondage of confusion, suffering and illusion...

## Mental Time Creation

All thinking of the mind is past; all thinking comes from past conditioning and experience. Even thoughts of the future are created from past-thinking itself and when you imagine something that 'might be' in the future, you can only imagine it based on pictures, images and ideas that were carried over from previous experiences and conditionings. For instance, if I asked you to imagine what a future world would look like, you could only ever imagine something that you have already previously seen somewhere. What you would imagine may be different from anything before, but it would be a mixture of bits and pieces of many previously seen things. So, the fundamental way to let-go of mental time, is to discard the past which no longer exists, also previous memories and experiences and to stop looking and judging the world based on the filters of the past. We must also stop ourselves from constantly acknowledging the perceived passing of time through clocks, calendars and dates.

However, using a clock or calendar practically to say 'I am going to be here or there at such and such a time,' is not the issue. In fact this is extremely useful in our daily lives but the real problems begin when we store that time in our minds and begin to mentally create the perception of time and regard it as a real, solid entity that we are bound by. This often happens when we mentally countdown the minutes, hours and days to get to some other imaginary point, created in our head, the imagined future. How many people at work constantly watch the clock wishing they were somewhere other than where they are and wishing that 'time' would go faster or maybe wishing that they were still in the midst of some previous, pleasant experience that is now long-gone, never to return?

Oh, how all seven days of the week are kept in the forefront of our minds, planning, scrutinising, looking forward to, or maybe even dreading the days ahead. This constant mental focus on what has been and what may be is what seems to remove us from ourselves in the moment. I say 'seems to,' as the reality is that we can never be taken away from the 'now' as it is the only constant and it is the 'now' moment from which all else is experienced and takes place.

There is an old Buddhist saying: 'present moment...only moment.' Everything that is occurring, occurs in the present moment and occurs now. Everything that is remembered is remembered now, in the present moment and everything that is imagined is imagined only in the moment too.

No matter how vividly the mind appears to transport us to some daydreaming 'land of memories and imaginations,' the body and reality is always here waiting for us to pay attention once again to its beauty and wonder.

And so when we see that there is no time other than the present, all we have to do to experience it fully is to notice it...

## Your Current Experience in the Moment

Allow me to ask you some questions about things that may or may not be obvious to you. Please take the time to answer these questions from your experience in the moment.

Are you conscious right now?

By being conscious, would you agree that you are having some kind of experience right now? (Experience meaning that you are aware of things that are taking place, for example, breathing, thinking, seeing objects in the room around you and reading for example.)

And so, in this instant right now, how many experiences are you having at this moment?

## The Secret Self

If we include everything that is going on around you or within you right at this actual moment, how many experiences are you having right now?

You are having one total experience at this instant, with many other possibilities taking place within it. Can you see this?

Please do not think too deeply about it but instead, look around and see, use your sight to see. Do not think about where you are and what you are experiencing, instead just notice and observe what is happening in front of you, right now.

So here is a deeper question: 'Who is it that is having the experience, who within you is the experiencer?' Please observe and contemplate this carefully.

The truth is that we are always in 'the moment' and our current experience, but our minds constantly wander-off into reflections of previous events and contemplation of possible 'soon-to-be' experiences. In other words, we and our bodies are in the present moment always...while our minds drift-off elsewhere.

Our constant focus on the worries of the future and the regrets of the past leave us feeling ungrounded and disconnected from the moment and therefore from ourselves, as we can only be located in the moment itself. No matter what may appear to face us in the next moment or what has been experienced in the previous one, it is always more than possible to be fully centred and aware in the here and now.

The story of the man and the tiger:

> *'A man travelling across a field encountered a tiger. He fled as the tiger ran after him. Coming to a mountain precipice, he caught hold of the root of a wild vine and swung himself down over the edge. The tiger sniffed and roared at him from above.*
>
> *Trembling, the man looked down to where, far below, a thousand foot drop awaited him. Only the vine sustained him.*
>
> *Two mice, one white and one black, little by little, started to gnaw away at the vine. The man now facing instant death saw a luscious strawberry near him. Grasping the vine with one hand, he plucked the strawberry with the other. Oh how it tasted so delicious and sweet!'*

The man in the story was still able to be in the moment and enjoy what was available to him, even facing imminent death.

Even if the next moment appears to show challenging circumstances we can always enjoy and be present in the moment as it is the only true existence that there is. To the mind, this appears to be most unrealistic as the mind believes it knows exactly what is to come, but in truth, we can never say that we know exactly, one hundred percent, what is going to happen in the next moment and so why waste time thinking about that which we cannot ultimately know? Why not instead enjoy this moment?

A Zen story of the Present Moment:

> *A Japanese warrior was captured by his enemies and thrown into prison. That night he was unable to sleep because he feared that the next day he would be interrogated, tortured, and executed. Then the words of his Zen master came to him,*
>
> *"Tomorrow is not real. It is an illusion. The only reality is now."*
>
> *Heeding these words, the warrior became peaceful and fell asleep.*

Stress, worry and fear happen only because our bodies are here 'in the moment' and our minds daydream and contemplate that which is not real, the past and the future. This creates a separation and split of body and mind. Most of our mental turmoil occurs when we focus on things that are not within our current experience and we then begin to say or think things like 'what if' or 'I hope this does or does not happen.' In other words, we become fixated and overly invest our attention towards that which is but a mirage of the mind, nothing more than a holographic construct projected in the mind, and therefore fail to recognise what is happening in the present moment.

The awareness that is 'you' is undergoing an experience in the body and this body is locked solidly into the present moment without escape.

I would like you to try this right now, wherever you are at this moment. Please try your very hardest to escape your current experience in the present moment, do that now...

Were you successful? No, I do not believe that you were. Why is this? Because it is impossible to escape 'the moment' and our current experience as we are always within our current experience and 'the moment.' Only when our attention becomes fixated on the past and future thought process do we seem to lose it, but in reality we can only think in the moment, and we can only remember whilst within our current experience. Please continue to observe your own thoughts and all that is around you to confirm that what I am saying is true in your own experience.

When we eventually concede and realise that the present moment is the only moment in existence and that 'you' are immovable from within it, our perception will begin to shift considerably.

## Time, Karma and the Mind

There is a thread that links time, mind and karma together. Firstly, the mind is the dimension of time. Time as we perceive it, happens in the mind and is created by the human mind. The human mind created clocks in an attempt to measure time, which is impossible, as ultimately there is no time built into the fabric of existence, everything is just motion and change, not time. So time and mind are one, because without the mind there is no sense of time and it is the backwards and forwards thinking of the mind that creates the mirage of linear time. When we move out of the mind, we move out of time, we elevate to a timeless dimension of consciousness that exists beyond the realms of space and time.

Karma is also the mind, it begins in the mind and ends by going beyond the mind. Karma begins with memory, memory of who we think we are and who we are through what we have experienced, which is ultimately false. When we begin to believe that we are our experiences, they become stored as memory at both a cellular and soul level. This memory or past sense of self, then initiates more streams of thoughts which lead to our intent and desires, following which our intentions and desires feed back into the loop of creating more karma. In other words, identity with past and future thinking, memory and intent, creates karmic imprints in the body and soul which are to be repeated again. Karma is memory and is re-imprinted by thoughts of the future. So to end karma for the awakened one, requires us to step-out of the mind which in turn brings us into a dimension of consciousness beyond time. If you believe that you are a particular identity, with certain beliefs, thoughts, opinions and you believe you are the experiences that you have witnessed, and they have become part of your identity, then you will be subject to repeating those things again and again because you are holding them to be your own. This is karma, but if you let them go and be aware that they are not 'you,' then you end all karma for the soul.

So by noticing the present moment, and allowing it to become our primary reality, we end mind identity and time. This does not mean that we cannot still use the mind or use clocks to plan and schedule things in daily life, it just means that our primary reality is in a dimension of consciousness that is not bound by time, mind and karma. This place is pure freedom.

## Fresh Moment

Each moment is a fresh new moment. It has been said in some scientific research that atoms blink in and out of existence, billions of times per second and this suggests that physically we are not the same from moment to moment, and that if we choose we can shift to a different state of being. So quite literally, we are physically 'brand-new,' each moment. Take that a step further from what we know about the present moment being the only moment that exists, and we literally have no past and no future, and so what this means is that we can begin afresh right now. In other words, when we let go of our past idea of who we think we are, and who others think we are, we are reborn.

A line from a song that I love, is from the band, *'Faithless.'* The song is, *'We Come 1,'* which refers to the mind coming into harmony. There is a line in the song that is extremely powerful and caught my attention... *"The Power to Begin again from right now ... in you."*

We all have the power to begin again and reset in each moment. This is constantly taking place in each atom, and we can achieve the same result if we let go of our past ideas about ourselves and others. The ego mind lives through the past, it judges people and situations based upon its past experiences and identity and when we understand that there is just now, we will then see that the mind is a complete hoax, and that the only one holding onto ideas that do not exist is 'us.' Because other people are also living in the past, they will try to remind us of who they think we are, and will refer to previous experiences and characteristics, and many often submit to the pressure and believe-in and become attached to who they think they are, based on how they were in previous moments. Those moments do not actually exist, and if we can let go, we would be completely free and fresh, ready to begin over again, without regret, shame or guilt. If we can see that we are brand-new in this moment, then we will be totally free. If we do not, then we will continue to refer to ourselves and others through the eyes of the past, which does not exist. Just be here now and see the truth of your freshness.

## One with the Moment

*"Enter by the narrow gate; for wide is the gate and broad is the way that leads to destruction, and there are many who go in by it. But small is the gate and narrow the road that leads to life, and only a few find it" Matthew 7:13*

The path of the mind is a wide gate that leads to destruction, because it focuses on the illusion of past and future and creates all manner of problems because of it. But when we pass through the narrow gate of the present moment, a whole new, beautiful world opens up. This is the path to life and the REAL you.

You cannot be located in the future and you cannot be dug up in the past, only 'now' exists, only now does life exist and so that is where you are also. You can only be discovered in the moment. When you look closely you will see that you are as one with the present moment and there is no escaping it. See if you can try right now to withdraw yourself from the now moment.

*Did you succeed?*

You and the now are one and the same, and when you notice the present moment you are recognising and connecting with your true self also.

## Practicing being Aware of the Moment

*'As the rate of mind activity is reduced, our awareness of the present moment becomes more greatly enhanced.'*

Essentially we become more aware of the present moment when our 'rate of thinking' is significantly reduced. This happens because as the mind appears to quieten and become still, the present moment is revealed to us and becomes more visible. The mind's constant thinking activity and concentration on our yesterdays and tomorrows, camouflages our ability to notice the moment in its fullness (please see diagram below).

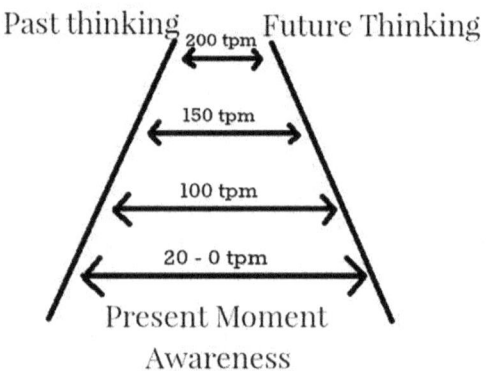

As the diagram above demonstrates, as our rate of 'tpm' (thoughts per minute) reduces, our perception widens to accommodate the present moment awareness. In other words we ground ourselves in the reality of the 'now moment' by not being distracted by the memories and imaginings of the mind. From our own experiential point of view, it is almost like being transported to another dimension and in essence this is true, as we are then accessing a higher and truer dimension of existence.

So, comprehending what has been discussed above, our methods of experientially entering the present moment must consist of that which can redirect our awareness from the constant, ongoing ramblings of the mind. As we discussed in the previous chapter, we must lay a foundation of regular meditation practice in order to help us reduce the level of mind activity and travel beyond the mind itself. This in turn, will make it easier for us to access the present moment in its full entirety, in a more effortless way.

That being said, remember that we are already 'in the moment,' it is simply the case that we are not paying it any attention. There are two main ways to access the 'here and now' in our experience, the first is to use the body and the other is to use the moment itself and all the elements within it, as a point of awareness.

## The Body—a Rock in 'the Now'

As we discussed earlier, our bodies are always in the moment while our awareness is often focussed on the past and future musings of the mind. This means that we can use the body like a rock or lead weight to ground us experientially in the instant now. And of course the advantage of the body is that it is always with us, everywhere we go in our waking life and it is something that we can always depend upon, to practice with.

Aware of the Body

Here is a simple mindfulness technique for the body, to try now:

*Breathing in, I'm aware of my whole body.*

*Breathing out, I'm aware of my whole body.*

Quite simply, as we breathe in we become aware of our whole body in that moment and as we breathe out we again become aware of the whole body. If we wish, we can say this either in our mind or out aloud as a sort of mantra that reminds us to breathe and become aware of the entire body. Allow the words to be a reminder to you to pay attention to the whole body and to feel it fully. If we do this throughout the day at intervals, it will dramatically increase our level of self-awareness and our awareness of the present moment. You and the present moment will come alive!

Sensing your existence

Here is another simple exercise we can do anywhere, at any time, to keep in touch with your being, in the moment. Can you sense your own existence?

*Breathing in, I feel my aliveness.*

*Breathing out, I sense I exist.*

Do not 'think' about existence or your existence, but instead can you sense it and feel it. Can you feel the aliveness within each cell of your body; can you feel the vibrant alive energy within?

When you sense this aliveness within, it takes-away your awareness from the thinking ego mind and plants it within the foundations of the body, and when you are in the body and not lost in the mind, you become more alerted to the here and now. Whenever you become lost in the mind and you are immersed in stressful thoughts, bring your awareness to the feeling of 'aliveness' within you. It is a pleasant feeling and is that most basic sense of 'I exist.' Whenever you sense it, you will become grounded in the moment.

## Noticing the Now

The reason why we seem to lose the present moment is because of our inability to pay attention to it. Through the mind we have become so accustomed to digress into the imagination and memories, that the present moment rarely sees a glimpse. This is a great shame as it is the only moment that there is and therefore the place where the whole of reality happens. So what we must do is to become more experientially aware of the moment by paying close attention to it and all the elements contained within it.

Here is a powerful exercise we can do to first establish ourselves in the moment:

> *Breathing in, 'I am aware of the present moment right now'*
>
> *Breathing out, 'I am here and now'*

It sounds very simple ... and it is, but this is simply a reminder to bring our awareness to the moment and not become distracted by compulsive thinking. We should allow the words to lead our awareness into the present moment. You see, the art of being aware first lies within reminding and practicing, as this takes us from the unconscious, 'autopilot' mode to the heightened perception of being conscious.

## Your Royal 'Here-ness'

Be aware of your 'here-ness,' that is to say, be aware of the reality of your being right here and right now. When you get lost in remembering yesterday and projecting the future, just remind yourself of you're here-ness within the moment, notice how it feels and how it looks to be here.

How does it look, smell and feel? What does it sound like and what is the texture and quality of this moment? When thought becomes too overwhelming and appears real, step into you're here-ness.

## Notice Objects in the Now

Another way to practice being aware of the moment is to focus on the things contained within it. What often happens is that we let ourselves get so 'fenced-in' by paying attention to the mind, that we miss all of the beauty and wonder around us? I remember many years ago that I used to drive on a particular route to work every day but eventually as I began to become more conscious, I noticed for the very first time a particular office building that had been there all along! I found this difficult to comprehend as I had passed this point so many times and never noticed it before. I found this really surprising and it made me ponder on what else I may have missed throughout my life. I soon realised however, that this all sprang from the fact that I had not been paying full attention to my experience in the moment and therefore I was missing most of what was within it.

Can you understand what this means? It means that most of us are in effect sleep-walking through life, even when we believe we are fully awake, because the mind is constantly daydreaming. When we are aware, we notice all within the moment and we also come to understand and see everything more clearly. But when we are mostly unaware, it is as though many things become invisible to us. However, as soon as we become alert and pay attention, it is as though dimensional doorways open-up to us and allow everything to be seen as the doors of perception open.

So here is another exercise to become aware of the moment:

*Wherever you are, pay attention to the objects that surround you. For example, pay attention to a tree and the shape of the tree and its colour and texture. Look at the tree (or any object) as if seeing it for the very first time.*

*Pick any object and observe it with utmost interest and wonder. You can say, 'I know not what I see'.*

One of the obstacles we may face with this practice is resistance. Resistance may occur because our minds believe that they 'know' what they are observing and that it has all been seen before. You see, we were taught from a young age to 'label' objects and therefore when we look at an object we dismiss its wonder as we merely see the label we have attached to it. So the mind will say, 'this is silly, I know exactly what it is.' But as I said previously, a label cannot be the object itself and the object can never be the label. So what exactly is it? Teach yourself to become curious like the child you once were and focus all of your attention upon the object in question. This will focus your attention on the present moment.

Simply observe the object without labels and be conscious of the minds tendency to insist upon labels for objects. Relax all pre-conceptions and observe the objects with interest, noticing the shape and colour of the object and so on. Try to observe the object and all of its attributes from a purely visual point of view, in other words do not become fixated on descriptions and labels.

# Stillness

Stillness is as it implies, a place of inner still. To be 'still,' means the absence of any inner movement, where we withdraw from the mind and enter into the natural place of calm and silence within, a place where no activity is present.

It is the place within us that is beneath the activities of the body and mind, just as the depths of the ocean are completely motionless, despite the extreme motion of the waves above. Stillness occurs when we slip into this place beneath what is being thought, believed and felt in the moment. It is a timeless and deep dimension of Intelligence within, which can only be experienced in the moment.

One way that we may be in touch with this stillness, is to listen to the silence within and all around and we should listen to this silence as often as possible. Listen to the pure silence within a quiet room, notice the silence in between each tick of the clock. Notice the silence prior to a car passing outside the window and as silence returns, once it has disappeared.

Also when in a noisy environment, listen to all the different noises and notice from where these noises appear, and to where they disappear.

*All sound arises from silence and descends back into silence, notice this and hear this...*

*Can you hear the soundless sound in between sounds, contemplate this...*

*We can also pay attention to the silence in between words and thoughts, as we speak... Be aware of your silent spaces and pauses in-between your words...*

As you listen to others be aware of the silent spaces in their speech. As you think, watch and observe any quiet gaps, no matter how tiny, in between each thought and see if you can notice from where each thought arises and to where each thought disappears. Notice this.

Anytime we become aware of silence, it is an opportunity to become very still within and connect with our true nature beyond mind. This silence and stillness may also be witnessed through being conscious of our breathing. Simply notice the stillness in the moment of holding the breath... in between the inhalation and exhalation of the breath. Take a moment to be aware of it now.

The thinking mind and breathing are very much connected. When our minds are erratic and busy, our breathing often becomes short and fast but when our minds are extremely relaxed and calm our breathing is often very slow and deep. When we stop breathing for a moment and hold it, our minds will stop also. Please check this out.

Firstly notice how your mind and breath is at this moment and see if they match...

Now breathe in and out three times, with long slow deep breaths. Then take a deep breath and hold it... Make sure to relax your body as you do so...

As you hold the breath in, turn your attention towards the thinking mind, notice what thoughts are in the mind... if any... and just be aware of them without judgement...

As you hold-in the breath, become aware and look for the spaces of silence within... Allow yourself to rest within these silent spaces...

*Use this daily technique as often as possible to establish contact with the stillness and silence within you and the now moment.*

Make silence your friend and it will reward you with the gift of your own natural being, in its entirety, depth and fullness.

## Moment to Moment Noticing

*"Live moment to moment."*

Another way to notice the present moment is to observe the passing of one moment to another. By this I do not mean simply sit next to a clock and count the seconds as they go by. As we have mentioned already, clocks are man-made inventions that run independently of us and have no real connection to the present moment and nature itself. Instead, try to discern exactly when one moment moves on to the next one. You may be quite shocked at what you find, but I will leave that for you to experience for yourself.

This is a great way to become aware of the present moment, as it takes a good degree of inner 'stillness' to experience this phenomena, which will inevitably bring you an awareness of the moment. So, at this point, does life seem to move in staccato fashion from one moment to the next or is there a smooth transition whereby each moment seems to blend into the next? Please observe and contemplate this.

## Pay Attention

Last but certainly not least, we should always pay attention!

We should be very attentive to each moment. We should always give it the full focus of our awareness by widening our eyes slightly and focussing but also relaxing too. Have you ever been driving a car on an intensely foggy night, or maybe during a heavy snowfall?

Remember how much you focus and concentrate on the task in hand at these moments . . . almost as if nothing else exists?

This is how we must always act in the 'moment.' When we are attending to any task at all, we should always give it our undivided attention. If we are unaware of precisely what we are doing in every instant, then we are not living in the present moment. This Zen story about living each minute to the full, illustrates this extremely well...

> *Zen students are with their masters at least ten years before they presume to teach others. Nan-in was visited by Tenno, who, having passed his apprenticeship had become a teacher. The day happened to be rainy, so Tenno wore wooden clogs and carried an umbrella. After greeting him Nan-in remarked: "I suppose you left your wooden clogs in the vestibule. I want to know if your umbrella is on the right or left side of the clogs."*
>
> *Tenno, confused, had no instant answer. He realised he was unable to carry his Zen every minute. He became Nan-in's pupil and studied six more years to accomplish his 'every-minute Zen.'*

We must always be 'aware' one hundred percent of the time in order for the present moment to become truly 'realised' and 'lived.' In order to make this happen, we should try to focus our attention upon the 'smaller' elements of our daily lives, things such as feeling each footstep as we walk in the grass or on a pavement or the feeling of our touch as we pick-up a cold glass of water and proceed to move it towards our mouth before putting our lips around it and tasting its coolness as it enters our body. Becoming aware of the sounds and sensations of our stomachs as they are digesting the food we ate. If we can become acutely aware of our body and the present moment itself, our whole world will open-up as never before, we will be happy, satisfied and more efficient in everything we do. The one thing that seems to distract most of us from the experience of the moment is fear...

# Chapter 4
## Have no Fear

*"The whole secret to existence is to have no fear." Siddhartha Gautama (The Buddha)*

One of the most debilitating forms of thought that humanity faces is fear; our belief in certain fears prevents us from fulfilling our goals on more endeavours than anything else, and can become a catalyst for unhappiness and in preventing us from seeking our true nature. Fear can literally immobilise us, but it only exists within the ego mind and never in the true self. And it only exists in relation to the contemplation of the future, not by remaining grounded in the present moment.

## Fear and the Ego

*"The ego loves to know what is in the next moment because it seeks full control; it seeks control because it fears being out of control, and being out of control could mean its annihilation"*

Can you imagine living without fear, without any slightest fear or insecurity whatsoever? Is it even possible to live without fear?

Oh yes, it is certainly possible and just imagine what could be done without fear holding us back from achieving what we want to achieve and being who we are.

What we refer to as 'fear' is a mental and emotional reaction to a perceived threat or danger, and in today's world our mind has been conditioned to perceive many things as potential threats. That which the mind perceives as a threat, is often not and most of what we perceive as a threat exists only in our imagination. In other words, we often project into the future and see what is not real and has not happened, and then become fearful about what 'could' happen.

You see, fear is simply a product of a limited sense of identity, believing we are just the body and mind, a finite reality. This creates a need for self-preservation as we believe that we, as a body, needs to be saved from anything that could potentially harm it, because to harm it would be to harm us ... or so we believe.

This need to preserve ourselves is not just a need to protect the body from harm or death, but also a need to protect our mental identity, our mental sense of self (ego). This is why fear does not just simply come in the form of a fear of death, but also in the form of what other people think about us and also whether or not people disagree with our beliefs or perceptions. When one is identified with the body and mind alone, fear will follow us around like a bad smell.

From this limited sense of self and need for preservation, our thoughts try to steer us on what we believe to be a course that will keep the body/mind and ego intact. This means that the mind will always project forwards into the imagined future in an attempt to protect itself from possible threats. Fear derives from an 'over-assumptive' mind as we convince ourselves of the possibility or even the inevitability of certain future scenarios. Through imagination and mental projection the mind will assume a particular outcome and then from that assumption, fear will be the result and this can then trigger the release of adrenaline within the body, thus reinforcing our belief that what we are assuming could be right. This unpleasant, nervous feeling then leaves us fearful and creates a mental block further reinforcing our fears—and all because the mind has imagined and assumed what may happen. In other words, our fears arise from false evidence which has the distinct appearance of being real. How can the mind possibly know exactly what will happen next, how can it predict the future? Of course the answer is ... it cannot.

Please reflect now, from your own experience, how many times have you thought and imagined that something was going to happen in a certain way, only for it to turn out completely differently to your expectations? In other words, how often do your worst fears and worries actually become reality in exactly the way your mind assumed it would?

If we are being honest with ourselves, we may all say that for the most part things do not happen in the exact way that the mind assumes it will. So given this truth, why do we continue to torture ourselves with fears about an imagined future based on our assumptions only? Maybe it is because it has become an unconscious habit created by our limited sense of identity and wondering mind.

All fears are a reaction to something you believe to be true, you don't have a feeling about anything if you don't first have an assumption or belief about that thing, that circumstance, or situation... That's what fear is for, it is there to tell you—you have a belief that is out of alignment with who and what you truly are. In other words, the belief or assumption that you are holding about this particular thing you are imagining... is damaging. Only the ego mind can create this illusion, the pure self just stays with the reality of 'what is' in the moment and doesn't assume what it cannot ultimately know.

> *'Fear is not real. It is the product of thoughts the mind creates. Danger is very real, but fear is a choice.'*

This Zen story about fear told by the Indian Mystic Osho illustrates well the current state of mind of humanity...

> *"A man walking in the night slipped and fell from a rocky path. Afraid he would fall down thousands of feet, because he knew that just at the edge of the path was a very deep valley, he grabbed hold of a branch that was overhanging the edge. In the darkness of night all he could see below him was a bottomless abyss. He shouted and his own shout was echoed back—there was nobody to hear him.*
>
> *Can you imagine that man and his night of torture? Every moment there was the thought of death below, his hands were becoming cold, he was losing his grip...but he managed to hold on and as the sun came out he looked down...and he laughed! There was no abyss but just six inches below his feet there was a rock ledge. He could have rested the whole night, slept well—the edge was big enough—but instead, the whole night was a nightmare.*
>
> *From my own experience I can say to you:*
>
> *The fear is not more than six inches deep. Now it is up to you whether you want to go on clinging to the branch and turn your life into a nightmare or whether you would love to leave the branch and stand on your feet. There is nothing to fear."* Osho

It is our clinging to life, people, people's opinions, material possessions and circumstances which blocks our true awareness from shining through and therefore obstructs the natural flow of energy being circulated throughout the body. Our life force then becomes weaker and doesn't reach its full potential by connecting with source energy (pure consciousness). This has implications on our wellbeing, relationships with others and our ability to use the instrument of the body to achieve our full potential.

This is mainly because of our mistaken identity with the ego (conditioned self) and the ego fears its termination, it fears death. Fear comes from the ego and the ego at its root is identified with being a separate self, separate from the totality of existence. When we believe we are fragmented from the whole of existence, our primary motive is self-preservation, translated as 'how can I survive?' This creates an underlining sense of fear and the reason we tend to hold onto things so tightly and desperately is because we are unconsciously trying to stabilise and balance our energies by leaning-on and being dependent upon other sources externally.

Most people exist in a kind of quiet desperation, trying to hold onto the material things of this world because they fear the body's demise and they believe it would be *their* demise, and so they hold on just like desperately holding onto the branch in the short story above. We are simply not aware that there is an abundant well of energy within us that completes us and keeps us fulfilled at all times, an intelligence within us that is vast, immortal and connected to the deepest core of existence.

## The Fear of Death

*"To fear death, my friends, is only to think ourselves wise, without being wise: for it is to think that we know what we do not know. For anything that men can tell, death may be the greatest good that can happen to them: but they fear it as if they know quite well that it was the greatest of evils. And what is this but that shameful ignorance of thinking that we know what we do not know?"- Socrates*

Firstly, it is apparent that death is the most natural thing in existence, it is inevitable is it not? Think of the billions that have passed before us and the billions that will pass afterwards. It is the natural cycle of existence; we observe it everywhere, in how the animals, insects and even plants pass. But ironically the fear of death is the singular biggest fear that the majority of humanity possesses yet its occurrence is an absolute certainty, the biggest certainty we face in our lives. With birth eventually and inevitably comes death, we each owe one life and that debt is paid upon our passing.

As briefly touched upon earlier, this is largely due to the sense of separation and our fear of it being the possible end of our existence, believing we are just the body alone. The fear of death remains for many also because of the fear of not knowing what (or what does not) await us when we pass. We often think we fear the unknown, but ultimately this fear of the unknown is not a fear of what we don't know but of what we 'think' may or may not happen. This fear of the unknown occurs because our minds have a natural tendency to wonder and ponder upon all of the scary or unpleasant things that could await us. But these wild imaginings are never based upon reality, they are always simply projections of the mind and assumptions of unknown possibilities. In other words, we often pointlessly worry about and fear what we do not know. Would it not stand to reason that if a person cannot possibly know what awaits him, that any assumption is a pointless one, being unworthy of the energy expended in thinking negatively about it? If we are to assume negative things about that which we have no knowledge, would it not be preferable to assume the most positive outcome instead... if any? At least that way we are able to imagine a more positive, fulfilling experience leading up to the point of where our soul leaves the body. Nevertheless, we will later briefly discuss the importance of contemplating the leaving of the body as meditation practice.

Another large contributory factor to our great fear of death is our societal conditioning regarding the concepts and traditions of death. So let us look closely and openly at these learnt perceptions, with compassion and respect for all views...

Firstly, most people automatically perceive this thing called 'death' as a largely negative event. Why? Well mostly because that is exactly how the media and culture portray it and indeed most people perceive death as an ending. Does that sound reasonable to you? Now think how most people react, when someone passes; most people say things like, 'oh isn't it terrible?' or 'what a waste' or 'what a tragedy.' I assume that we have all heard these kinds of comments before?

Now of course one can have compassion and respect for someone who died without feeling 'bad' about it. This is quite reasonable but most of us automatically associate death with bad feelings as though it is compulsory to be hurt in some way and we will investigate this more deeply as we talk about death and the reality of the grieving process.

So our negative reaction to death derives from our association of the word, that is we perceive death as an end (the end of I), a point of no return and so we often interpret it as an automatic loss, a loss of the essence of a person. We only need to take a look at the societal rituals we undergo upon someone's death to confirm this. Everyone wears black, and avoids discussing it, hiding death away as though it is in some way shameful or too outrageous to speak of openly in polite company. Furthermore it is considered morbid and people's earthly remains are often buried and hidden away in dark forbidding cemeteries that most people do not frequent. It is almost as if our whole culture, especially in the west, is about the denial of death, a determination to not face death, to not look death in the eye, to not accept it.

We only need to look at how western culture often encourages us to try and stay young forever to confirm this as a fact. It is a very common occurrence to see men and women who will go to extreme measures such as plastic surgery in order to stay young. This often derives from believing implicitly in a need to stay young and avoid the inevitable, as if we are desperately trying to hold onto who we think we are. But is this the only way to look at death? Do all peoples of the world perceive death as a loss?

> *In India the Hindu people honour their ancestors as far as seven generations back -- which is a really long time. They begin by bathing in sacred ponds and rivers, and continue by offering prayers and food to their ancestors as they return from the afterlife for the night to feast.*
>
> *In Japan they have a Buddhist holiday which has been celebrated in Japan for 500 years. Families gather to clean and decorate the graves of their loved ones, and then release lanterns to help guide their spirits. The holiday also features a traditional dance.*

*In Mexico they celebrate the 'day of the dead', on this night, families gather to clean and decorate the graves of their loved ones. It's also known for its skeleton decorations, candies, and elaborate costumes.*

*The Mah Meri tribe in Malaysia, who make up a small minority of the country's population, celebrate their dead with a day of dancing that is steeped in tradition. Shamans offer blessings before the ceremonies begin.*

*And in Korea 'Chuseok' is a three-day harvest festival, but it's also the holiday during which Korean people honour their ancestors. Each year, about 30 million people in Korea visit the hometowns of their ancestors to pay homage. People pray, clean the tombs of their immediate ancestors, and offer them food and drink.*

So, we can see that many of the world's cultures celebrate and honour the deceased, which means that they do not see the leaving of the body as an end, but only as a new beginning. If we can step out of our own culturally conditioned norms to an alternative view of the leaving of the body, it will help us achieve a greater acceptance of this thing we call 'death.'

Non-acceptance of death comes at a hefty price; the price of fear and terror of one's own demise. Imagine what horrors go through the mind of someone about to die, yet who cannot accept death—and the internal struggle and pain that must thereby ensue. Trying desperately to cling-on to what they believe themselves to be, the body and their worldly chattels, what suffering there must be? Conversely, now think of those that have been more accepting of the inevitability of death, those that have given up the struggle against it. The peace and grace that comes to those beings who have surrendered themselves to what awaits is an inspiration to witness. The difference is stark, almost as if these people are somehow lighter in being, relaxed and able to 'let go' of their earthly ties without a struggle. Sometimes you will see that those who are preparing for death begin to change in a positive way, they become glowing and radiant almost.

Please allow me to recall here, a story of a friend of a family member who had a brain tumour... (We will call him 'Bill' for the sake of privacy)...

## The Secret Self

A relative of mine recalled Bill being such a relaxed and laid-back person. He had the ability to deal with any situation in a totally calm, unhurried manner and on one particular occasion, whilst at work, Bill was reading a newspaper on his break when a colleague rushed through the door, threw some keys on the table and said, *'Bill, go lock-up gate no. 11 now.'* Bill, without even looking-up from his paper, slid back the keys to the end of the table and said in the most calm and confident tone possible, *'I'm on my break at the moment.'* He never moved a muscle and his facial expression never changed but yet his whole demeanour and tone certainly put the message across in no uncertain terms. What could his colleague have said to that? It seemed as though Bill did not really mind whether he kept his job or not; how could he be so fearless? So the colleague turned around and went back through the door without another word and Bill continued to read his paper as if nothing had happened.

My family member knew why Bill was so relaxed and confident; he knew that he was pretty much fearless. Apparently a couple of years previously Bill had been diagnosed with a brain tumour which he was told was terminal and that he had only around six months left to live. That whole six month period of his life was filled with worry and fear of his impending death and in time his condition became worse and worse until he was admitted to hospital for the anticipated remaining few weeks of his life.

Bill recalled, *'...things really got put into perspective for me, I mean I used to worry about so much trivial stuff, and now I was here facing my last weeks of life. All of that other stuff that I used to worry about just seemed to fade away into insignificance.'*

> Then one night something powerful hit Bill and according to him, *'I was sat there in my hospital bed extremely anxious about my situation, when I looked to my right hand side and became aware of a former priest who was also on his last legs, near his end, too. I contemplated for a moment and then looked to my left side and already knew that this particular patient who was also dying was a wealthy businessman. Then I realised something on a deep level that had not really hit home before; I suddenly knew that no matter what your*

*status, income, religion or achievements, no-one can escape death and no matter what you do, the inevitable will happen.'*

This proverb came to mind... *'At the end of the game, the king and the pawn go back in the same box.'* Suddenly Bill relaxed; he accepted where he was and what was to come, knowing that it will come to us all. As he relaxed his mind relaxed also, all the worrying thoughts that were going through his mind suddenly faded into the background and he says that, *'...something changed in me that night, I suddenly let go of all fears I had been carrying, I felt at peace with myself.'*

Remarkably, Bill recovered and his brain tumour shrank. Many of his family and colleagues noticed how he displayed a vastly different attitude and approach to life from that point on and he seemed to take everything in his stride, was never worried or fearful and never took things personally. When asked about his new approach to life, Bill said, *'Why take anything personally, everything is borrowed and we give it back eventually anyway. I don't feel I need to possess anything anymore, I just enjoy what comes to me, and the only difference now is I'm not scared to lose it. What's the point of getting upset about things so trivial? I now appreciate each day and live it as though it is my last.'*

It is perhaps easy to understand now why Bill was so relaxed about what happens at work. When one has overcome the fear of death, all smaller fears, worries and concerns seem laughable, would you not agree? Once that most basic of all human fears is overcome, a being is really ready to live and to live as if there is no tomorrow. It is only when we can fully accept death that we become reborn and truly live. This is the paradox, we must die to truly live.

Fear is a product of the ego and belongs only to the thinking ego mind. Fear always relates to the future and what 'may' happen in the future. We never fear the present moment, because the very instant that the mind tries to think about that moment, it is already in the past.

We can use the acronym below to remember where fear originates from...

FEAR

- False
- Ego

- Appearing
- Real

Whenever fears or insecurities arise, always remind yourself that it is only the ego that does fear and that fear is always what we imagine about what we do not ultimately know. Fear is the false ego appearing real, so remain in the moment, as the true self.

## The Fear of Other's Opinions

*"The moment we begin to fear the opinions of others and hesitate to tell the truth that is in us, and from motives of policy are silent when we should speak, the divine floods of light and life no longer flow into our souls."* Elizabeth Cady Stanton

Another huge fear that most people have, in many ways more so than death, is the fear of other people's opinions, the fear of what other people think about them. This often blocks and erodes many people's confidence and desire to achieve particular goals in life. Many people have dreams, dreams to achieve something significant, yet the fear of what others may say can engender a mind-set whereby they are even afraid to try, just in case of potential failure. As a result of this most people's great potential is never fulfilled. Many enter the grave without ever having tried to achieve their dreams and often times we will even convince ourselves that there is a good reason why we did nothing instead of doing our best, regardless. Some will say 'the time just wasn't right' or 'if only I had more money, then I would have given it a try.' Through fear of failure, the mind will invent any justification to warrant inaction.

What is really happening below the surface of the subconscious mind is terror of how others may judge us. You see, a major part of our societal conditioning has been to overly care and take to heart what others say about us or our work and because we live in a competitive society where comparison and measured performance is taken very seriously, we tend to compare ourselves and our endeavours to others, as if any two paths can ever be the same. But this is our conditioning and so we judge and scrutinize each other constantly to see who is best. The real pain is felt when we judge each attempt at something as a very personal thing and so most people by default take everything they do very personally. When we take things personally, the result is pain and inner suffering because if something does not work-out as planned, we believe it is a reflection of who we really are, as it hurts the ego we are identified with and the false persona.

And so the result is that we arrive at the end of our life with most of our potential unfulfilled and most importantly with the crippling fear of what others may say or think about whatever we do. This is no way to live and leaves us with an almost permanent undercurrent of unhappiness, as we cannot be truly happy and ourselves as long as we are a prisoner of the mind, with fear as the padlock. This reminds me of a story I once heard from a friend...

My friend had been reading an article in which dying people were being interviewed and one of the questions these people were asked was, '...if you could have done anything differently, what would it have been?'

One particular man answered very adamantly by saying 'I wish I could have been true to myself.' A very powerful statement indeed. We often sacrifice what we really want; our happiness and true nature by trying to conform to others' expectations, through fear. We become insincere and end up 'living a lie,' and the price we pay is the ultimate price, the price of our inner freedom, happiness, our dreams and true nature.

Is this what you want? Do you want your whole existence to be a lie because of being led rather than being yourself? If you opt for the way of fear, then that will be your path. If you completely let go of fear, then total freedom will be your reward, the freedom to have full choice and to be yourself. Which would you rather have?

It is illogical to care what other people think; there are over seven billion people on this planet, each with a completely different perception of the world, none identical to another. There are always slight differences; no one sees the world in exactly the same way, everyone looks at the world through a unique perception. So out of those seven billion different perceptions, whose perception is the correct one? Bearing in mind that most of humanity's perceptions have been tainted with some form of conditioning, like wearing a pair of rose-coloured spectacles and seeing pink wherever you go. So is your perception right? Is your neighbour's perception right? Is the child in China's perception right or the woman in Brazil's perception right? Is a dog or cats perception right?

So all that matters is *your* perception, all that matters for you is *your* experience. If you try to live your life through other people's eyes, then you're going to be disappointed every time. This actually reminds me of an old Sufi story...

*There was a father with his son and they were walking with their donkey into town. As they came close to the town they passed a group of men and the men began to snigger and chuckle at the young boy and man. One of the men said, "...if a donkey is not to ride upon then what is it for." So the man upon hearing this decided to suddenly climb upon his donkey and the boy walked at the side of the donkey and they continued on their way.*

*Then later they passed a group of women and one of the women said, "...look at that poor boy having to walk while that rotten man saves his feet by riding the donkey." So the man now hearing this immediately jumped off the donkey and proceeded to place his son on the donkey. Further up the road they walked past two men and one of the men said, "...look at that young boy, fit and healthy and he's riding the donkey letting his old tired father walk. How bad is that?"*

*Now the man, upon hearing that, decided that he would climb on the donkey with his son and so both he and his son rode on the donkey and continued on their journey. They then came upon another group of women who said, "...look at that poor donkey, with two people on its back, how cruel is that?" The man upon hearing this became completely distraught and did not know what to do and so he got off the donkey and took his son off the donkey. He pondered for a moment and then he got a long pole and decided to tie the donkey's legs to either end of the pole and then hoisted up one end of the pole onto his shoulders and got the boy to hoist the other end of the pole onto his shoulder, with the donkey now upside down, strung between them. They walked a short distance to a bridge which they began to cross, but suddenly the donkey broke free one of its legs, the boy couldn't help but drop his end of the pole and before they knew it the donkey had fallen into the river and drowned.*

Christopher J. Smith

*An old man walking behind them said, "...you fool, please all, and you will please none.'*

This is what most people are trying to do on a daily basis; they are trying to please everyone else. Rather than trying to please everyone else, we should always be true to ourselves by listening to our own intuition and ideas instead of the opinions of others. Again, this is programming that we must overcome before life passes us by and overwhelms us. Please do not become that person (persona) yourself.

People tend to think one thing today and another tomorrow, so do not ever take their views personally, as most of us judge only through our own programming. Most people's opinions are not their own, they have been 'given' to them. Many years ago, I remember seeing a TV documentary about death and one comment from the narrator that really stayed with me was *"Isn't it amazing to think, that on a long enough timeline, all that you ever did won't matter."*

Now to the ego (separate self) that seems like a depressing thought, but to the true self that is infinite and vast beyond space and time, it is extremely liberating. Why is this? Because it takes away the pressure that the ego usually places upon us, the desperate need to succeed, impress others or leave some kind of legacy. This realisation is very humbling. When we drop these false needs, we relax and achieve a great freedom and inner peace with the realisation that the whole of the world will continue just fine without us as individuals. We only need a very brief look at reality to realise that this is true. You see, life is so intelligent and in 'synch,' that even if Gandhi for example, had never existed, someone else would have risen to do what life needed to be done in that situation (ending the British rule in India).

We often get caught in the trap of thinking that we as an individual self (the ego self) must do everything to affect change in our world, completely forgetting that there are so many other forces at work and therefore so many other factors that make a situation or event happen. At the core of all existence is intelligence so powerful that pervades everything and this is the ultimate driving force underlying everything.

Have you ever felt so compelled or inspired to do something that it felt as though 'you' were not doing it alone, just as though something had pulled you in that direction and felt so natural? This is the divine will within us that is connected to the source of all creation, the pure Self within and when this intelligence needs something to be done, it will often act through those that are most receptive towards it and that allows it in to transform them and inspire their actions. Life will always find a way and if Gandhi, that is his individual self, had not been available, then life would have responded through the next individual that was receptive enough. Life will always bring forward a 'master' at the appropriate time, so to speak, someone that has the ability to move existence to the next level.

We are never alone. Even when we appear disconnected from this physical realm, the 'source' is always with us, acting through us. Whenever we face challenging circumstances in our lives, these challenges are not meant to punish us but to inspire change and transformation within us in order to allow us to connect to a deeper level of existence within. Once we are able to understand this, what is there to fear? Trust life, because life is intelligent and moves as it needs to move, when it needs to move and through whom it needs to move.

## Phobic Fears

*"A man that flees from his fear may find that he has only taken a shortcut to meet it" JRR Tolkien*

Phobic fears can often be more intense than a fear of not paying the bills on time for example, or more even than the fear of not being loved. But phobic or not, a fear is still a fear and therefore a product of the mind. Why then do phobic fears seem to stop people dead in their tracks?

Phobic fears differ slightly than other fears because they often have their origin in a strongly negative past experience. An experience of this kind can trigger a particular emotional response in us and this negatively emotional memory is often stored in the mind at the subconscious level, just waiting to be triggered by a similar experience.

I remember a family member of mine once mentioning that they detested liver and onions and when I asked why that was, they explained that as a child the school they attended used to try and literally force the food down their throat and would insist that they eat it. It is very easy to see why even many years later this person cannot eat liver and onions and even the thought of it makes them feel physically sick. In fact, it is simply the thought of it that triggers the memory which then triggers the emotion we associate with it, the feeling of fear.

As I have mentioned previously, fear is but a feeling in the body which often comes in the form of an adrenaline rush or a sickly or fluttering feeling in the gut. When we experience strong thoughts or mental images, this sends a signal through the nervous system to the area that best deals with a threatening situation, the adrenal gland causing the release of chemicals which produce certain side effects within our bodies such as dry mouth, thumping heart and sweaty palms. So in essence, it is not a particular experience that causes the fear, it is the feeling engendered by the body's response that we find unbearable. Not knowing that fact, we often assume it is the external object itself causing our discomfort, when in reality it is the body's chemistry which causes various mental and physical reactions.

As I will cover in a later chapter, nothing or no-one ever causes us turmoil, it is always the mind's conditioned reaction that does this and that triggers our internal suffering. Memory and emotion can be very closely tied together. Have you ever listened to a particular piece of music that seemed to trigger a memory of some past experience, which then in turn generated a particular emotion within you? Yes we all have experienced this as music is one of the most powerful stimuli for creating emotion.

In a similar way, any powerful past experience (both pleasant and unpleasant) can create a particular feeling or emotion within us in the present moment. This is a driver for phobias especially and it is not that we really fear the object of our terror; it is more that we are associating it with a previous experience that we did not enjoy and it is actually our beliefs and thoughts of it that really cause our reaction.

In order to minimise this effect, we must look at life in a clear and honest way, which requires us to look at an experience or object truthfully without a mental layer or interpretation overlying it. Because when we observe through a layer of conditioning and mental dialogue, what we see becomes distorted. If we are judging something now, based on a past experience of something similar, then we are not really seeing this new experience before us in its true light. Instead we just accept the minds past experience and all the emotions and mental images attached to it.

Expanding on the example of the food phobia above, indeed when any strongly disliked meal is placed before us, the mind registers all information associated with it, the smell, look and taste of it and this then enters the mind via the sense organs. As the sensory information reaches our subconscious, a judgement occurs within the thought processes and for most people this happens automatically through 'second nature' because this is how we have been programmed and thus developed to function.

However this mental dialogue is really just a choice on the conscious level, in other words we do not have to judge or engage in a dialogue about it, to be able to experience it through the sense organs. When we experience something without a mental interpretation of it, this is 'mindful awareness,' and the ability to see and experience life or the object in question just as it is, without the labels and false interpretations.

So in regards to a phobia, it is not the actual external object that is creating the fear, it is just simply our thoughts and anticipations of it—or what the mind *believes* may happen—that is creating the phobia. So, put simply, if we can observe this internal process that is taking place every time a phobic fear arises, then we can break that cycle through our conscious awareness of it and eventually we will be able to overcome any fearful phobic thoughts. Fearful thoughts can only take us over when we are unconscious of them and as soon as we become aware of them and don't believe them, they will simply melt away and begin to lose their power over us. When we are conscious, we have full control and power over what we perceive and it is only when the mental processes go unobserved in our unconscious, dreamy haze that they seem to have the power to take us over.

When we see these thoughts as just being reactive patterns that are not related to who we are, we can be aware of them, observe them and begin to pay them less and less credence. Once we remove our identity from thought and belief, they have no power any more.

# Practicing 'No Fear'

Ultimately having no fear comes from certain realisations about the nature of what we are not—the body and mind. However there are some powerful practices we can use to overcome fears and to become more aware of the thoughts that create it.

If we really want to let go of all fear then there is only one real way to achieve this and that is to fully accept death and die daily, yes die daily. So what does to 'die daily' entail? Dying daily means two things; firstly we must contemplate and meditate on the nature of death and the impermanence of existence itself. Secondly we must surrender more and more that which is not ourselves, that which will eventually leave us and fall away. I am speaking of the body, the mind, our persona/ego and all the things of this world to which we cling so tightly. We must accept and remind ourselves of our mortality. If we can never surrender these things in our minds and be willing to accept the inevitable, then how can we lose fear? It is the very mental attachments that we have to our false identities and the things of this world which are holding us hostage to the chains of fear, the fear of loss.

## The Art of Dying

Firstly it must be said that the following is not to be believed, nor is it to be disbelieved, it is a perspective that some people have acquired through their own inner understanding and experience, and is best not taken at face value. Instead you should search for these truths within your own experience in order that it become the truth and reality for you.

The art of dying is no more than the art of letting go, it is a relinquishing of that which is ultimately not you. Once you do this, then you may realise that actually there is no real death, that death is an illusion to those who have not found the everlasting life within them. Death does not exist for anyone who has discovered their true immortal nature. Instead all that they experience is a simple leaving of the body, and their true essence continuing on into other dimensions of existence beyond human perception.

## Dying Consciously

There are two ways to die consciously. Firstly we may die consciously at the time of bodily death, in other words, when the body's natural cycles have run their course. For instance, when the body becomes too old or ill to continue functioning. A conscious being will have prepared for this death of the body through their own conscious understanding and acceptance that they are ultimately not the body and are not afraid of death. We may achieve this through the contemplations and meditations at the end of this book and this will prepare us for the death of the body, reducing the sense of shock and allowing us to die peacefully and gracefully.

It is said in some of the ancient spiritual traditions, that how you die and leave the body is very important, because it can set the precedent for the 'state of our being' when we 'cross-over.' If we cross-over in a distressed state because we are unwilling to leave and let go, this can cause much suffering. The conscious way to die in peace is by first practicing surrendering and letting go and then through total surrender and letting go. You see, true surrender and letting go is beyond practice. When faced with death of the body, which is the time to truly let go, we either let go or we do not. This will lead to true peace and therefore a conscious death.

There is another way to die consciously which is considered in the many yogic traditions as the ultimate form of conscious death, and that is through what is called Mahasamdhi. This is the conscious process of picking the time you will die and then leaving one's body in a conscious fashion. This process is something that may be undertaken when we achieve a certain level of enlightenment, enabling us to leave the body at will. This is the 'greatest' form of conscious death because we are able to consciously choose when we will leave on our own terms, rather than by waiting for the body to deteriorate. In order to practice this form of 'ultimate death,' we must firstly awaken to the ultimate life within. If we really wish to reach the highest levels of consciousness in all areas of life and be the masters of our destiny, then we must awaken the spiritually enlightened self and then the reward will be a conscious mastery of all our life-energies and destiny. Once we are able to choose either two of these ways of dying, consciously, then we have overcome the fear of death and may live our lives to the maximum.

Now, the following practices may shock the conditioned mind and you may experience some stout resistance from the mind as the mind always tries to keep itself 'alive' and in control. The ego is very controlling, while the true self is surrendered in divine will as it is connected to a deeper power that is at the source of all creation. When the ego dies, what is left is the merging with the pure divine will of the universe and the un-manifest dimensions of existence. From this merging we become aligned with a divine will that is both you and acts through you. We still retain our decision making abilities; it's just that now it is empowered by the 'big boss' itself, so to speak.

Your mind may find these mediations disturbing, but know that these practices if contemplated in detail will liberate your mind and lead you along with other things into a massive, inner awakening. These types of meditation have often been referred to as 'negative visualisation' and they are a powerful way to liberate our mind from the restrictive ties of mental attachments.

## Meditation #1—Life's Passing Nature

Find a quiet place where you will be undisturbed and lay down, either on a bed or sofa, or maybe on a comfortable floor.

Now, as you lay on your back, bring your hands on top of your stomach, palms and fingers down. Simply take a few deep breaths-in through the nose and out through the mouth and notice how the stomach rises and falls as you do this. Continue to breathe until you feel more relaxed.

Now, stop controlling the breath and just allow it to happen naturally. Watch the natural movements of the breath with the rising and falling of the stomach.

Next be attentive to this contemplation, begin to reflect on the impermanent and constant changing nature of life. Think about how the plants, trees and various animals and life forms transform and die away...

Reflect on how many humans have already passed away on this planet, all those famous and historically renowned people and all of those persons whose name you never knew, who you never knew existed, so many of them...

Now contemplate all of the thousands of people who are dying on a daily basis from all around the world. The men, women, elderly and children that are passing away every day...

Then think of all the beings that are alive today that will also one day die and how their bodies will decay in the ground and become one with the soil. Think of how this will happen to your neighbours, friends and family, your sons, daughters, brothers, sisters, mothers and fathers etc...

And finally, remind yourself how your body is not excluded from this proposition...

When you are finished, bring your full attention back to your breathing and slowly open your eyes in your own good time.

*Points to note:*

Remember to go into as much detail as possible, the more you do this the more you will be transformed as it registers deep into the core of your being.

Also, please allow yourself to feel any emotions that may arise. For example, if you feel like weeping, then please do so. Often, this can be very cathartic as crying often allows us to release previously pent-up and hidden emotions that we have been suppressing in the subconscious mind.

When you finish the practice, please pay attention to how you now feel and if you notice any subtle changes in your perception, maybe you will feel lighter and your perception more free and expansive. Remember to be open-minded towards whatever may occur.

# Meditation #2—The Death of Your Body

Once again, find a quiet place where you will be undisturbed and lay down, either on a bed or sofa, or maybe on a comfortable floor.

Now, as you lay on your back, bring your hands on top of your stomach, palms and fingers down. Simply take a few deep breaths-in through the nose and out through the mouth and notice how the stomach rises and falls as you do this. Continue to breathe until you feel more relaxed.

Now, stop controlling the breath and just allow it to happen naturally. Watch the natural movements of the breath with the rising and falling of the stomach.

Next be attentive to this contemplation, begin to reflect on the fragile nature of your life, on the times you have become ill or times of helplessness...

Allow yourself to reflect on all the ways in which your body could be taken away from you, by illness, accident or other threat. Think of how you could die at any moment or time by all of the different possible ways that people may die every day, such as by plane or car crash and cancer etc. Think of how the body will begin to break down and age over time, and how eventually nothing you do will be able to prevent its ultimate demise.

Now with your eyes still closed imagine yourself, whether old or young, ill and at the point of death, lying on your death bed. Imagine yourself looking from the perspective of this death bed, see your friends and family around you and contemplate how you feel at this moment.

Look at your family and friends around you and imagine what they might say, how sad their faces may look or whatever other expressions may be etched upon their faces.

Next, imagine yourself in a helpless state becoming weaker and weaker, slowly fading away and your senses slowly closing down, your sense of smell leaving you along with your sense of touch, taste, sight and then sound, all of them completely shutting down. Do not fight it, instead surrender to it as you take your final breath. Imagine leaving this whole world and everyone in it behind and allow any thoughts or feelings that this image brings to you to be heard and felt. Notice them carefully.

Now imagine you have passed away and are watching your own funeral. How does the funeral look exactly? Who has attended your funeral and how do they look?

Now, please visualise yourself looking out from the coffin, watching as family members and friends file past to pay their last respects to the shell of your lifeless body. This is the final time they will see your body. Try to visualise it all. How does that feel?

Allow whatever thoughts and feelings to occur naturally, be they feelings of fear, regret or pain. Give them the space they need to express themselves and if tears begin to flow, then let them.

When you are finished, bring your full attention back to your breathing and slowly open your eyes in your own good time.

Finally, maybe take a few moments to appreciate how lucky you are to be alive and how grateful you are for every moment of life and just how grateful you are for those around you in your life.

*Points to note:*

Once again remember to go into as much detail as possible, the more you do this the more you will be transformed as it registers deep into the core of your being.

Also, please allow yourself to feel any emotions that may arise. For example, if you feel like weeping, then please do so. Often, this can be very cathartic as crying often allows us to release previously pent-up and hidden emotions that we have been suppressing in the subconscious mind.

When you finish the practice, please pay attention to how you now feel and if you notice any subtle changes in your perception, maybe you will feel lighter and your perception more free and expansive. Remember to be open-minded towards whatever may occur.

As you continue to practice these meditations, you will find that your whole view of life takes-on a new meaning. Your level of happiness and joy will increase along with your appreciation of life. We often treasure most what we know we can lose at any moment and will eventually lose in time and the more often that you remind yourself of these facts, the more you will cherish each moment of your life experience here in this body. Eventually, all the small things that we once took for granted will be transformed into beautiful experiences, filling you with immense gratitude for what you have. The petty things that used to bother you so much will also become insignificant to you in comparison to the gift of life itself.

As this transformation occurs within you, you will find yourself becoming more and more content and relaxed in the present moment.

> *Daily practice—firstly reflect on any fearful thoughts and feelings you may be holding onto. Take a moment and look deep in your mind, shine the light of your awareness on any fearful thoughts, then when you're ready repeat the declaration below with meaning. As you say it relax and let the energy of fear melt away. Trust that the declaration will do its work, as what you say becomes true.*

Repeat this Declaration daily—*'I let go of all fear, I am fearless'*

Allow yourself to become more and more fearless as you accept death and let go of all fears. As fear begins to melt away you may find your level of happiness and success becomes greatly enhanced.

*'Once you become fearless, life becomes limitless'*

# Chapter 5
## Letting go of Guilt

*"Guilt is anger directed at ourselves because of what we did or did not do"*
*Peter McWilliams*

Most of us live in the past. We carry over memories (whether pleasant or unpleasant) from past experiences, with us into the present moment and this colours the way we see the present based on past conditioned filters. We often refer to ourselves and others through the memories of the past and keep those identities and ideas alive through the constant recalling and referencing of them.

Nothing is more burdening to our minds than carrying a negative experience from the past, but it only becomes 'heavy' if we choose to lug it around with us. Most people do this unconsciously day-in and day-out, for most of their lives. We often see this burden etched upon a person's face or in their body language or posture. For example, they may appear older than their actual physical age and display the 'wear and tear' of carrying this negative energy within their whole cellular structure.

Maybe you know someone such as this? They often refer back to the past, talking about what was done to them, about the injustices others did, maybe holding long-standing grudges or regrets? Or maybe they live through their past achievements and always feel the need to bring them up in the present moment. They just cannot seem to let go of the past, almost as if it is still happening and relevant to right now.

I remember a friend of a friend who I met some years ago; she had split up from her partner several years previously and the conversation turned to relationships. This person then began to automatically speak in a negatively passionate way about her ex-partner and how she had been so hurt by their breakup and how it was all the other person's fault that she was still depressed by it. I thought that maybe her rant had been triggered off by the conversation on relationships, but according to my friend this was a regular normal occurrence for this person to speak about what had happened all those years ago. Maybe you have also encountered some people that exhibit similar behaviour to this? What a mental and emotional prison this can be for such people, spiralling them into inescapable states of both depression and anger.

This is what can happen when someone becomes attached to past memories whether positive or negative. Even the constant need to live through a positive past with pleasant memories can be an escape from the present. When a person feels the need to constantly refer to the past, it means that they are not fully focussed and satisfied with their present reality or paying attention to what the 'only moment' in existence right now has to offer. It means in many ways that they are struggling against life itself, because they cannot seem to align themselves with what the present reality contains, it never seems good enough.

There are many different forms of 'past' that people cling onto, causing them to be trapped in a state of constant suffering, never really experiencing the pure joy of the Self in the moment. And one of the greatest barriers to this pure joy is 'guilt.'

# Guilt

Guilt is a powerful, yet extremely negative emotion. It is impossible to experience true joy or happiness whilst feeling guilty and it is true to say that the more guilt we hold onto the less joyful we become. In a subconscious way, it is as though we do not allow ourselves 'permission' to be happy as the guilt takes precedence over all else. Then as the guilt builds and accumulates there is a danger that we can be drawn into bouts of depression as a result.

Guilt always derives from a sense of us having done 'something wrong' and as we have no doubt all been taught from childhood, when we do something wrong we should feel bad and thus be punished in some way. Often, it is we that punish ourselves in various different, subconscious ways.

As per the quote at the beginning of the chapter, guilt is caused by anger directed at ourselves from something we did or did not do in the past. Every time we have guilty thoughts about the past it can be likened to us taking a baseball bat and smashing ourselves around the head for no apparent reason. Ironically, we 'beat ourselves up' because of something that is now no longer in existence—apart of course, from a persistent memory.

So, does this mean we should never feel guilty about anything? Well, it all depends on whether or not we have done something badly that could have been done better or something that harmed someone unnecessarily. If this is the case, then initially we may well feel guilty, but instead of wallowing in that guilt we would better serve ourselves and others by using this experience as a 'lesson.' If we can learn from our mistakes and do things differently next time we are confronted by a similar situation, then this can only be regarded as a positive step. We can then remove the guilt and its associated bad memories as it would no longer serve any purpose whatsoever to retain that association. The fact that we have learnt the lesson would then demonstrate a conscious recognition of our own failings and confirm our disengagement from the ego and a clearer understanding of the situation. Holding onto guilt benefits no-one, not even those who may have been harmed by something bad that we did to them. Learning to be a better person as a result of negative experiences removes the whole reason for guilt and its unnecessary mental anguish.

Also when one constantly retain guilty thoughts and feelings, we are less likely to do anything positive to remedy our wrongdoings next time the situation occurs. This is because we may be too busy feeling bad about our actions and this makes it more difficult to muster the energy to actually change ourselves or a situation, because guilt held onto long enough can soon turn into low self-esteem and can lead from there into depression. Anyone that has suffered with depression will tell you how much more difficult it is to change yourself or a behaviour when in that state.

The only thing for which past experience in the form of memory is useful, is to learn from it. That is all that is required of memory. We learn to drive a car or ride a bike by memory and we can do many other practical things with it and indeed it is needed for Human-evolution, but to use it in any other way generally leads to problems due to the strengthening of the 'ego self,' which is completely composed of past experiences.

So once we learn the lessons from something we did or did not do, we must then let it go as it will no longer benefit us. In other words, *'once we get the message, we can then put down the phone.'*

## A Zen Story

*Two travelling monks reached a river where they met a young woman. Wary of the current, she asked if they could carry her across. One of the monks hesitated, but the other quickly picked her up onto his shoulders, transported her across the water, and put her down on the other bank. She thanked him and departed.*

*As the monks continued on their way, the other one was brooding and preoccupied. Unable to hold his silence, he spoke out. 'Brother, our spiritual training teaches us to avoid any contact with women, but you picked that one up on your shoulders and carried her!'*

*'Brother,' the second monk replied, 'I set her down on the other side, while you are still carrying her.'*

## Daily practice 1 ...

Firstly, reflect on any unpleasant past thoughts and memories you may be retaining. Take a moment and look deeply into your mind, then when you are ready, repeat the declaration below. As you say the words, relax and let all the energies of past unpleasantness melt away. Implicitly trust that the declaration will work its magic ...

*'I let go of all unpleasant past experiences'*

Let it go! What is done is done. Learn the lesson if needed and then move on, do not weigh yourself down with unnecessary pain, carrying it with you on the rest of your journey through life. Lay it down and put it to rest. 'Be' in the moment, right here, right now.

## Addictions

*"The only way anyone ever quits an addiction, is that they come to a place where the desire to be free exceeds the desire to use"*

Throughout our lives, the average person will experience some kind of addiction with or without being aware of it. Many people are addicted to coffee, cigarettes, alcohol, drugs, food, video games, sex, gambling, exercise, relationships and many other things but some addictions are physically a little healthier than others. For example, being addicted to exercise is generally healthier than being addicted to cigarettes, but to our state of consciousness, all addictions are damaging, because when suffering from an addiction we are being controlled by it, and if we are being controlled then we are not 'fully conscious' beings.

The object or activity itself is never what controls us, it is the mental relationship to it that exerts that control. In other words, it is our identification with it through the ego that determines our relationship with it, and with everything else, for that matter.

Through the ego we have developed a relationship with the object of our addiction because we are receiving something back, in return from it. The question is, 'what exactly are we receiving from it?'

If we can understand why we suffer these particular addictions, then we will understand the root of the issue and can begin to remedy it. This awareness is always the first step towards change, because only by being aware will we then be able to make a conscious choice to go beyond it.

## Why Addictions Occur

All addictions occur because we receive something in return from them, and the common factor of all addictions is that they, however temporarily, make us 'feel good.' No-one would persist with any addiction, if it did not provide this 'feel-good' factor and bring us pleasure or satisfaction in some way.

This 'feel-good' factor comes in two ways. Firstly, the addiction brings us direct, pleasurable stimulation such as sex, certain drugs and exercise, for example. Addiction through the 'adding' of some element, in effect. And secondly, an addiction may make us feel good by 'removing' something. For example, alcohol can remove tension and mental stress. It achieves this through its anaesthetising effect on the brain, and by removing that which may be causing us inner disturbance. Once this disturbance is gone, what remains are 'good feelings.' The absence of suffering is happiness, and this is what remains when all inner turmoil is removed.

So, all addictions begin because of their perceived 'benefits' to us. The ego mind begins to latch onto whatever feels good and then soon craves those feelings again. The ego is separate from the natural self that we really are, and so we only seek pleasure when we are not experiencing the natural peace and joy of who we really are, radiating through us. Whilst we are in the ego mind, negativity becomes all too apparent, but when we are in alignment with the True self, a natural pleasantness and satisfaction prevails. So, at the root of all addictions, is the fact that they manifest only because of our lack of connection and alignment with the pure natural self. And when we are isolated from the true joy of being, being the self, the ego masks the pain it feels by searching for other things to temporarily numb its pain. When we are trapped in the ego mind, it feels unpleasant, but all of the joy, pleasantness and satisfaction we could wish for will only come to us by connecting deeply to who we are. Who we truly are, is the ultimate joy, peace and bliss.

# Beyond Feeling Good or Bad

There is a place beyond feeling good or bad; the home of pure consciousness within. This is who we really are, beyond the body and mind and therefore not subject to the physicality of feeling good or bad. Searching for physically good feelings is subject to the 'pendulum effect.' Everything in the universe is part of an overall 'balance,' where opposites, positives and negatives serve to counter-balance each other, such as male and female, night and day etc. This is also true within the body itself. When we ingest something into the body in order to make us feel good, this 'high' will always be followed by a 'low' to balance it. And when we experience extreme pleasure, it does not last forever and will eventually subside, leaving us with a great sense of anti-climax, or in other words, a 'low.' Take the example of an alcohol 'high.' After the short 'high' of intoxication for several hours one evening, there may follow twenty-four to forty-eight hours of feeling terrible, an extreme 'low.' This is the pendulum effect, but it only applies to the material things of this world. If we take part in this game of ups and downs and pleasures and pains, we will ultimately be unhappy and suffer, because the artificially induced 'good feeling' can never be sustained permanently.

Addictions occur because the ego will always try to sustain the 'high' and will seek for the next 'fix' to retain it. The longer we remain in an unnaturally high state, the greater the fall will be, and so ultimately this is a foolish game to play. It will never satisfy our urges and as a result of this will eventually lead to self-destruction. What we 'are' is essentially beyond the body and mind and is a neutrality that can be stepped-into at any moment. It allows us to reside in a place of natural sweetness, a sweetness that remains unchanged no matter whether good feelings or unpleasant ones are felt on the surface. This sweetness is forever complete and satisfying as it is and is very deep and smooth by nature. It is not subject to the up and down feelings of pleasure and pain, yet at the same time, should we choose to, we may 'ride the waves' of the pleasant feelings yet remain merely a 'watcher,' unaffected by the unpleasant ones. In this place of sweetness we will experience the best of both worlds. If we feel good, that is positive but should we feel unpleasant, that is fine too as we are ultimately beyond that unpleasantness, remaining in the 'sweet spot' of pure consciousness.

## The Agitated Mind

Often the mind may be agitated by its desire to sustain its addiction. A feeling may arise which instigates thoughts of satisfying that addiction, or the mind itself may develop certain patterns of thought that lead to a powerful urge to quench the thirst of addiction. This may happen either or both ways; thought then feeling, or feeling then thought, and each one will feed the other in a 'snowball effect.' When the mind is agitated, this feels very unpleasant, but when we satisfy its cravings, the agitation will stop and then we feel good temporarily. However, this is short-lived as the agitation will soon return. For example, suppose that we feel a strong urge to drink alcohol, we may find that until that happens, strong, recurring thoughts will 'sell' us the idea of a drink in many different ways until we succumb to temptation. We may receive a stream of thoughts convincing us of how good it would feel to take a drink or receive mental images of how good that alcohol will taste or smell, or how great it will make us feel. We may then have thoughts of pleasant experiences associated with alcohol, such as partying with friends, or losing all our inhibitions. In other words, the conditioned mind will bombard us with many different thoughts and images in its attempt to elicit the response it needs.

What we need to realise is that this thinking and conditioned thoughts, is not who we are. We are only the witness of them, and this therefore means that we have a choice, we can take it or leave it. We can believe these conditioned thoughts to be true, or we can accept that these thoughts are not representative of who we are, they are just old, habitual, conditioned thoughts that keep recurring in order to get our attention. In other words, we realise that it is just the ego looking to fulfil its lack of satisfaction, and attempting to remove its misery or unpleasantness. The ego needs its 'fix' to feel good whereas the pure self that we are, needs nothing to feel good. When we refuse to believe all the mind-chatter, we will feel good and already be within the 'sweet spot.' All we must do in order to be the one who is free within, is to recognise that sweet spot.

## The Guilt of Addiction

Addictions and guilt are very closely linked together, and may actually feed each other and in effect, trap the ego mind. If we enjoy a certain pleasure that we have been taught is wrong or taboo, the conditioned mind will experience strong feelings of guilt, and this will trigger the 'looping effect.' This arises because when we feel guilty we feel even more unpleasant, and so we revert back to the addiction, because the addiction 'feels good,' and so the cycle continues on. In other words, the guiltier we feel, the more likely we are to revert to what makes us feel good. For example, someone who struggles with their weight through overeating will often seek comfort food. This is because when they are feeling guilty about their weight, they turn to the very thing that gives them most pleasure in order to lift their mood; in this case their favourite foods. And so the cycle perpetuates itself in this way, as with all addiction cycles.

Because of what we are taught, we often believe that we should feel guilty for doing the things we are told are wrong. But we do not have to feel guilty just to recognise the obvious, in this case the obvious being that addictions are not in our best interests. So my suggestion would be to simply release all guilt about all addictions. Do not worry about what is right or wrong, instead just simply become aware of whether this is the best thing for you and those around you. Ask yourself, do you enjoy being a slave to an addiction? And simply recognise that all addictive tendencies emanate from the ego mind in an attempt to cover-up the pain it feels, the pain of not having contact with the ultimate source of satisfaction. This source is your true aligned nature beyond body and mind identification, the pure consciousness within that is not subject to the ups and downs, or the suffering that the mind incurs. What the ego truly yearns for, is the true nature of consciousness, it longs for the unlimited self. When you awaken to your true nature and become ever more deeply connected in it, you may find that instead of having to overcome an addiction that the addictions just dissipate without you needing to do anything. All that is needed is your awareness, as your awareness expands, the addictions will just fall from you like leaves falling from a tree in autumn. You may even find that you outgrow all addictions. Does that mean that you will never engage in any of those activities again? Not necessarily, it just means that you will be completely free to take them or leave them. It just means that they will no longer have any hold over you. Discover your true nature and the neediness and attachment that was once there, will disappear and you will be free to enjoy them if you choose and completely free to let them go if you choose that too.

## Self-Forgiveness

What we must realise is that everyone is doing the best that they can, with the degree of awareness that they have. Most people operate from the subconscious mind over 95 percent of the time because the subconscious by its very definition, means 'below the threshold of the mind.' This means that people's thoughts, beliefs, desires and motives, that take place there, remain hidden from them and so people are mostly unconscious of their actions and motivations, in a kind of 'autopilot mode' and are never really in full control of themselves. If someone is sat in a boat on a lake looking up at the sky, how would they know all the different activities taking place in the water below them? The only way to know would be to put their head below the surface and take a look, otherwise how else can one be conscious of that which they cannot see, without looking?

Most of us have never ever been taught to look within our own minds, we have only ever been taught to look outside of ourselves and so most people's inner depths and mind-content remains undiscovered.

The first step towards changing any behaviour or belief is to firstly become aware of them. Only then can we make a choice as to whether or not to change it, otherwise we are simply lost, fumbling in the dark and bound by the unseen dungeon of the thinking mind with all of its associated horrors. So, the first step to self-forgiveness (and to forgive anyone for that matter) is to recognise that we have made mistakes because of our unconscious tendencies, which for the most part remain hidden from us and tend to take us over, outside of our control. We have only ever been able to operate in the best way we could at the time, from the level of intelligence we had at any given moment (Intelligence meaning awareness).

Have you ever witnessed in a person a tendency that you recognised in them yourself, but that seemed oblivious to the actual individual themselves? Maybe something such as a habit of which they were unaware? This happens because most people are only semi-awake, and being semi-awake can lead to mistakes and accidents. Anyone who has ever had an accident in a car can confirm that one lapse of attention will spell disaster. People, because of their general unawareness and unconscious tendencies, often lack this acute attention to detail and so are really blameless if doing something without awareness. It is similar to blaming a small child for never having heard of the planet Jupiter when they have never been taught astronomy. How would they ever know of its existence when it is not something that is already within their sphere of awareness?

We like to think that adults would know better, but the fact is that it has nothing to do with age but everything to do with how conscious a person may be, compared with how unconscious they are. If we do not know something, then we cannot be responsible for it, but the minute we do know it... well, now we become completely responsible as long as we remain conscious. The ability to be fully aware gives us the ability to make conscious choices and if we are not aware then we do not really have a choice because we are simply having unconscious tendencies and therefore it is no longer a choice but rather an automatic, built-in response, similar to that of a robot.

So, having this understanding can make us more compassionate towards ourselves and our mistakes and towards others and their mistakes also, because it is easier to forgive when we realise the truth—that most people do bad things from a place of unconsciousness as opposed to a clear state of consciousness and that we have also made mistakes based on our unconsciousness too. As long as we learn the lessons, we can forgive and move forward and develop ourselves to become more and more conscious of everything we do.

The word 'forgiveness' ultimately means to 'give-up' in the sense of giving 'something' up. In this case it is to relinquish guilt by forgiving ourselves for whatever we did to cause that guilt. The truth is that guilt can only exist in our life because we are holding onto it and yet as soon as we become aware that we are retaining something unwanted and that does not best serve our purposes, we should let go of it... permanently.

> *You see, it takes so much more energy to retain something than it does to let it go. To relinquish something is almost effortless... we just simply release our grip on it and it will disappear forever.*

> *So, release your grip on guilt and just let it go right now, let the past go and start afresh immediately. Each moment is a pristine, new beginning.*

> *What is done is done. Learn the lessons and then move on in a light-hearted and carefree way, fully-focussed on where you are in the present moment.*

## Daily practice 2...

Firstly, reflect on any guilty thoughts and feelings you may be retaining. Take a moment and look deeply into your mind, then when you are ready, repeat the declaration below. As you say the words, relax and let all the energy of guilt melt away. Implicitly trust that the declaration will work its magic...

> *'I let go of all guilt as I forgive myself'*

Allow yourself to be genuine and open when repeating this declaration. Sometimes negative emotions will arise in order to be cleared away and do remember that it is fine to do this as clearing away the old burdens will set you free.

*'When you finally let go of guilt, you will find that something better comes along.'*

# Chapter 6
## Ending Shame

*"Shame happens when you believe something negative about yourself that the outside told you."*

Unlike in the days of the ancient Samurai when the Japanese would commit suicide if they were shamed or felt shame, shame today does not cause the same, extreme reactions. However shame, even in recent times, has been known to lead to suicide but it still plays a role in our culture and can have a damaging impact on our sense of self-worth and happiness.

When we hold shame it can dampen our confidence and hamper our will and drive for life. Guilt and shame may seem very similar on the surface, however guilt is based on anger, regret and ill-feeling toward ourselves for something done or not done, whilst shame is a negative we feel about ourselves based on what others (or society) says about us or our actions or who we are.

Not too long ago (and still in some parts of the world) to be of a homosexual or lesbian persuasion was considered unacceptable by society and therefore the majority of people would condemn people who fell into that category. When society frowned upon this it would often bring feelings of great shame to those who felt an attraction to those of the same sex. However, times change and most people have now become more tolerant of this practice and those who used to feel afraid and ashamed of their behaviour, now feel more confident in openly expressing their sexuality without fear of ridicule and the feelings of shame that this engender.

So, the catalyst for shame appears to come from 'outside,' based on what society may say about us or our actions, thus triggering our inner thoughts and feelings of shame. However, as we investigate this more deeply we may uncover something surprising...

## Shame Creation

Here is a short story of the Buddha and an angry young man...

*It is said that one day the Buddha was walking through a village. A very angry and rude young man came up and began insulting him, saying all kind of rude words.*

*The Buddha was not upset by these insults and instead he asked the young man, 'Tell me, if you buy a gift for someone and that person does not take it, to whom does the gift belong?'*

*The young man was surprised to be asked such a strange question and answered, 'It would belong to me, because I bought the gift.'*

*The Buddha smiled and said, 'That is correct. And it is exactly the same with your anger and insults. If you become angry with me and I am not insulted, then the anger falls back on you. You are then the only one who becomes unhappy, not me. All you have done is hurt yourself.'*

It is often a truth hard to bear that is overlooked, the truth being that shame is not actually generated by the outside as it may appear, but that we actually create a feeling called 'shame' within ourselves based on what we think and how we react to the outside 'perceived pressure.' In other words...we feel shame because we received the gift, as opposed to leaving them with it.

Have you ever wondered why two people can be faced with the same circumstances but yet they react to it in totally opposite or different ways? Why is it that one person experiences shame yet another may not be affected as much, or may not be affected at all?

One major thing that we must take responsibility for in our lives is our reaction to the outside world and other people. We have often been led to believe that when something happens to us or when someone says something to us that there are in-built responses of how we should react, that we should feel upset, sad or happy when particular things happen or are said to us. The truth is that life has no fixed meaning, in other words it is us that creates the meaning (or just sees things neutrally without a particular meaning) as opposed to life automatically bringing one.

As an example, two people may be involved in a car accident in the same car and one will react in a certain way to the accident and may be reluctant to get back in a car for a long time afterwards. However, the other person may feel fine about it the following week, without exhibiting any fear whatsoever. Why would this be? Obviously the accident was physically the same experience for both, but yet they reacted differently. This clearly demonstrates that the accident itself had no fixed meaning, otherwise they would have both reacted in the same way. So what was the difference? Their reactions were the difference. And where do most people's reactions originate? They come from conditioned responses, thoughts and beliefs that we acquired from the outside world or from the ego's interpretation of life's rich experiences.

This is where the role of conditioning enters our lives. Conditionings are in-built responses, beliefs and thoughts we have developed over time as we have grown and matured. These conditionings were accumulated by us from many different sources—as we have already covered in the previous chapters. It is our firm 'belief' in these conditionings that create our suffering and in particular, as relevant to this chapter, our innate sense of shame.

The outside world is not really to blame for our sense of shame and we are not to blame for our sense of shame either, because we would not inflict it upon ourselves would we?

So who is to blame? Actually no one or nothing need be blamed, but the culprit is the in-built conditionings we have unknowingly taken on and bought into. It is these conditionings with which we identify, that control our emotional responses to life situations.

If we feel ashamed about something it is usually because we have 'acquired' certain ideologies or 'norms' of society and have then responded with shame when we believe that we have somehow transgressed them. If we believe that our being black-skinned or homosexual is wrong, then we will also, at some level, feel ashamed of our existence and that will be further emphasised should other people confirm their similar views, to us.

So as you may by now have concluded, this whole book and the spiritual journey contained within its pages, is in and of itself all about taking full responsibility of our perceptions, mind directions, emotions, actions and responses to life, without blaming others or a society for our own shortcomings or the pain and suffering we may be feeling. Ultimately, we create our own suffering by the ideas and beliefs we have about ourselves, others and life in general. There is no-one or nothing to blame for our sufferings, they are simply created because of our unconsciousness to self and life and we suffer because we believe falsehoods of ourselves. Once we stop blaming others for where we are and what we feel, only then are we taking full responsibility for our life and state of being within the present moment.

**Daily practice 1 ...**

Firstly, reflect on any shameful thoughts and feelings you may be retaining. Take a moment to look deeply into your mind and then when ready, repeat the declaration below. As you repeat it, relax and let the energy of shame melt away. Implicitly trust that the declaration will perform its own magic.

*'I let go of all shame'*

Do not allow yourself to carry shame any longer as it no longer serves you on your journey to truth, self-empowerment, happiness and self-responsibility.

# Worthiness

*'If you find yourself constantly trying to prove your worth to someone, you have already forgotten your value'*

When shame overtakes us we can often feel unconfident of our own self-worth. We may then begin to try and convince others of this worth, when ultimately all we need do is remind ourselves that we already have it within us and without condition.

From the earliest age, most of us were brought-up with a sense of inadequacy as though just being ourselves was somehow not enough in itself and that we must constantly strive to prove that we are adequate and therefore acceptable in the eyes of society in general. This creates a dynamic within us that says our sense of self-worth can only be attained by what others or the world may say and whether or not others validate us. This has the effect of setting us up for a great fall, as when someone disapproves of us or our actions, we are likely to feel shamed by it.

The truth is that every single being on this planet has in-built worth that is not dependant on any outside or internal conditions. Just because a society or person may say that you are worthless unless your bank account is full, does not make it any truer than saying the sun only shines when the sky is clear. In fact the sun always shines, regardless of whether the clouds are there or not, just as you are always worthy despite what others or your minds conditionings may say. Life is such a powerful, intelligent and magical thing that the very fact that you were born at all, shows how inherently worthy you are. Creation 'chose' you as an organism, to express itself in a unique way that no other being can precisely replicate.

We do not have to do anything at all to be worthy, instead just recognise that our very existence here is already one of worth as we are life and life is us. We are not separate from life as we all may have been taught, but we are a child in the bosom of the very great existence itself, and our existence validates us as worthy, automatically. We all bring a unique flavour to this life that can never be exactly identical to that of anyone or anything else. Please just contemplate on that for a moment or two...

## Daily practice 2...

Firstly, reflect on all the ways that you are worthy and how you are naturally worthy in the eyes of life itself. Take a moment to look deeply into your mind and then when ready, repeat the declaration below. As you repeat it, relax and let the energy and feeling of it uplift you... Implicitly trust that the declaration will perform its own magic.

*'I am worthy because I exist'*

There are no conditions attached, no rules, no living-up to someone else's expectations of you. Very simply, we are all 'worthy' because the very universe validates our right to exist and be the unique flavour that we are. Stand tall, be confident and humble at the same time. Our expression is the universe's expression also and as we thrive the universe thrives and therefore life wants us to stand tall within our own worthiness.

*'Your crown has been paid for, put it upon your head and wear it'* Dr. Maya Angelou

# Chapter 7
## Understanding Grief and Trauma

*"Initial grief is natural, overcoming it is a matter of choice"*

Grief is a trauma that can affect us all at a deep mental and physical level. The mind and body are so tightly connected that when we face any challenging situation such as the loss of a loved one, abuse or the breaking-up of a relationship, it can leave a mental, physical and emotional impression within us that becomes stored in both the subconscious and conscious mind levels and which can terrorise us for the rest of our lives. Whilst it often seems that facing challenging situations leaves us with no choice but to bear the psychological and physical scars for the rest of our lives, we must understand and accept that not only is it well within our control to overcome the prolonging of grief and trauma which can ruin our lives, but also to discover exactly how to handle these challenging situations in a more effective way as they arise.

Once we realise what is really causing our grief and suffering on an initial and prolonged level, we can place ourselves, through self-awareness, in a position to alleviate our suffering.

## Prolonged Grief and Trauma

It is certainly not uncommon for people (maybe ourselves also) to continue to relive traumatic events of the past and in doing so live a life of internal strife and suffering. So, because this may have been a common occurrence in our lives, we tend to just believe it is a very natural process for a person to grieve for so long. It is true to say that whatever we believe to be true, becomes true for us and so not knowing any different, we will continue to suffer for a very long period of time.

Have you ever heard the saying 'time heals?' So what is the correct length of time it takes for a person to heal? That is like asking 'how long is a piece of string?'

There is no set-in-stone answer. There is no definitive or 'correct' time. We would therefore have to come to the obvious conclusion that it must depend on the individual and how they are able to deal with their own traumas. But what is it that distinguishes one individual from another in dealing with such things? It is their degree of consciousness; consciousness meaning their ability to be aware of the mind, body and its various thoughts and emotions of the moment.

You see, any recollection of the past is based on memory and memory is a thought stored in the mind. If this memory has certain mental attachments in the form of ideas and emotions, then when we reflect on such a memory it will generate strong emotions and thoughts within us which can create intense suffering.

Remember how the process works? Thought creates a feeling and a feeling can lead to an emotion, and then the mind will interpret the emotion as good or bad, creating a continuous, yet repeating cycle.

So if we do not have much self-awareness or indeed any awareness of this process, then we will continue to be 'lost' in the mind via memories of the past which in turn will cause unpleasant sensations through particular thoughts and emotions. The more aware we become therefore, the more control we will have and the more we will comprehend the insanity of constantly creating suffering for ourselves, especially from events that have already passed us by.

The harsh truth of the matter regarding our prolonged grieving for a loved one is that this occurs not because we are grieving for the other person anymore, but because we are grieving for ourselves and **own** loss...

Please consider this carefully and I am sure you will agree that this is in fact the case. If someone close dies in a way that caused that person suffering, then initially we may grieve for their suffering, but as time goes by and their pain is long-gone, our continued grieving evolves into a 'selfish' grieving for ourselves and for what we feel 'we' have lost. This may sound almost sacrilegious at first hearing but the more we examine this statement, the sooner we begin to understand that this is absolutely the case and that we have transformed those original, empathetic feelings for another, into the self-indulgent feelings of our own personal loss. Most people are unaware of this and believe that they are simply grieving the loss of their loved ones, but by becoming aware, the sooner we can end the self-suffering. The mind will tend to resist this truism, because it is so deeply ingrained within us that the conditioned mind will always struggle to accept it. We should always look deeply into ourselves and recognise and reflect upon the truth.

Another strong contributor towards prolonged suffering or grieving is that we often do not allow ourselves to fully experience our own emotions naturally, as they occur. In the typically 'western' cultures of the world, we have been raised and conditioned by our societies with a tendency to withhold our emotions at times or to maintain a 'stiff upper lip' in the face of adversity as this is perceived as being a 'strength.' We may all have noticed, at funerals or when conversing with traumatised people that individuals will tend to hold their feelings and emotions in check, thus suppressing these thoughts and emotions, which will then only have to be confronted at a later time, thus postponing the inevitable. One of the most effective strategies for ending this otherwise prolonged suffering, is to 'feel' whatever we 'feel' in the moment, with 100% intensity. If we feel the need to weep, then we should not hesitate to do so and experience the emotions completely, thereby allowing us to rid ourselves of the pent-up emotion naturally and quickly and this course of action is far more beneficial to our mental wellbeing.

When this occurs we often find that something strange happens. On the surface, we may think that this would be a 'bad idea' because it may completely take us over, but something rather different happens when we allow ourselves to feel an emotion completely. It will release itself quickly, as you experience it...

You may have heard the saying, 'what you resist persists.' This is similar with thoughts and emotions; the more we try to stop them, the stronger they become and the more suffering we feel. When we 'invite them in' fully and accept them, whilst at the same time being ready to experience their intensity, the result can often be like watching an explosion from a distance. The very act of ending our struggle against them, allows them to pass through us quickly and express themselves in a more 'controlled,' almost disposable manner. In this way the thoughts and emotions are soon released and do not linger long, whereas when we attempt to block them or numb them with drugs, alcohol or inner resistance, they are stored in the body and mind instead.

So, the lesson is that whatever challenging situation comes your way, do not resist it, instead accept it and allow it to be experienced fully. Whether it be tears, emotions or thoughts, allow them to express themselves and in this way you will transmute them into something 'higher' as they are transformed by the illumination of your consciousness.

When it comes to the death of a loved one, one of the things that we have been conditioned to believe is that grieving is a sign of showing our love for that person and that if we stop grieving 'prematurely' then this somehow demonstrates that we did not care enough for that person. In other words, the more you love someone, the longer you should grieve. But this is not true at all. Please tell me, do you believe that remembering the person with great love and affection is less powerful than grieving itself? Surely, it is **more** powerful is it not?

To be joyful in the moment with love in your heart for that person, showing how much you loved them and how much you love yourself is absolutely the best way to honour yourself and their memory.

> *"Grief is natural she said. Overcoming it is a matter of choice"* Jeffery Eugenides

Overcoming our grief and trauma is simply a matter of choice. However, when we allow those feelings to take us over, it is because we feel powerless, a victim of circumstances, but in reality it is well within our power to change this. All it takes is self-awareness and understanding.

Prolonged grieving demonstrates that we have made the issue about ourselves rather than the person who should be the subject of our grief, whereas to be joyful and remember the person with love in our hearts right now in the moment means that we are paying the highest respects to them and ourselves. We are celebrating their life and who they were by 'having a party' within ourselves and inviting them into our hearts to join us. To live our life earnestly and happily in the moment is the best thing we can do for all concerned. We must let go of all the bad memories and live in the moment with love, as love and awareness heal all things.

## Initial Grief and Trauma

When first faced with a challenging situation such as the passing of a loved one, physical or mental abuse, the breaking-up of a relationship or an accident, it is our mental reactions that determine how we feel and therefore how we respond.

The initial grief we feel at the death of someone close or the ending of a relationship is completely natural. After all, we are merely reacting to and coming to terms with our loss. When we have lost someone that completed our identity, we feel the reduction of that energy when we are deprived of it. However, the only reason that we feel this so powerfully is because our energy is very strongly attached to those we have lost. Remember when you were a child and had your favourite toy taken from you, you would cry and grieve its absence. This is because as a child we were taught that certain things are 'mine' or 'ours' and therefore we became attached to them believing that they are actually a part of us. The same thing happens when we are older; it is that attachment to people and things which creates intense suffering and a feeling of loss once we are deprived of them for whatever reason.

So, the initial grief we feel when a loved one has passed is twofold. Firstly we grieve for what the person themselves must have experienced at the time of death, especially if their deaths involved trauma or intense suffering. And secondly our grieving derives from the sense that 'we' have lost something that 'belonged' to us and if we were strongly attached to that person for our sense of identity and happiness, then we will feel an intense sense of emptiness within us because of our mental attachment to that person. If it was simply death alone that makes us respond in that way, then why do we not feel the same way when a person down the street dies or when a complete stranger dies?

This in itself proves that it is not the act of death itself that automatically brings us grief-related thoughts and feelings; it is the level of attachment to that person that makes the difference. Contemplate this...

Think about anything that was ever taken-away from you in your life or when you were deprived of something you were dependant on for you happiness. Maybe you were distraught, but yet when something else was taken away on which you had no particular dependence. Were you moved to grief? I suspect not.

It may sound quite 'cold' to dissect our feelings in this way, but these are simply the facts of the matter. It is our mental and emotional dependence on something for our sense of happiness which can determine how we feel when it is taken away. The aim here is not then to become cold and detach yourself from people, instead it is to simply realise the truth; the truth being that our level of grief is often determined by how much of a mental attachment we have to that person and if there is a strong mental attachment present, then our minds will create more inner suffering and grief for us.

So what is the solution? The solution is to simply be aware of the mind and its processes when confronted with these situations. Whatever thoughts or feelings arise, allow them to develop naturally and do not try to hold them back. Allow them the leeway to take their natural course and remain un-curtailed. In this way, should we need to grieve, it will happen more naturally in a way which will not completely consume you and create unnecessary inner-strife. Once we are fully conscious of what is going-on inside our minds and bodies, they cannot dominate us and there will then exist a degree of separation which allows us to become more aware of our feelings and emotions. The more we become 'watchers of the mind,' the more we will be surprised by what we see and be overtly conscious of how our minds and bodies really work.

One last point to remember about grief and dealing with the death of a loved one is that as we spoke about earlier (chapter 4, on have no fear), is that understanding that leaving the body is the most natural thing in the world, will allow us to become more prepared for it when it happens. Contemplation of death and dying daily will not merely help us prepare for our own death but to prepare for the death of those around us, instilling within us a greater acceptance of the fact, when the time comes, and acceptance equals a more peaceful transition period.

Here is a short story which assists in reminding ourselves of the fleeting and changing nature of life . . .

> *A revered Zen teacher once approached the king's palace late at night. Because they knew him, the guards did not stop him as he made his*

> *way inside to where the king was seated upon his throne. The king recognised him too.*
>
> *"Welcome, sir. What do you want?" the king asked.*
>
> *"I wish to sleep in this inn tonight," said the teacher.*
>
> *Taken aback, the king snorted, "This is no inn! It is my palace!"*
>
> *The teacher politely asked, "If I may ask, who owned this palace before you?"*
>
> *"Why, my father, of course! He is dead now."*
>
> *"And who lived here before your father?""*
>
> *"My grandfather, naturally. He's dead too."*
>
> *"This building where people live for some time and go away, did you say that it is not an inn?"*

This short story clearly shows us how we easily become caught-up in believing that things will somehow last forever but reminds us that life constantly changes, people and things come and go. If we can come to terms with this on a deeper level and accept it, then we will find ourselves more at peace with the things that also come and go in our life.

I would like to say that dealing with the death of a loved one can often be a challenging affair and is not something that is always easy to deal with but the more we contemplate and understand this thing called death, attachment and how the grieving process works and how it is created, the more that will help us become more consciousness and therefore attain greater strength to deal with it.

The most important thing to remember is to not carry a sense of grief around with us for the rest of our lives.

Below is a daily practice to help us let go of any grief in our relationships or with regards to dealing with the death of a loved one.

## Daily practice ...

Firstly, reflect on any thoughts and feelings of grief you may be holding onto. Take a moment and look deep within your mind and then when ready repeat the declaration below with meaning. As you say the words, relax and let the energy of grief melt away. Trust that the declaration will do its work, as what you say goes.

*'I let go of all grief'*

*"Grief can be the garden of compassion. If you keep your heart open through everything, your pain can become your greatest ally in your life's search for love and wisdom"* Rumi

# Relationships

Dealing with the break-up of a relationship is much the same as dealing with the death of a loved one. It all comes down to our level of mental and emotional attachment towards that person for our sense of happiness.

You see, from the earliest age it was always hinted to us by our elders that we were somehow incomplete within ourselves and as a result, most of us came to believe that. We were then encouraged to believe that the answer to our becoming complete was in the external world, in people, relationships, possessions, status and achievements and so on and that the accumulation of these things would eventually lead to our completeness and happiness. Through this belief we have systematically spent our whole lives, whether consciously or unconsciously, in the pursuit of 'completing ourselves' and in the pursuit of happiness, only to realise that we never really achieve it. Even when we do appear to attain happiness or contentment, it never stays for long and so we are then compelled to move onto the next phase of our lives to chase the unattainable dream again.

With this sense of incompleteness in mind, we have all commonly been taught that one of the answers to our problem lies in finding a partner to make us 'whole,' and so most people pursue relationships from this sense of internal lacking, looking for another person to fill that imaginary void that we believe exists in our life.

When both people enter into a relationship with this need to be fulfilled and they place the responsibility upon the other person to live-up to all of their expectations, this is most often the beginning of a misaligned and rocky relationship. Why exactly is this?

Firstly, we must understand exactly what it means for a person to be 'incomplete' when beginning a relationship. We all have an attraction to an opposite energy, whether that person is male, female, different or same sex makes no difference, it is a particular type of energy (often the energy we are ourselves missing) to which we are most attracted.

Consider the two sides of the brain, the right brain which is the more emotional side and the left brain which is more the logical side. The emotional side has been more traditionally prevalent in women, whilst in men the left, logical side has been more dominant. The logical left side is more related to the 'masculine energy,' whilst the right, emotional brain is connected to the 'feminine energy.' Please remember though, that we are talking about a quality of energy here and not necessarily a gender type. However, men have traditionally been more oriented toward the masculine energy of the 'hunter-gatherer' type and women more towards the nurturing, homemaking energy of the feminine. But this situation has now begun to shift radically in today's society.

In other words, both sides have traditionally been operating from just one side of the brain, or one energy type but for a human being to be 'complete,' both in the left and right brain (the masculine and feminine energy) there needs to be a balance whereby they are both working together in synergy. It is this holistic balancing of the two sides of the brain and their respective energies which makes us a level and complete being, endowing in us a sense of inner completeness, satisfaction and holistic function.

Many people have a constant battle raging in their heads. This battle is between the emotional and the logical and when the two brains are not in synch and balance, war breaks-out in our psyches as a result. In the very same way, when two people enter into a relationship without their logical and emotional selves in balance and are largely coming from a one energy polarity perspective, relationship conflict often occurs. 'Women are from Venus and men are from Mars' comes to mind. This is why, throughout history, men and women have often struggled to understand each other and why conflict and relationship breakups can happen so easily. When a person is too logical they can often struggle to understand a person's emotional perspective and conversely when a person is too emotional they often reject rational reasoning.

Then, when these two incomplete energies come together it can create a euphoric feeling that we all recognise as 'love' but often it is physical attraction misinterpreted as love and a false sense of wholeness that cannot last. It is the joining for the first time of the two complementing energies. This first relationship phase of usually three to six months can often be complete bliss, as each person in the relationship is revelling in the freshness of their joining together and the feeling 'wholeness' it brings to them. However, what often happens next is that each of the people in the relationship, representing one dominant side of the energy polarity begin to try and exert control over the course that they believe the relationship should take, because now the two complementary sides are making a 'whole' and this is where conflict often begins.

How many relationships have you been part of or witnessed in others the strong need for each individual to have their own way or fulfil their own desires, even if that means using emotional blackmail or manipulation to get it? Often times, relationships will descend into petty squabbles, just like two children arguing over who is going to play with which toy. Have you ever experienced or witnessed this yourself? This is the manifestation of what the ego will do in order to fulfil its idea of what it thinks it needs.

Another source of conflict is the bringing of expectations into a relationship. Especially in today's world, it is becoming more common for people to have unrealistic expectations of their prospective partner and this is largely because our society often encourages us to have high standards when choosing our partners. Often, people will have a 'virtual' tick-box with all of the different qualities people must possess before they are accepted as good enough to be a potential partner. This outside influence is largely due to our conditioning from today's invasive media and entertainment industries and these ideas are often seized upon by the ego and this can then result in unrealistic expectations instead of us accepting people as human and as being imperfect and having faults.

When we enter into a relationship with unfeasible expectations, we are being grossly unfair on our partner by placing unreasonable pressure on them to be as *we* expect them to be. In truth, no-one can be expected to constantly 'live up' to all of the expectations we set and sooner or later these expectations will go unfulfilled and this is when conflict occurs.

As a result of this the partner will then often in turn try to manipulate or control their 'other half' usually resulting in a 'looking elsewhere' to have their desires met. This is the reality of entering a relationship from the egoically incomplete perspective of expecting our partners to satisfy all of our emotional and physical needs. Conversely, when we already have a sense of wholeness within, we will not feel the need to become complete through our loved-ones' fulfilling all of our innermost desires. Instead we will just be content to enjoy the relationship and spending time with the person without constantly trying to derive our happiness from their reaction to us.

When we begin a relationship looking to the other to make us whole and fulfil our ever whim and desire, we do not really 'see' that person anymore, instead we more readily see what we are trying to extract from them for ourselves.

Please take time to reflect on the above and observe yourself and also the relationships of others around you and notice how they function...

So when a relationship ends and we feel a sense of pain or loss it is often because we have placed a disproportionately large amount of importance on the other person in that relationship for our happiness and have made them the focal point of the fulfilment of our own desires. In other words we have created a mental attachment whereby without them we feel an incompleteness. When our relationship ends, it is not necessarily the parting of ways with that person that automatically hurts us, it is the thought of losing all the things that we believe the person brings us that is hard to bear. And this is simply because we have invested all of our sense of happiness within that person, in other words we are once again grieving our own loss.

Please contemplate...

## Conditional Love vs. Unconditional Love

*"If you love a flower don't pick it up, because if you pick it up it dies and it ceases to be what you love. So if you love a flower, let it be. Love is not about possession, love is about appreciation"* Osho

'Love' is a word that has come to mean many different things to many different people, but love in essence is a much more simple phenomena than it would appear to be at first glance. In the initial stages of meeting a person we often mistake physical attraction for love, the magnetic pull towards a different energy and also a mental attraction based upon conditioned ideas that we have come to believe are attractive qualities, for example the persons status, income bracket and fashion sense or a type of personality that we find appealing at that time.

Our attractions at a genetic level are based on what person will be best for procreation, who will be the best provider or child bearer; these are the attributes that the body is unconsciously drawn towards. To continue the right genetic code in order to give the lineage the best chance of surviving and passing on one set of information (DNA) to the next generation is all the body requires in its selection process.

Then there is a level of attraction that comes from the mind, being attracted to a certain personality that seems to mesh well with our own. This may often be sabotaged however, by the mental conditioning we acquire from society and society's ideas of who is attractive and relationship-worthy and who is not. It is noticeable from generation to generation that our perceptions of what is and is not attractive in a partner, changes. For example, a person wearing clothes in the style of the 1940s and speaking with the affected received pronunciation in the manner of a BBC presenter of sixty to seventy years ago, would not be seen as attractive or desirable to the people of today.

Nowadays, we are often bombarded with so many messages telling us what we should be looking for in a person and a relationship. We have TV, films, glossy magazines and our family's expectations, all of which tend to influence our decisions when choosing a partner. The conditioned mind can very easily be swayed towards finding what it expects and finds palatable in another person. Be aware of the egos expectations and ideas...

What is often misnamed as 'love at first sight' is largely governed by the above factors. It is these attributes of attraction, through the body and mind that we often mistake for love, itself.

Once we are in a relationship, what we call 'love' eventually begins to change somewhat and the feeling of attraction towards the other person can begin to wane dramatically from its earlier intensity.

As stated earlier, our innate sense of incompleteness drives us on to become 'one' with the other person. This is actually the act of sex itself, the act of desperately trying to become one with the other person, being as close to each other as possible, like two single cells trying to merge as one. But obviously no matter how hard we try it can never actually happen and in fact the closest we can ever get is to create another cell that is partly 'he' and partly 'she.'

So now that our quest to find 'Mr or Miss Right' has succeeded through our mutual attraction, the conditioned mind's next goal is often to wholly possess that person, to make that person 'mine.' This is why marriage has been so popular throughout the ages. Marriage is a contract that 'binds' us together through law, both 'legal' and 'religious' and is often entered-into through the fear of losing this person and not always because of love as we may think. And so the act of declaring the relationship 'official,' is often an attempt to bind the other person into the relationship, so that no other person can possess what we believe and feel to be 'ours' by right.

You see, what we refer to as 'love' (conditional love) is really nothing more than how the other person 'appears' to give us a pleasant feeling within ourselves. When a person looks the way we like them to look (physical attraction) and does the things we like them to do (mental attraction through expectations), an overwhelming feeling of 'well-being' is generated within us, which we believe has emanated from the other person, but in essence it has actually been generated within ourselves on behalf of our partner. As they continue to behave in a way that we want them to behave, this triggers warm feelings towards them, in essence generated through our own ideas and responses.

In other words, we feel 'good' when our partner is meeting the expectations that our mind has set for them but as soon as they stop living-up to these expectations our 'love/attraction' for them begins to dwindle dramatically. How many times have you seen or experienced this yourself? This demonstrates clearly that what most people call 'love' is nothing more than conditional love or love with set conditions that must be met. As soon as those conditions are no longer being met our so called 'love' can often turn to hate or dislike and if love can turn to hate so easily, this proves that it was never really 'love' in the first place, because real love is unconditional and does not discriminate based on someone's actions or lack of them. Real love is not part of a love-hate duality as most of us may have now come to regard it. In fact many of us believe love and hate are at opposite ends of a scale and this is why we often refer to a 'love/hate relationship' with someone or something. What they are really speaking of here are likes and dislikes which have nothing to do with real love. Real love always stands alone as an ever present force of understanding and freedom.

An example of real, unconditional love may be seen in the way that a parent shows constant affection for its child, they will always feel love for that child no matter what the child does or does not do and that is true love. True love is also an understanding, the understanding that I am you and you are me, it is the ability to see and appreciate the familiarity in all things, to see that the essence in another person, a tree or animal is ultimately the same essence that is at the source of all life and within us all. True love has nothing to do with a relationship in and of itself; it is a kind of reverence and respect for all life and things and is also the ability to look deeply and directly into another being and see the core of who they are (who we all are) beyond roles, judgements, labels and experience an intense appreciation of them. So, if you can say you truly love your partner regardless of what they do, then you are displaying a true, unconditional love of them. You may not always approve of what they do, but unconditional love will always overcome this and enable you to see the real 'them' at the deepest level and without being negatively influenced by their actions and the inner misconceptions of your mind.

Put more simply, unconditional love is love without conditions, guidelines or requirements for that love. Whether you are with that person or not, you are able to continue to show appreciation for who they are at the deepest level. That is true love indeed.

Please contemplate these things...

Real love is not necessarily how your partner affects you or what you receive from them, but more how you see them and appreciate them for what they are and without any expectation of receiving anything in return. Often, the 'learnt' mind expects to receive the same back in return for what it gives, but this can easily become a motivation for doing those things only for the purpose of receiving. Giving, then no longer becomes genuine.

Conditional love often demands that we entrap and possess our partner, but once we attempt to possess them in this way, we restrict them from freedom of movement and expression. Freedom is the bedrock of love, love is freedom. Whenever we try to make something ours, we are removing the freedom of the very thing that we are trying to possess and that we tell ourselves we love. Love cannot be gained through control and possession; love can only be demonstrated and returned through freedom, giving the other person freedom to express themselves in a natural way, uninhibited and unlimited by another. Freedom is the basis of all love.

Sometimes in a 'rocky' relationship that does not seem to be working for either partner and where only pain ensues, we must let that person go, understanding that it is our love for them that is putting them first and that it will be the best for all concerned if we part. I am sure we have all witnessed a painful relationship that was being prolonged unnecessarily and painfully because both people in the relationship were too scared to release each other. But sometimes, if we truly love the person, then we have to recognise our own selfish motives in wanting to keep them and we have to relinquish our hold on them, knowing that it will be the best thing for all concerned.

Please contemplate this ...

Fundamentally, love at its source is pure connection, the connection of the deepest aspect of ourselves connecting with the deepest aspects of others and of the existential reality itself. When we recognise the source in all things, we wish to give those things freedom, appreciation and the gift of our understanding. If we can enter all relationships with this deeper knowing, then all of our relationships and the people within them will flourish.

# Hate

*"Holding onto anger is like drinking poison and expecting the other person to die" Siddhartha Gautama (Buddha)*

The above quote by the Buddha is referring to the negative power of holding anger, but feeling hate towards something or someone also applies in the same way. Hate is a very unpleasant and low vibrational state in which to exist. It is a persistent, intense form of dislike towards someone or something and when we continuously or even temporarily hold onto such a feeling it can really drag-down our state of consciousness and literally cause physical harm to our bodies.

Sometimes people may say things like 'oh I just hate doing the dishes.' But in this example, they are really referring to disliking something as opposed to hating it. Hating something is when that dislike has reached its peak of intensity, almost like a combination of extreme dislike mixed with anger. Hate derives from a gradual build-up of dislike; for example when someone does something that we dislike so passionately it can soon build into a lasting feeling of hatred towards that person or situation.

When we 'hate' a person or situation, it is directly because of how those things make us feel but what we really hate is the feeling within us and not necessarily the perceived object of our hatred. Whenever the person or situation triggers these unpleasant feelings within us, we direct our hatred towards that person or thing because we tend to view them as the root cause of our unpleasant feelings. In other words, our 'hate' is really about the fact that we do not like how we feel and so we then direct our malice towards those who appear to have caused it. Once again we must take responsibility for our own actions and understand that it is our reaction that has caused the way that we feel and not the outside influence. Looked at another way, incidents happen and then we respond to them in either a pleasant, unpleasant or neutral way. However **we** respond will determine how **we** feel, because our mental response creates a tangible physical response (emotion/feeling) in the body. So, our hate is fuelled by how terrible we feel inside.

Let us take an extreme example, such as a loved one being murdered or someone being abused as a child. Once again, I would like to say that none of this is particularly easy or pleasant to speak of, but if we wish to become a powerful, joyful and awakened being then we must take full responsibility for all of our mental, emotional and physical responses to life. In fact that is what the word 'responsibility' actually means; the 'ability to respond' and we can only take responsibility the more we understand and become conscious of our inner responses. So let us now understand more of what is taking place within us.

If someone close to us is murdered, we will grieve and may even feel completely distraught. The length of time it affects us and intensity of our feeling towards the event, depends greatly on our degree of self-awareness. When we feel so distraught inside and feel bad for the suffering our loved one may have endured, our natural response is to blame the murderer for what has happened and whilst it is true that the murderer created the situation, it is also true that we can positively or negatively affect ourselves by the way in which we personally 'handle' the intense situation. Of course everyone reacts differently to any given situation but if we harbour an intense feeling of hatred towards the person who has caused so much pain and wish them harm in the same way they caused harm to our loved one, then we need to understand that ultimately this makes no sense. When we retain hatred for someone within us, it actually causes us more pain than it does those to whom it is directed. Is this not a true statement?

When these negative feelings are retained too long they can create a bitterness and resentment and ultimately that only serves to damage us and those around us. The same is true if we have been abused or raped, we may find ourselves holding hate and resentment against those that wronged us, but it is that same hatred which can destroy us and our life. So, if we cannot find it within our hearts to forgive whoever did what was done, we should at least rid ourselves of our hatred for them for our own sakes and the sake of those around us. The more conscious we become, the easier it will be to let go of the past and to do what is right for your own state of wellbeing.

This short story called 'destroying the enemy' speaks of the solution to hatred...

> *"How many enemies—boundless as the sky—might I destroy," wrote the Buddhist poet, Santideva. "Yet when the thought of hatred is abolished, all enemies are destroyed."*
>
> *"How," asked the Buddha, "will hatred ever leave anyone who forever thinks: 'He abused me; he hit me; he lied to me; he robbed me?' There is an enduring law: hatred never ceases through hatred; hatred only ceases through love."*

Find it within your heart to set yourself free through love.

Christopher J. Smith

# The Power of Forgiveness

*"To forgive is to set a prisoner free and discover that the prisoner was you"*
*Lewis B Smedes*

When we hold something against someone, we actually hold ourselves prisoner to it. To forgive ultimately means 'to let go,' to let go of that which is holding us in bondage, that which is plaguing us and causing us suffering. Forgiveness does not just heal us, but it heals those that we offer it to.

A powerful true story comes to mind of the convicted serial killer Gary Ridgway who was known to have killed at least 48 people. Gary Ridgway was in court listening to his victims' family member's statements; a woman came forward and said she wished him a long, slow, suffering death. Then a mother came and said that she hoped he would go to hell where he belongs and Gary just sat there stone-faced and emotionless.

Then a father of one of the victims took the stand and said *"Mr. Ridgway there are people here who hate you . . . , I'm not one of them. You've made it difficult for me to live up to what I believe . . . and that is what God says to do . . . and that is to forgive . . . you are forgiven sir."* Suddenly something amazing happened, the stone-faced and emotionless Ridgway broke-down into tears.

I am unsure as to whether or not the enormity of what happened was really understood by those that witnessed it. How is it that an act of forgiveness was able to penetrate a cold and hardened exterior that no one else could get through to, a mental wall that appeared to be as thick as the doors of Fort Knox?

When a person's humanity has been covered-up and obscured for so long, only an act of humanity can bring out the humanity in another. It is almost like an unspoken language; hate either draws out more hate or erects a barrier, but when we express our humanity to another being it often touches the humanity in them also. It is one heart reaching out to another heart and no matter how much that heart seems to be buried; an act of humanity can unearth it.

All people, whether convicted serial killers, criminals or everyday people have inherent good within them and our task and the task of our societies should be to find the best way to bring that out in all of us, especially those that need help most of all. You see, lack of understanding breeds fear and this is why so many people say things like 'lock them up and throw away the key,' because it is so much easier to do that, to pretend that it is not our problem. This type of mentality is born from the fact that we often cannot see or understand how to truly help these people but it is high time that instead of turning our backs or hating them, we start to try to understand what causes people to commit crimes or behave anti-socially and then seek out an appropriate solution that reveals the humanity in them. This is where the fields of neuroplasticity and epigenetics could help greatly. They are sciences of transformation that could help us realise that anyone can change for the better if we are prepared to work with them.

Here is a story from my own experience, from the time when I used to work as a nightclub 'bouncer' (doorman) . . .

I remember one night a man was extremely drunk and was causing some issues at the bar and it was down to me to escort him from the premises ('escort' is a euphemism meaning throw him out, bodily if necessarily) and so I took hold of him and began to walk him out of the building through one of the side entrances. As I was holding him and walking him through the building to the exit, he was calling me several unpleasant names, struggling and implying that when we got outside he was going to attack me. As this was going-on, I very gently but firmly spoke into his ear with zero aggression and in a totally relaxed way . . . *"OK mate,"* I said, *"don't worry about it, you have just had a little too much to drink that's all. I know you are a good bloke and only wanted a good time."*

Suddenly he relaxed and stopped speaking. As I released him just outside the exit door he slowly turned around and apologised to me, admitting that he was acting like a complete idiot. I replied that it was totally fine and he thanked me, shook my hand and was soon on his way.

What had happened in this case was that I did not try to use aggression against aggression, or anger against anger and I did not try to make him appear to be wrong and myself to be in the right (that is a trick that the mind usually plays) and so all the conflict was removed from the situation. Instead, I looked for the humanity within him and in the situation (the situation being that alcohol was obscuring his humanity somewhat) and as soon as I encouraged that humanity it was immediately uncovered and sprang forth from within him. Finding the humanity within a person or situation does not necessarily mean that we agree with or approve of what was done, it simply means that we should always look for the humanity within anyone, by demonstrating our own first. Life is often like a mirror and what our attitudes are often reflects back. Search for the goodness in someone and you will find the goodness, look for the badness you will find the badness, look for truth and you will certainly find truth.

When we come from a place of hate we see only hate and this can often bring out the hatred in others. When we start from a place of goodness we see goodness and it can bring out the goodness in others. When we start from a place of truth we see truth and can bring out the truth that lies within others. Could it be any simpler than that?

Please contemplate this...

Forgiveness of others is actually a form of self-cleansing. When we hold onto hate, bitterness or resentment it is we that feel its burden, day in and day out so do not carry that burden but instead set yourself free and if you can find the courage within, then also offer the gift of your forgiveness to the one who may need it most. Forgiveness does not necessarily have to be spoken in words, it can be simply released in the quietude of your own 'space.' The releasing of this forgiveness will cleanse you from the inside so that the light of truth shines strongly within you. Forgiveness also does not necessarily have to be directed towards another person either; it is sometimes more about letting go of the recurring negative thoughts and feelings about someone, that we may be carrying with us. Amazing things can happen when we do this, because as we let go of the negative thoughts and feelings about another person, we will then begin to see that the cause of our distress was not the actual person but instead the constant negative mental attitudes and feelings about them.

Please contemplate this...

All the ills of the world happen because of our unconsciousness. Unconsciousness means that we are unaware of what we are doing, that we have been taken over by the mind and its conditioning; that we have been taken over by hate, anger or bitterness. Those people that commit crimes are often just a little more unconscious than the average person, and so the mind takes them over just a little more. As soon as we are taken over by the mind and its conditioning, we are finished, we are lost in a place without self-control, but as soon as we become more self-aware and break free from the clutches of the mind, nothing can be done within us without our nod of approval. So if someone acts unconsciously does this mean there should be no consequences? Certainly there should be consequences and life will always provide them even if human law does not, but we all suffer and do things that later we wish we had not done. All the ills of the world occur because of our ignorance. Ignorance is the only darkness and awareness, truth and understanding are the lights which will heal and eventually prevent all ills in the world around us.

Allow me to share this story of the Thief and the Zen master with you...

> One evening, Zen master Shichiri Kojun was reciting sutras when a thief entered his house with a sharp sword, demanding "your money or your life." Without any fear, Shichiri said, "Don't disturb me! Help yourself to the money, it's in that drawer." And he resumed his recitation.
>
> The thief was startled by this unexpected reaction, but he proceeded with his business anyway. While he was helping himself to the money, the master stopped and called, "Don't take all of it. Leave some for me to pay my taxes tomorrow." The thief left some money behind and prepared to leave. Just before he left, the master suddenly shouted at him, "You took my money and you didn't even thank me?! That's not polite!" This time, the thief was really shocked at such fearlessness. He thanked the master and ran away. The thief later told his friends that he had never been so frightened in his life.
>
> A few days later, the thief was caught and confessed to, among many others, his theft at Shichiri's house. When the master was called as a witness, he said, "No, this man did not steal anything from me. I gave him the money. He even thanked me for it."
>
> The thief was so touched that he decided to repent. Upon his release from prison, he became a disciple of the master and many years later, he attained Enlightenment.

Because of the master's shocking kindness and firmness the man decided to change his ways. This illustrates how powerful we are when we speak from truth and understanding. Kindness is often thought of as a weakness, but kindness is only a weakness when we are not grounded in our own firm power. For example, have you ever met a person that was always very kind to people but when that kindness was thrown back in their face they crumbled? However when we 'really 'know who we are,' we do not really mind and are not affected by whether someone is grateful for our kindness or not, because we are fully grounded and secure in who we are. Let it be known that your power and kindness can change lives.

Below is a powerful meditation on forgiving others. A part of this meditation is to remember that all of us at some time or another have hurt or harmed others through our own thoughts, words, actions and deeds and we have all done this through our own unconsciousness and ignorance at the time.

> *To practice forgiveness meditation, let yourself sit comfortably, close your eyes and allow your breath to be natural and easy. Let your body and mind relax. Breathing gently into the area of your heart, let yourself feel all the barriers you have erected and the emotions that you have carried because you have not forgiven others. Let yourself feel the pain of keeping your heart closed. Then, breathing softly, begin asking for and extending forgiveness, saying the following words, letting the images and feelings that arise, become stronger as you repeat them.*
>
> *FORGIVENESS FROM OTHERS—There are many ways in which I have hurt and harmed others, have betrayed or abandoned them, caused them suffering, knowingly or unknowingly, out of my pain, fear, anger and confusion. Allow yourself to remember and visualise the ways in which you have hurt others. See and feel the pain you have caused out of your own fear and confusion. Notice and feel your own sorrow and regret. Sense that finally you can release this burden and ask for forgiveness. Picture each memory that still burdens your heart. And then to each person in your mind repeat: 'I ask for your forgiveness, I ask for your forgiveness.'*

# The Secret Self

*FORGIVENESS FOR THOSE WHO MAY HAVE HURT OR HARMED YOU—There are many ways in which I have been harmed by others, abused or abandoned, knowingly or unknowingly, in thought, word or deed. Allow yourself to picture and remember these many ways. Feel the sorrow you have carried from the past and sense that you can release this weight of pain by extending forgiveness when your heart is ready. Now say to yourself: 'I now remember the many ways others have hurt or harmed me, wounded me, out of fear, pain, confusion and anger. I have carried this weight and pain in my heart too long. To the extent that I am ready, I offer them forgiveness. To those who have caused me harm, I offer my forgiveness. I forgive you.'*

*Let yourself gently repeat these two Meditations for forgiveness until you feel a release in your heart. For some deeper pains you may not feel a release but only the burden and the anguish or anger you have held. With those pains be gentle. Be forgiving of yourself for not being ready to let go and move on. Forgiveness cannot be forced; it cannot be artificial. Simply allow yourself to continue the practice and let the words and images work gradually in their own way. As you work with this meditation you may find it becoming a regular practice in your life, letting go of the past and opening your heart to each new moment with wisdom and kindness.*

## Compassion

*"Love and compassion are necessities, not luxuries. Without them humanity cannot survive" Dalai Lama*

A significant component of compassion is the ability to see things from a different perspective and the ability to put ourselves in the position of others. As the saying goes, 'don't judge a person until you have walked a mile in their shoes.' Our conditioning often encourages us to judge others at face value, looking from the outside in, but real compassion comes only when we look from the inside out and can imagine ourselves in the other person's situation. Compassion is also about showing respect for all people, treating all people equally despite what a person may have done or not done. Even those that have made mistakes no matter how great, deserve respect because we all make mistakes and most mistakes come from ignorance and unconsciousness. People do not have to earn our respect just as we do not have to earn the respect of others. Respect comes when we first show respect and we can only fully show respect when we respect every aspect of ourselves.

Compassion often grows within us as a result of our own sufferings. Through those sufferings we learn that our suffering is very much the same as our neighbour's. Despite slight differences in all of our issues and sufferings, basically they all derive from the same kinds of beliefs, thoughts and feelings.

As the Chinese Proverb says, *'To know others, know yourself first'*

When we understand ourselves more clearly and recognise the suffering we have endured ourselves, it helps generate empathy and compassion for those around us. Through self-understanding we come to know the mind and every trick the mind can play, intimately and understand that we were also once lost in the unconsciousness of our own conditioning and so can empathise with others that are lost within it too. When we stay connected with our true nature, beyond the conditioned mind, we will find that it is very natural for us to show compassion and kindness to others. It is only when we reside in the learnt mind (separate identity) that we will find ourselves thinking and reacting from a place of fear and therefore kindness will not be easy to display, because we will be looking at the world from a perspective of self-preservation. As mentioned previously, when we do not understand something, we can tend to fear it and when we fear it, we are less likely to act in a humanitarian way.

Here is a Zen story regarding the nature of things...

> *Two monks were washing their bowls in the river when they noticed a scorpion that was drowning. One monk immediately scooped it up and set it upon the bank. In the process he was stung. He went back to washing his bowl and again the scorpion fell in. The monk saved the scorpion and was again stung. The other monk asked him, "Friend, why do you continue to save the scorpion when you know its nature is to sting?" "Because," the monk replied, "to save it is my nature."*

So the lesson is, do not concern yourself too much with the nature of others, simply be the natural 'you' beyond the ego mind and the right action will be forthcoming as and when necessary. The reward for this type of noble action is the reward of your humanity and the humanity of others, but when we follow the path of fear, the consequence is more ignorance and more fear.

> *"Compassion will cure more sins than condemnation"* Henry Ward Beecher

A compassionate world is a peaceful world. If a person is told often enough that they are evil and insane, then they may well believe it and become the person they are told that they are. Often when someone is labelled with particular negative traits, they will endeavour to live up to that label, as they believe that everyone sees them that way in any case. Conversely, when people are constantly regarded as someone of a truly benevolent nature then they will also adopt those traits to an even greater extent. It is our attention that is the key and whatever we focus on becomes more magnified. If we label someone as 'bad,' then we will be more likely to see bad in them and they themselves will be far more likely to become bad, because they will begin to believe it themselves. This demonstrates the power of our beliefs and also the power of the encouragement of such beliefs.

When we awaken to our true natures and the love and compassion inherent within all of us, all the self-limiting beliefs we have about ourselves and others will soon dissipate and pass, leaving us feeling light, free and expansive.

Feel the powerful effects of love and compassion with this meditation...

Please take your time to reflect and contemplate in detail at each stage of the meditation.

> *Find a quiet place and sit comfortably in a position where your back is straight and body relaxed. Allow your eyes to close and turn your attention inwards.*
>
> *Begin to notice your breathing and how this breathing is taking place naturally...*
>
> *Now take three large, deep conscious breaths. Breathe-in through the*

*nose ... hold it for a few seconds ... and then exhale out through the mouth.*

*Again in through the nose ... and out through the mouth.*

*Again in through the nose and out through the mouth.*

*Allow your body to fully relax. If any thoughts enter your mind ... let them pass straight through like clouds passing in a clear blue sky.*

*Now begin to imagine someone you love very much ... this may be a partner or a son or daughter, or a parent or friend. Anyone. Hold their image firmly in your mind.*

*Now just become aware of how much you love this person.*

*Notice how strong this feeling is and hold it on your heart.*

*Become aware of what you would do for this person? And how much you would help them if needed ... And when you feel this love, recognise that you are both one, together and connected by that love ...*

*Stay with this feeling of love ... begin to feel it expanding and soothing your entire body ...*

*Now feel the strong energy of love reaching and filling the entire room ...*

*Allow this energy to expand and move in every direction ... imagine its reaching every corner of the globe ... being felt by every being along the way ...*

*Now imagine this energy of love covering and hugging the whole world ... with great reverence for every being ... including man, animals, trees and seas, holding all in equal regard ...*

*Feel in your heart how much you love the natural beauty of this planet and every being within it ... then realise that true love is the ability to see yourself in another whilst realising that there is no other ...*

*The actualisation of this is true love, true peace ... true bliss ...*

*Then, when ready, concentrate once again on your breathing, and in your own time open your eyes.*

## The Secret Self

The continued repetition of this meditation will eventually open our hearts and provide us with a greater sense of compassion, love and connectedness to all beings and things in life.

It has been said that the heart is like a garden. It can grow compassion or fear, resentment or love. What seeds will **you** plant there?

# Chapter 8
## Genuine Self-Expression

*"Success in any endeavour depends on the degree to which it is an expression of your true self" Ralph Marston*

Let us now consider some of the obstacles to genuine self-expression. Firstly, we can say that genuine self-expression occurs only when we are not operating from a limited consciousness perspective. In other words, when we are not functioning from the learnt ego self, as the ego's expression is often rigid and formatted as opposed to being fluid and adaptable when coming from the true self.

Self-expression then only occurs when we are aware of who we truly are, the unlimited self, experiencing this seemingly physical existence. When we recognise the role of this apparent physical existence, we are then able to express ourselves to our fullest capacity and demonstrate the uniqueness of the pure awareness clothed in a human body that we actually are.

When we are locked into a limited personal identity, we tend to express ourselves in a disconnected and rigid way, the way of a conditioned-self that carries many insecurities and fears and from that a need to control and manipulate others. And when we derive our sense of self from the conditioned mind, we tend to act in ways we learned from others, believe the same things as others and even think the same way as others. This then means that we are not being true to ourselves, but instead acting as a carbon copy of those with whom we interact . . . from a collective ego 'hive mind,' so to speak. In other words we are not as truly unique as we may have believed.

Also, being our authentic selves means not succumbing to peer-pressure and behaving in ways that are not faithful to who we really are. So many people often act in certain ways in certain situations, in the way that they believe that they 'should' behave, based on what society or certain people proscribe, and will often bow to the pressure of conformity and thus relinquish their true self-expression for an expression that falls in line with societal norms. One sure way to deny your own true self its freedom to express its own unique way is to 'toe the line' with the rest of the world and never question your own motivations. In order to demonstrate a true expression of who you really are, the 'real' you, requires a great degree of fearlessness, especially in not heeding what other people may think or say. Our fear of what other people think of us, places imaginary barriers around us, preventing us from showing our real natures to the world and the full expression of the unique beings that we all truly are. All of the heroes of history were fearless enough to follow their own paths instead of the one more regularly trodden and their reward and humanity's reward was a radical new way of thinking or a new idea or invention, something that brought humanity to a new level of development. We should all thank God for the fearlessness of these people.

Often, we may believe that we are acting in our own unique way when in reality our behaviour and sense of identity is based on society's standards or a particular role model. We may also place ourselves into a category, such as *'I am this or that type of person'* representing a particular character trait we may for example, have noticed in someone else and then adopted as part of our own identity. We also will often associate ourselves with recognisable groups, especially as younger people, identifying ourselves as being a 'rocker,' 'Goth,' 'hippie' or 'punk' etc., or any number of other identities, all of which 'pigeon-hole' us as being a particular character type. I remember as a child often imitating particular movie characters that appealed to my way of thinking at the time, thereby reinforcing my belief of who I was or who I was becoming. With so much influence in the world from all forms of media, religion and society in general it can be very easy for the mind to be influenced and therefore acquire particular identities that we mistakenly believe is 'who we are.'

True genuine self-expression happens and is experienced only when we are able to release all the external influences on our psyche and are able to become an expression of whatever emanates naturally from within, allowing us to express the true meaning of inspiration (coming from the place of spirit). The ability to recognise and tap-into that deep reservoir of silence, intelligence and creativity within, is the truest form of self-expression and the greatest contribution we as individuals can give to the world. Be willing to be yourself and play on the edge of societies norms.

## The Inner Conversation

As discussed previously, most of us are subjected to an inner conversation that takes places in the mind and when we believe ourselves to be this 'thinking' dialogue, it forms what is known as the 'ego self.' This ego self is a mixture of conditioned thoughts, belief systems and a sense of separation from the rest of creation. When we allow this constant noise in the mind to become 'us,' this can be the cause of many of our troubles, whether this be trouble communicating with others or in the sense of creating unnecessary inner suffering and turmoil for ourselves. If this inner voice with which we identify ourselves is not in alignment with who we really are at the core of our being, it creates a 'war within,' an inner battle of self-sabotage. Often our inner dialogue will tell us something, but then it will either not be expressed outwardly in the same way as the original thought or it will be repressed through peer-pressure or fear and thus will our external behaviour be different and self-modified for conformity. In other words, we will not be being true to ourselves because we are adopting a behaviour that is not ours.

For example, there are many people that dislike or even hate their jobs, but yet despite this they may have conflicting thoughts that urge them to continue in it because of the fear of what family or friends may think if they quit. So, this then causes a misalignment of their internal energies which creates suffering through suppression of the thought: 'I dislike this job and don't want to continue with it.'

This is in fact, a form of disingenuousness, because essentially we are lying to ourselves. In other words we are not being true to who we are or what we really want from life. There is then a distinct danger that we will then seek control of others, all because we have a lack of control within ourselves through this misalignment inside the body and mind. When the ego feels itself to be out of control it will often seek to control the outside through the misperception that this will bring control and stability. But the truth is that it never results in self-control, but only a false sense of control and this need for control can often turn into manipulation through various means, twisting another person's words or using emotional blackmail and tactics in an attempt to achieve its own ends.

It is this same need for control that results in an urge to lie to others as the mind uses lying to either get what it wants or to try and protect itself from a damaged self-image. Sometimes lying becomes a self-defence mechanism in order to protect our sense of self and self-image. The need to protect our sense of self only arises when we do not actually feel fully aligned and secure within our own self. You see, if person is being true to themselves, then they will not feel a need to lie because they would have nothing whatsoever to hide. To be yourself, one-hundred percent means 'laying all your cards out on the table' in plain sight without holding any close to your chest so that others cannot see them. We only feel the need to obscure those metaphorical cards if we are somehow insecure in who we are.

Please contemplate the following...

Daily practice...

Firstly, reflect on all the times you may have lied to others and told yourself lies. Take a moment and look deep in your mind and then when ready, repeat the declaration below with meaning. As you say it relax and let the energy of lies melt away. Trust that the declaration will do its work, as what you say, goes.

Repeat this Declaration daily—*'I let go of all lies'*

Do not allow yourself to lie any longer as it no longer serves you on your journey to truth and self-expression.

# Depression

Depression comes from suppression and therefore creates compression, a compressed and condensed state of being. If you have ever observed the body posture of someone that is going through depression, their posture is often slumped and contracted and their state of consciousness is often more condensed also, as often people with depression have a kind of 'brain fog' or haze, preventing them from functioning normally. Depression may occur when the body and mind enters a compressed and 'tightly-wound' state and this is often a result of the suppression of thoughts and words; in other words the lack of true self-expression and the ability to release our thoughts freely into the world, without fear of criticism or rejection from others.

When depressed we have a tendency to withdraw within ourselves and suppress bodily and verbal expression. It is almost as if we slowly begin to lose our voice and inwardly contract through a retraction of outward energy resulting in the retraction of both physical action and verbal expression. This often happens when are fearful of what others may say or when we feel isolated and have no-one in whom to confide and so we cut ourselves off from the outside world. This 'bottling-up' of our thoughts fears and emotions spreads more 'dust on the mirror of the mind' thus creating more distortions, confusion, contraction and therefore extreme unhappiness.

All of these suppressed thoughts and emotions are stored in the subconscious mind and therefore lodged in the body, just waiting for their chance to be released. This is why people with depression or those that tend to suppress their natural feelings, will often experience a huge 'burst' of anger or an emotional meltdown because the body and mind has a metaphorical 'release valve' with which to 'blow-off steam' so to speak. But this can be dangerous for obvious reasons. When we undergo this uncontrollable burst of emotion then we often have no control over where or to whom that energy might be directed or what the consequences may be.

So it is much more natural to speak to others about our innermost emotions or to share our thoughts and feelings than to retain them within ourselves without confronting their long or short-term consequences. There are certain meditations and methods for releasing thoughts and emotions that allow them to be confronted and dealt with when they arise and these will be covered later chapters. When we feel reticent about confronting certain thoughts, feelings or situations, they are often relegated to the subconscious mind where they must be processed and released at some point. If they are not dealt with or released, then our subconscious mind activity will begin to affect and influence our choices and behaviours in the conscious mind, and thus may unconsciously become the controlling influence in our lives. One of the ways we can release our pent-up thoughts and emotions is to channel that energy into some kind of creative endeavour, project or activity...

## Self-Expression through Creativity

One of the best ways to discover and unveil self-expression is through the medium of creativity, for example through various activities such as martial arts, dance, painting, videography, music and writing to name but a few only. Our capacity for self-expression through creativity is only limited by what the mind can conceive, as almost anything may be turned into a creative endeavour through which we can express ourselves. The meteoric rise of the internet and technology now also provides us with a significant tool for creative expression and gives us the ability to take creativity and expression to platforms and levels beyond those ever seen before in human history.

However we should also be aware that as regards to art and creativity, we may imitate or subconsciously use the ideas of others. This is acceptable and we may often use those ideas to create a framework within which to work in our own chosen fields, but true self-expression comes when we are able to drop preconceived ideas and allow our natural selves full expression in the activities we undertake.

In the wide world out there, there are thousands of photographers or actors etc., but it is our capacity to express ourselves fully without censoring our thoughts and actions that makes the difference. This 'expressive consciousness' is the true self and not the ego self. Often we may believe that we are expressing ourselves naturally when in truth we are only expressing ourselves through preconceived programmes and ideas already present within the mind. This is the expression of our true selves that extends beyond the physical body and mind and when we are able to just let-go and be ourselves fully, in the moment, then a richer and greater intelligence can shine through and enhance our creative abilities. Whichever point of spiritual awakening you are at, just allow yourself to flow freely without censor whilst at the same time continuing to journey deeper within the true essence of your being, this way you will continue to be yourself at every step of the way.

## Martial Arts for Self-Expression

One of the best ways for genuine self-expression is through martial arts, as these, like dance and many other physical activities give us an opportunity to truly express ourselves through the medium of the human body. When we relax our muscles and they become more fluid, the body develops an intuitive movement which when combined with specific training in these skills, will create the perfect foundation for their being put into practice. This is an excellent way to *be* ourselves and to express ourselves freely and also to relax. These disciplines allow us to add the essence of our being into the freedom and diversity of movement that these activities promote. A 'good mover' of any kind, whether a martial artist or dancer is 'stillness in motion,' they will move with their mind empty, because only when the mind is empty is there an absence of the censoring and blockage of thoughts. If we have thoughts in the mind that say, 'I cannot do that, or move this, or that way,' then that greatly limits our self-expression.

Expression truly occurs when there is no internal censor erecting artificial barriers up, and so in this sense the access to the secret self is the missing key to freedom in respect of bodily and mental freedom. This missing key is one that will unlock the body and mind, allowing it to achieve its full potential by removing all 'inner censoring.' This is a symbiotic relationship. Just as discovering our inner freedom will free the body, freeing the body will help free the mind and allow us to access the secret self. The key to success is being able to move and express ourselves with our minds devoid of all of mental blockages. Martial arts combined with meditation and the secret self will bring about genuine self-expression and this will also have an effect on every other area of your life.

## Conscious Communication

*"Communal wellbeing is central to human life"*

Just as cells in a body must communicate with each other to function, so must human beings. Real communication is the absolute foundation of human existence, but so often miscommunication or the lack of communication altogether, takes its place. Why is this so?

Miscommunication often occurs because most of us do not communicate efficiently. Conscious communication only occurs when we are fully alert and awake in the present moment. If we allow our mental processes to aimlessly wander into the past and future then it becomes impossible to communicate properly and consciously with others. Conscious communication is all about intimacy and connection to the person with whom we are attempting to communicate. To 'commune' literally means to 'be with' and to 'be with' someone means that we need to communicate effectively at all times. In this case, 'we' refers to the core of who we are, which is beyond the conditioned and inauthentic self. Often, the inauthentic self, may be present with all its heavy baggage of past memories, conditioning and future anticipations and if we attempt communication at the deepest level with others under these circumstances then 'real,' effective communication is impossible.

To be fully aware and ready for communication means being one hundred percent present in the moment and giving our full attention and awareness to another person. Have you ever been with a person (maybe in a relationship) where you were sat quietly not doing anything in particular but yet that silence did not prevent you from feeling connected to the other person? Simply because you were both there, being aware of each other's presence created an unseen energetic connection. When we are silent and fully aware with another person, this creates a deep, emotional connection, but when we are 'lost in the mind,' the connection is far weaker. It may be compared to a telephone conversation where the line is distorted and fuzzy and the person at the other end of the line can barely be heard. This will also happen when we communicate with all kinds of preconceived ideas and 'mental baggage' present; we do not really hear the person correctly because of all the internal prejudices and mental 'white noise' taking place.

## Conscious Listening

*"The biggest communication problem is that we do not listen to understand. We listen to reply"*

Have you ever been speaking with someone but sense that they are not really listening to you? That maybe they are lost in thinking about something else or that they are just waiting for their turn to speak without really listening to what you have to say?

When this happens, the other person is not really listening to what you have to say but instead they are simply waiting to counteract your words with their own thoughts and this in effect means that they do not really hear what you are saying, but are only hearing their own mind's interpretations of your words. It is impossible to focus our full attention on listening when part of our attention is concentrating on how to respond. Our attention becomes divided and we will fail to understand the entirety of what has been said. This is the root and meaning of the phrase 'give our undivided attention,' because when we become lost within codes of thought and mental interpretations, our attention becomes split and therefore weakened. It requires a great degree of inner silence and stillness if we are to have a clear and empty space from which to receive the ideas and thoughts of others because if our mind is full of 'noise,' then how can we truly receive? If a cup is full then how can anything else be added but if the cup is empty and therefore receptive, how much more can be added? So, true listening is about receptivity that is how receptive we are to what is being given to us. If we are unreceptive because we are not really there in mind, then anything being received will be blocked-out by our mind.

Try this practice when in communication with another person...

> *When listening to the other person speak, see if you can remain empty and still inside, maybe by bringing your attention down from your mind into your heart level in the chest and focus on their words and the sounds of the words as opposed to mentally trying to interpret them. Allow the person's words to be received naturally, and allow yourself to feel the words instead of mentally processing the words in your mind.*

What we may notice with this practice is just how often the mind tries to 'grab' the words and make sense of them and how it wants to automatically respond immediately. At first this practice may feel quite strange, but the more we try to 'feel' the words, the response will be pleasantly surprising and the other person will also feel more deeply connected to us. When people feel they are truly being listened to, they are more likely to open-up and develop a stronger bond with the person with whom they are communicating. This practice is also excellent in developing the capacity to become more aware of the deeper level of stillness within and at the 'being' level of who we are. The more intently we listen, the more meditative and 'silent' we become.

# Conscious Speech

*"Communicate, even when it's uncomfortable or uneasy. One of the best ways to heal is simply getting everything out, because if you live bitterly then you will live a lonely existence"*

The key element of conscious speech is the actual intent and ability to speak even when we may not feel like speaking. If our 'not speaking' is something that brings us closer to the core of who we are inside, then this sense of 'not speaking' is significant and should be considered, but when it is the mind and its fears and insecurities telling us not to speak, then we must either move into true inner silence or we must verbally express and communicate as this will provide a 'release' for the body and mind. So, the ability to go beyond the mental block of 'not speaking' is the first step towards actual conscious speech.

The second step towards conscious speech is to allow it to emanate from deep within our consciousness and to express it from that 'quieter place' inside as this helps bypass the conditioned state of consciousness and transports us into a place of pure 'being.' One of the simplest ways to allow ourselves to enter this 'quieter place' is to become more in touch with the body through mindfulness. When we are grounded and feel our bodies through mindfulness, we divert attention away from the busyness of the thinking mind and instead move it more into the body itself thus reducing the mind's activity and opening-up a space of greater silence and stillness within and from whence a more intense state of intelligence and expression can be found.

The third step is to be fully aware of the words we are speaking and to choose those words very carefully instead of just unconsciously saying the first thing that occurs to us. Have you ever said something hastily and without thinking and immediately afterwards wondered why you even said it at all? Or have you ever been with or around a person that constantly talks really rapidly without paying full attention to what they are actually saying? This is 'unconscious speech' in action and 'unconscious' means that we are not totally aware of what we are doing and so in this case we are speaking without really noticing what is being said. Below is a simple practice to undertake before speaking...

*Firstly, we need to make sure that we undergo the listening practice when hearing the other person speak, then rather than speaking ourselves immediately after they have spoken, take a deep breath and a short, silent pause before choosing the most brief and precise words with which to reply. In other words, we should try to speak in a more clear and precise manner without using unnecessary words.*

Often we speak unconsciously and therefore waste energy because we are not being mindful of our speech and the words we are using. When we practice the exercise above, we should find ourselves becoming more mindful and will no longer be wasting energy in using many unnecessary words.

In the renowned book *'The Yoga Sutras of Patanjali'* it states; *'Only speak what is pleasant and true, and if it is true but not pleasant then don't speak it and if it is pleasant but not true don't speak it.'*

This is an excellent way of remembering to speak consciously. So why only speak what is true and pleasant?

When we speak about things that are false, we only serve to steep ourselves and others in Illusions and therefore drive ourselves deeper into misalignment and the clutches of the limited, conditioned mind. It is nothing more than a form of lying to ourselves and others whether consciously or unconsciously, so learn and be mindful to speak only the truth at all times, but remember that the truth you speak must be pleasant.

When we speak of unpleasant things, we may bring ourselves and others down to a lower and more disconnected state of energy. We have all encountered (or have been ourselves) one of those people that are so pessimistic and negative that they seem to have the ability to lower the energy of an entire room as well as the energy of others by their very presence and the words that they speak. Conversely we have met those that have an uplifting and positive presence and always speak about things in a truthful and optimistic way. Which type of person do most people prefer to be around, do you think?

The conscious aspect of us is more attracted to those that operate on a higher frequency and to those that are more aligned with truth and positivity, but the ego will often unconsciously lean towards the unpleasant and melodramatic. This is the reason that TV soap operas, films, news and celebrity gossip is so popular, because the ego feeds on the negativity inherent within it all. It is an exact frequency match and so the ego is always drawn towards it. The conditioned mind loves negativity and drama and so is always looking to connect with whatever unpleasantness it can find, although unconsciously it does not know that it is seeking negativity, it is just addicted to that type of energy in the same way that an alcoholic needs his next drink. Because the ego is based on an identity of separation it loves the energy of negativity and because the basis of negativity is that which creates separation, it tends to destroy rather than create. This is why our media culture tends toward the negative, because the conditioned mind will identify with it and is thereby fuelled by it. The more we dwell in unpleasantness the more disconnected we will become from others and the further and deeper we will fall into the false 'ego self' and therefore Illusion.

If however, we continue to speak from a place of truth and pleasantries we will naturally be drawn toward more truth and pleasantness and those of this persuasion will unconsciously or consciously seek us out as like often attracts like. Unlike negativity, positivity is a force of connection; it is the energy of bringing things together and the basis of all positivity is truth and without truth there can be no real foundation for positivity, because the opposite of truth is illusion and illusion only serves to create more disconnection, therefore magnifying negativity. It is impossible to pretend to be positive, our demeanour and body language would betray us every time. However, positivity is often a by-product of our moving away from illusion into truth (see chapter 9 for the meaning of truth). As we move more towards truth, all the illusions begin to fall away and along with it, so does the negativity.

So does this mean we cannot speak about the more challenging events in the world like suffering, disasters and the personal issues we all must face? It is not always what we say, it is often the way we say it and the way we say it depends on whether or not we are in a place of truth and positivity or unpleasantness and illusion.

As an example, to talk about a disaster may not seem like speaking pleasantly, but if we speak about it in such a way that brings people comfort and optimism, then we are speaking in a truthful and pleasant way. Then, because we are leaving open the door for some optimism to enter the situation or we may be offering a positive solution of some kind, to the issue as opposed to creating fear or pessimism. Do you see the difference?

Speaking unpleasantly about a truthful situation can often just bring ourselves and others down further, whilst speaking about a truthful situation in a pleasant way through offering a solution or being optimistic often leaves us and the other person more uplifted and optimistic themselves. In other words it can help change their state of energy to a higher vibration.

So, the lesson is that we should only say what is pleasant and true if we wish to uplift ourselves and uplift others in our life. This will lead us and those around us on a fast track towards uncovering more truth and pleasantness within life generating an ongoing cycle of happiness.

Daily practice...

Please repeat this declaration every day, clearly with passion and purpose and allow yourself to become what you speak of.

*'I speak my truth clearly and positively'*

## The Unseen Power of Words

*"Words cast spells. That's why it's called spelling. Words with emotion are strong energy, use them wisely"*

There is an unseen, energetic power behind the words we speak on a daily basis. All words possess some power, but words with emotion have an immense power and transformative influence. Their transformative power lies in their capability not just to transform our own body and mind, but to potentially influence the minds of others and to influence the entire fabric of our world.

When our energies, intentions, emotions, words and actions are all in alignment, this then endows in us a great creative power. Our verbal power of expression also contributes greatly towards this end too and so we should always be very mindful of what we feel, speak and outwardly express in every moment. People will often say things such as 'I cannot do this' or 'nothing good ever happens to me' and there are so many more examples of the disparaging words people use on a regular basis and thus in effect, creates the reality they weave for themselves.

When we live 'in the moment' we are more conscious and able to express ourselves in a more mindful way. The most powerful way to speak and express is directly 'from the heart,' with honesty, clarity and passion and when we are in true alignment with who we really are, at the core of our being, this will happen naturally and we will suddenly find that positive things begin to happen to us. Through the medium of our words we are spelling-out our own realities and helping to influence and shape the fabric of our lives.

What follows is not just simply an ancient teaching or a metaphysical idea; it is a verifiable scientific phenomenon.

## The Power of Sound and Intention on Water

Consider the following stunning and surprising research from Dr. Masaru Emoto...

Dr. Emoto has proved beyond doubt that if human thoughts are directed at water before it is frozen, images of the resulting water crystals will be either beautiful or unattractive depending upon whether the thoughts were positive or negative. He found that this can be achieved through prayer, music or by attaching written words to a container of water. Since 1999 Emoto has published several volumes of a work titled *'Messages from Water,'* which contains photographs of water crystals within essays and 'words of intent.'

He has conducted research worldwide on the effect of ideas, words and music upon the molecules of water, and the descriptions below are taken from the book of his published results.

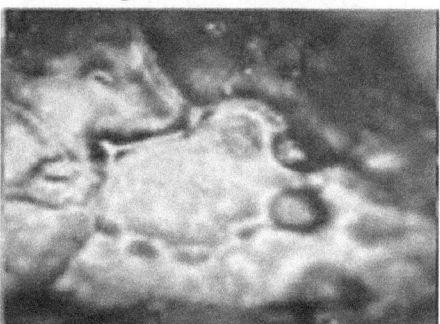

Fujiwara Dam, before
offering a prayer

The photo above is of a frozen water sample from the lake at Fujiwara Dam, in Japan. As you can see, the water's structure is dark and amorphous, with no crystalline formations.

After the above water sample had been taken, the reverend Kato Hoki, chief priest of the Jyuhouin Temple, undertook a one hour prayer session beside the dam and immediately following that, new water samples were taken, frozen and photographed. As you can see (below), the change is stunning. The ugly blob of the former sample has become a clear, bright-white hexagonal crystal-within-a-crystal.

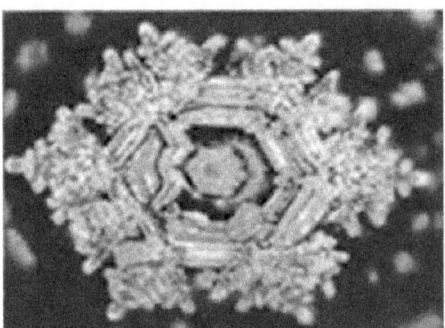

Fujiwara Dam, after offering a prayer

And here (below), are the results of taping the words 'you fool' to a container of distilled water. Interestingly, the pattern made by 'you fool' was almost identical to the pattern that emerged when heavy metal music was played. Masaru Emoto surmises in his book, perhaps heavy metal musicians look upon people as fools.

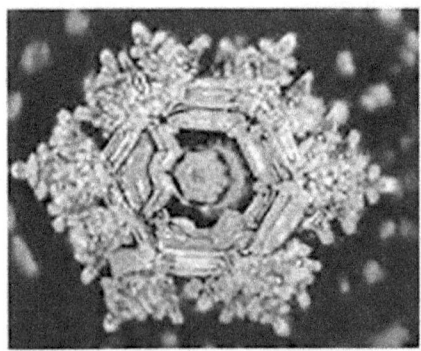

Words of love and encouragement are symetrical and pure like snowflakes

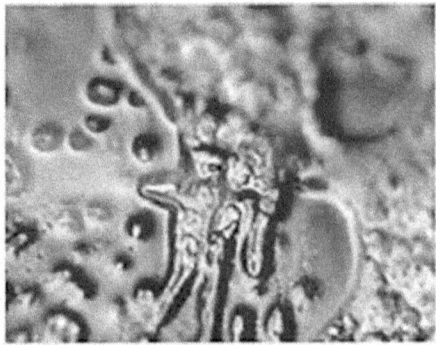

Words of hate, anger and criticism are discolored and malformed

Another instructive set of pictures (below) demonstrates the amazing difference between the crystalline patterns evoked by words of encouagement and discouragement.

So, we can perhaps deduce from this that what we tell ourselves and others, really does matter a great deal, as evidenced above. The pictures below show us the difference between positive states and intentions and those of ill intent and negativity.

Sometimes, when we cannot immediately see the results of our prayers and affirmations, we may think that we have failed. But, as evidenced by Masaru Emoto's amazing photographs, that thought of failure itself becomes represented in the physical objects that surround us and now that we have seen this for ourselves, perhaps we can begin to realise that even when immediate results are invisible to the unaided human eye, they still exist. When we love our own bodies, they respond and when we 'send' our love to others it is felt.

"I Love You."

Our own bodies at birth are 70% water, and the percentage of water in our bodies remains high throughout our lives. Also, the earth's surface is 70% water and now we have seen the proof that water is far from inanimate, as demonstrated conclusively above, it is actually alive and responsive to our every thought and emotion. Perhaps now we can begin to really understand the awesome power that we possess, through choosing our thoughts and intentions, to heal ourselves, others and the earth, if only we remember this truth.

> *"Every Intention sets energy into motion, whether you are aware of it or not"*

The words 'I AM' are profound and powerful and whatever we place after them becomes the embodiment of an intention. When we say 'I am this' or 'I am that,' we are making a statement of expression. Often we may say 'I am angry' or 'I am sad' and this embodies that emotion or thought within us. Conversely, if we say 'I am healthy' or 'I am happy,' we also embody that too. So which chosen expression do you prefer for yourselves and others? It is simply a choice; we only have no choice when we are unconscious. One option sets us on a path to greater health, happiness, truth, expansion and the ability to positively influence the people around us, whilst the other draws us into a negative, downward spiral of anger, unhappiness and depression and into a lower state of vibrational frequency. Our speech and self-expression has the power to lift ourselves and others up to the greatest heights as well drag us down to the lowest of lows. Which path would you choose?

Daily practice ...

Please repeat this declaration every day, clearly with passion and purpose and allow yourself to become what you speak of.

*'I am a positive influence in this world'*

Know that you are constantly moving closer to more and more truth within yourself as long as you are moving into a greater alignment with the truth of your own being. Express yourself both verbally and non-verbally, genuinely and honestly at all times and this will be a gift to yourself and help change the world for the better. Let go and be yourself one hundred percent of the time.

## Just be yourself in each Moment

*"The more room you give yourself to express your true thoughts and feelings, the more room there is for your wisdom to emerge"* Marianne Williamson

Wherever you are on the path, just be yourself in each and every moment, no more expressive than you are naturally, and no less expressive. Do not hold anything back but also do not force anything, simply relax and be natural. As you continue along the path and move deeper and deeper into your true nature, it will change how it expresses itself over the path. As you continue with your meditation you will become more of who you really are, and as that happens you will express yourself more genuinely within the moment, intuitively and spontaneously.

Do not try to 'live-up' to any ideals and do not act how you *think* you should, just express yourself naturally each moment. And as you achieve closer contact with who you really are, it will manifest differently within its range of expression. By releasing control of the mind into the pure self, the mind will no longer attempt to modify your behaviour and remove its alignment with what you are. The ego mind will tend towards this based upon its fears, insecurities and conditioned limitations so just relax and the ego mind will naturally fade into the background. Once this happens, then you will be free to just be yourself in each and every moment. Resist nothing and allow everything within you and around you to simply be as it is, within the here and now.

## Remain Unblemished

When we identify with being the ego mind, we suffer because each event or situation that happens within our experience has the potential to bruise the ego. This is because when we are 'lost in the mind,' we take things 'personally.' Many things we face in life tend to blemish us and seem to pollute our being, but when we remain as our natural selves, nothing can blemish us, nothing has the power to scar 'who we really are.' It is beyond the reach of our apparently physical reality, and when we remain our natural selves, as a pure neutral witness to all our experiences and life-events, we are in the safety of the divine. The body may be affected, the mind may be affected and even the soul may be affected, but the one who is beyond even the soul, continues pristine and unchanged. We all travel through life with many scars and traumas, and as a result the ego either becomes softened and victim-like, or becomes thick-skinned, hard as a rock and cold as ice, cut off from emotion and empathy. Neither brings us true joy or happiness, and neither serves our fellow man.

You may have noticed in yourself or through watching others, that when someone is hurt or affected by a challenging situation, then they are often 'broken' or 'softened' by it, or alternatively they may become hard and cold. The reason for this is our natural tendency to protect ourselves, say for example after a whole series of unsuccessful relationships. We may develop a mentality of 'I am never going to fall in love again,' as we were so hurt by our experiences that the ego decides to prevent this from ever happening again. This is the ego in 'defence mode.' However, when we remain as our true selves, the 'unaffected one' that is beyond being changed or modified by life's experiences, then we will remain in peace and joy and be of great service to those around us.

Everything in life we encounter is a potential influence upon us. People, astrology, environment, thoughts, feelings and challenges all have a potential energetic affect on us, but what determines whether we are affected or not, or changes our behaviour or not, is to what degree we are conscious. The more unconscious we are, the more influenced we will be. When we are fully conscious and standing in the naked truth of our being, we can never be swayed from that, we can never be influenced to be or act in a way that is not in alignment with who we truly are. We are completely grounded in our Ultimate Reality, and our destiny is in our hands.

Can you imagine being able to go through life in this way, where no matter what happens, we remain the same peaceful and joyful presence you have always been? Where you remain a joyful and peaceful 'rock,' a bright lighthouse and beacon of pure presence for others to take refuge with, when they need some inspiration and strength or when they need a reminder of who they really are and the pure power that resides within. We can all be that symbol, a hero of humanity. One who is joyful and of great service to humanity, must walk this world in the pure unaffected self, only then can we truly be of the greatest service, because if we have not conquered our own inner suffering, then how can we truly help another. However, when we become that joyful presence, we can positively influence all with whom we come into contact. So, be the one who walks unaffected and stays constant in your natural peaceful self. Of course, this does not mean that we will become hardened in some way...far from it. We actually will become like water, more fluid and adaptable, and able to 'roll with the punches' of life and also able to remain ourselves whilst being flexible in both action and mind.

In other words, nothing will ever put us out of alignment, because our inner connection to who we are is so strong, enabling us to prosper in any situation and without compromising 'who we really are.'

# Chapter 9
## From Illusion to Truth

*"The truth has never denied the seeker... it is the seeker who has denied the truth"*

There are over seven billion people on this planet—each with a unique individual perception from which they experience the world, not to mention all of the other creatures and life forms of this world and how they experience life. Imagine experiencing life through the eyes and senses of an owl, their individual experience must be so different to that of a human being. Even the difference between one human experience and any other must be immensely different, yet all are experiencing one and the same world.

Everyone's perception and experience is completely different from any other because of different conditioning, beliefs, emotions and even handicaps, which can all flavour and scent our individual experiences of the world. Yet despite all of this flavouring there is only one world being experienced, a reality that is being shared by all if only we could see it. Only when we remove the filters of perception, can we suddenly see life with crystal clarity, in all its full truth and honesty.

## We Suffer our Misperceptions

*Once there was a monk who specialized in the Buddhist precepts, and he kept to them all his life. Once when he was walking at night, he stepped on something. It made a squishing sound, and he imagined he had stepped on an egg-bearing frog.*

*This caused him no end of alarm and regret, in view of the Buddhist precept against taking life, and when he finally went to sleep that night he dreamed that hundreds of frogs came demanding his life.*

*The monk was terribly upset, but when morning came he looked and found that what he stepped on was an overripe eggplant. At that moment his feeling of uncertainty suddenly stopped, and for the first time he realized the meaning of the saying that "there is no objective world." Then he finally knew how to practice Zen.*

We suffer our own mental delusions and conditioning. Often times through our conditioned beliefs we imagine the world and situations to be a certain way when they are not, we often see things that are not there, and through this mirage we create inner turmoil for ourselves.

The Illusion of our reality...

> *"Truth is available only to those who have the courage to question whatever they have been taught"*

If someone had made us permanently wear a pair of red-coloured filtered contact lenses when we were young children, we would grow up believing that the whole world was tinted red would we not? And everything we saw would be perceived as being of a reddish colour, thus falsely creating the impression that everything **is** actually the way we see it, when in truth the removing of those red lenses would reveal a wholly different, new world as never experienced before. So, what if most of our lives we have been looking through false perceptions, thereby experiencing a distorted view of reality, and that a whole new world of truth awaits us if only we could see beyond the pre-conditioned filters of the mind? What if we have been living in Illusions created by the ego-mind itself? How sad it would be to never experience the real truth of our existence?

This is how conditioned beliefs, thoughts and emotional responses can act upon our perception of life and life situations, thus leading to our Illusions of thought and identity. Through a notion of ego identity we end up living our life from inside the 'box' created by our own experiences, a fictional self, made of ideas, concepts and assumptions which influence our experience of the world. The great illusion then is that we tend to always experience life from behind the fence of a conditioned false self, and therefore miss the true, essential nature of life.

Essentially this conditioning is information that has been gathered from our previous experiences and then held in the mind as memory, some of which has been translated into a part of our self-identity because we have retained it.

As an example, if we have had a number of previous relationships that did not work out well, we may well have firstly carried within us the idea that *'relationships don't work, or they are too much hard work,'* and secondly on a personal identity level we may have grown to believe, based on these previous relationship experiences, that *'I am someone who is unlucky in love'*. If we continue to hold these ideas about ourselves, we will soon begin to regard all relationships and relationship opportunities in that light, and will believe the mental fiction of *'I am so unlucky in love'*, thus adding a false idea to our identity.

And so subsequently we may be presented with the opportunity of a perfectly good relationship but yet are unable to recognise it because all we see are the ideas based on past experience, therefore distorting the reality of the situation in the moment. This may then lead to our reluctance to give the relationship a chance because we believe it will not work or alternatively giving the other person signals of insecurity because we believe that we are 'always unlucky in love,' thus being seen as unconfident and unworthy. And so in any relationship we always see the illusionary projection of the mind as opposed to the actual truth. This is just an example of what can and does happen in all areas of our lives when holding false perceptions and for most of us, this is happening on many different levels.

Losing the plot...

> *"The shortest distance between a human being and the truth is a story"*
> Anthony De Mello

One of the greatest illusions most of us maintain through the mental chatter of the ego mind, is the illusion of a storyline, plot or drama. We all experience a constant, interpretative conversation going on in our minds, a thinking, analysing and judging mental dialogue about everything all of the time. This is the expression of the 'ego self,' or the 'inner critic' as it has often been called. Most of us actually identify this voice in the mind as ourselves but unfortunately this locks us into the mental and physical levels from which only a limited portion of life can be experienced. When we identify ourselves as 'being' this internal chatter, it often causes us grief because the majority of the ego's ramblings are very negative in nature and based on a sense of separation and lack.

The often negative, mental story that is played over and over again in our heads can and frequently does cause internal suffering and can also distort our view of situations and people and our overall experience of reality.

Many of us will often say *'I am finishing one chapter of my life and starting another'* and this is based on the idea that through the mind we see our lives as a kind of story or movie that has a beginning, middle and an end. This 'life story' idea creates a strong sense of time and engenders the idea of time as being a very real, solid entity. Time is in fact a large aspect of what keeps the false ego-self alive in the mind, always referring to the past for its identity and to the future for its hopes and dreams of fulfilment thereby promoting the idea of a story and a character (us) and thus perpetuating the illusion and obscuring us from the reality of the 'here and now' as is its primary nature.

Any story, whether pleasant or unpleasant is simply that, just a story and not the actual truth of life in its natural state and appearance. A positive mental story is obviously more beneficial than a negative one but neither alternative gets us closer to the actual perceptual truth of existence. It may be good to have a pleasant, positive story playing in our minds but the basis for all positivity is truth and truth is the foundation from which all positivity can arise, without it being a false *fake it until you make it* positivity, which does not emanate from a 'genuine' place. The genuine place always needs to be one of truth and neutrality.

Once we access truth, then quite naturally and spontaneously positivity will arise. Truth brings everything else within us into alignment; our thoughts, words, emotions and actions will then all reflect our connection to inner truth. So for us to really connect with and see truth on its most subtle level, we must see ourselves and life beyond the mental story created by the ego-mind. The 'story' must take second place and only then can the real truth be experienced. Once we relinquish our mental stories and plotlines our perception clears and leaves us able to experience the vast truth of life in all of its greater glory.

However, the most damaging mental story is a negative one, a *negative* mental story will not only prevent us from seeing the truth of ourselves and life but it may also drag us down to a low level of consciousness and frequency, causing illness, depression and a general malaise. This in turn affects every area of our lives, relationships, work, health, state of mind and our ability to create that which we wish to experience in our reality. The more negative the minds mental story, the more negative and unpleasant our experience of life will be and therefore the more likely we are to find ourselves in situations and life circumstances that we would prefer not to experience, given a choice.

It is our engagement in mental stories of the mind that often leads to our energetic, karmic output and imprints, emanating a particular life-force energy and therefore allowing us to 'reap what we sow,' whether wanted or unwanted. The power of positive thinking is often praised, however it is usually very difficult for us to make an instant transition from a negative state of mind to a positive one and indeed this feat can often be too difficult to achieve at all. Attempting to transform a busy, negative mind into a positive one can be a near impossibility without firstly achieving a neutral state of mind. This neutral state of mind is the observer state which is most commonly accessed through thought-watching and sensory meditation and it is this observing state that provides us with the capacity to see truth and the ability to detachedly observe thoughts as they come and go. Therefore, the most powerful way we can become more positive is by developing an insight and a fundamental recognition of truth through the observer state.

## The True Essential Reality

*"It defeats truth to use words, since words imply that you know what it is that you are looking at. Instead, truth is an actual experience"*

Much has been said about truth, amongst which that truth is subjective or that truth is what the majority agrees upon. But truth in its essence is that which stands before us without individual mental interpretation. For instance, if two people sit in the same room and look around at the objects within that room, their conditioned minds will conjure various different mental interpretations of the objects being witnessed. One of them may look at a painting on the wall and say '*I like that painting, its beautiful,*' whilst the other person may say '*I dislike that painting its ugly.*' Both are looking at the exact same object, yet each one is filtering it through a uniquely different mentally-conditioned interpretation, which colours the individual view of the object being observed. The object itself is metaphorically 'colourless.' It is just simply '**as it is**,' the object being experienced without language, in all its base honesty. Even the word 'painting' is not actually an accurate description of the object. That is simply a conditioned label from the past, allocated by us in attempt to convey a convenient concept of what it is, to others. This label obviously has some relative truth to it, but the ultimate 'truth' of the object is well beyond mere words and labels.

It is the words and labels we apply to them that create a sense of separation between objects and these words can also create a subject / object split too, developing the sense that we are separate from all things. It is indeed words and labels that prevent us from 'seeing' the real truth of life and what we see before us, which is just 'what is.' 'What is' refers to the essential reality of all existence, as demonstrated by this short story...

> *"Zen master Fushan Fayuan (991-1067) entered the Dharma hall and addressed the monks... 'I won't speak any more about the past and present. I just offer the matter before you now in order for you to understand.' A monk then asked, 'What is the matter before us now?' Fushan said, 'Nostrils.' The monk asked, 'What is the higher affair?' Fushan replied, 'The pupils of the eye.'"*

In other words, life is just what is 'here and now' in our experience, without an intellectual understanding based on the past. It is the simple but profound reality that stands before us when we do not believe the mind's interpretation of it.

There is great beauty in seeing just 'what is,' and life often has vivid detail that is not fully appreciated by our conditioned minds. Our awareness is usually so engrossed in thoughts that we very rarely get to enjoy the full spectrum of life's pleasures, the richness of colours, smells and sounds, textures and tastes because our awareness is not fully tuned-into 'what is' but is instead tuned-into the mind's constant chatter about 'what is' or worse, completely lost in the past or future through memory and imagination. When we are lost in this randomised thinking of the mind it places us in a very limited state of consciousness from where all we see is thought itself and very little of anything else but as soon as we un-clutch from the mind we move into a more 'panoramic' state of consciousness that is able to take in everything. This is the difference between looking at a brick in the wall and only seeing that single brick rather than stepping back and seeing the entire wall and all the bricks in the wall together as one entity.

## Partial Truth and Total Truth

A partial truth is when we are looking at something from a more limited perspective; the conditioned state of consciousness is the limited perspective in this case and the total truth comes when looking from the unlimited consciousness that is beyond thought. Thought consciousness dissects and separates objects through compartmentalisation, whilst the unlimited consciousness beyond thought sees objects and life without these pigeonholes of perception. The barriers and boundaries that appeared between things from the limited consciousness perspective completely collapse when we view things from the unlimited consciousness perspective. This creates the difference between a perception of separation and a perception of oneness.

An apt analogy would be looking out at the world from the ground floor of a building. When we look out we see one part of the street but when we move to the top of the building we will see that this street is connected to a whole series of other streets that were invisible from the ground. Another example would be looking out at the world and believing it to be flat, but yet once we are able to see the view from several miles up into space, we will realise that the 'flat Earth' is spherical. The partial truth was seeing the Earth as being flat from a limited perspective compared to seeing that the Earth is spherical from a higher, unlimited perspective. This is exactly the same with thought consciousness and the unlimited conscious that is positioned behind thought, so to speak. We often begin to believe that things exist in a certain way based on what the mind is telling us about the object being seen but when we relax the interpretation, we actually see the truth of what is there. It takes awareness of an object without a mental interpretation to really 'see' the object and this is true with the whole of life. Life cannot be ultimately examined through thought but only through pure perception.

*"The only true wisdom is in knowing you know nothing"*

The only way to recognise the truth is when we are able to realise the enormity of *'knowing nothing.'* Only when we put aside what we 'think' we know can we actually arrive at a perception that can be open to truth and then suddenly all preconceived notions are swept away and the prime reality can be seen. Ultimately reality is not something that can be understood mentally, it is something that can only be known experientially.

Knowing Nothing . . .

> *A monk asked Zhaozhou, "I have come here and know nothing. What are my duties?"*
>
> *Zhaozhou said, "What's your name?"*
>
> *The monk said, "Huihan."*
>
> *Zhaozhou retorted, "A fine 'knowing nothing' that is!"*

All preconceived notions only act as a block to experiencing the actual 'exactness' of life. These preconceived notions form an obstruction in our range of consciousness and distort what we see. It is similar to looking through a frosted glass window and expecting to discern something on the other side in fine detail. So if we really wish to see the truth of existence then we must let go of all previous information, which is often the exact opposite of what we have been taught to do with regards to knowing and understanding life. Only when we drop all previous information does the mind relax and reality be born.

> *"If you're brave enough to say goodbye, life will reward you with a new hello"*

It is often been said that we must lose ourselves to find ourselves. Only when we lose who we think we are will the preciseness of life and self be revealed, otherwise this quest will always be blocked by our false perceptions of self and the world. Only when we completely relinquish the idea of ourselves and the world that we carry within, can we wipe clean the slate of the mind like a dusty mirror. Then and only then will we really see the true reflection of who we are.

Christopher J. Smith
# The Truth is Now and Enlightenment

*"Realise deeply that the present moment is all you ever have" Eckhart Tolle*

As we have covered earlier, life is simply just 'now' and everything moves and operates only in the 'now' moment, even when we are thinking about what may happen tomorrow or what happened yesterday, this act is also taking place only in the moment and there is no escape from it. Try to escape it right now... even if you try to think about memories or imagine something different you cannot elude it, it is right here all the time and all we need is to be aware of it and bring our attention to it. The paradox is that even if we are not aware of it, it is still the only place we can be. The question simply is 'are you conscious of it...?'

So 'the moment' is our primary reality, it is the ultimate truth that all other truths are contained within, once we align our awareness with it we are synchronising ourselves with the ultimate truth of existence. Where do you think our true self is located? Yes you guessed it, right here and now. You and now are one and when we become conscious of our match with reality, we will find ourselves consciously aware of all truths, or 'what is.' When the now moment becomes our permanent state of being, we will be securely grounded in the truth of reality and find ourselves nestled firmly in the whole of existence, as the whole of existence itself.

> *"Enlightenment is: Absolute cooperation with the inevitable"* Anthony De Mello

The inevitable is 'what is.' It is the essential reality before us that is already in place and when we align ourselves with the 'is-ness' of the moment, which is in effect cooperating with the inevitable (what is) and allowing everything to be as it is, then we can begin to move in total harmony with life as life, in a nondual flow with life. In fact we become the wave in the sea that recognises it is actually as one with the entire ocean. Suddenly a great force will move us and express itself as us; we become life itself and this merging through the recognition of the wave which sees it is the ocean and therefore flows and cooperates with the ocean is the magic of enlightenment. Enlightenment is the true union of all dimensions of life together in a synchronistic cooperating flow, whereby we 'melt' into 'what is' and the moment. Existence is like a colour that is deep and moves into ever more light and subtle shades until it is completely transparent. We will then lose our sense of a separate self in the cosmic soup of all existence and will swim in reality where there are no borders or cut-off points between us and the universe. The experience of oneness and peace is then born and enables us to realise that we are nothing and everything. We will have become the space in which all is appearing and happening on the screen of pure consciousness, this 'knowing' eliminates all illusions.

Eloquent Space

> *When the old warrior Hosokawa Shigeyuki (1434–1511) retired as daimyo or territorial lord of Sanuki Province, he became a Zen priest. One day he invited a visiting scholar-monk, Osen Kaisan (1429–93), to see a landscape-painting he himself had brushed in ink on a recent trip to Kumano and other scenic spots on the Kii Peninsula. When the scroll was opened, there was nothing but a long, blank sheet of paper. The monk Osen, struck by the emptiness of the 'painting,' exclaimed 'Your brush is as tall as Mount Sumeru, black ink large enough to exhaust the great earth; the white paper as vast as the Void that swallows up all illusions...*
> 
> *(From a story related by William Scott Wilson, 'The One Taste of Truth: Zen and the Art of Drinking Tea' 2012)*

Our true nature and the nature of the universe are one, it is the great space that exudes as all things.

> *"There is no other greater ecstasy than to know who you are"* Osho

When we know who we truly are, which is the same as saying we know the truth of 'what is,' then peace, joy, bliss and even ecstasy can be the result and all struggle melts away into the ecstasy of life itself. Struggle and pain only arise when we are resisting the natural flow of life within us and our life situation and this is why cooperation with the inevitable 'what is' is essential to stay aligned with life and live in comfort. One of the things that prevent our alignment with life is the need for fixed assumptions and definitions through engaging in judgements and discrimination of people and situations within our experience...

Christopher J. Smith
# Non-judgement and Discrimination

*"Judging a person does not define who they are, it defines who you are"*

The way we think and make judgements in life is simply a reflection of what opinions we ourselves are holding at that moment. It is almost like holding-up a mirror to our psyche and when we judge a situation we are not seeing 'what is' but only our definition of 'what is' which is not necessarily correct and can never be ultimately true. This subjective judgement therefore is telling us more about where we are at and what we are holding onto ourselves as opposed to who or what the situation is. Every time we judge something negatively it demonstrates that we perceive life in a sense of lacking and every time we see the positives in any situation we are proving that our mind 'sees' life optimistically and when we cease all judging and just see life exactly as it is, we are in touch with true reality at that moment.

So our judging or non-judgement reveals to us where our perception is and whether or not we are aligned with truth and the 'is-ness' of the moment. Once we are connected to the true non-discrimination of the moment we will then have a strong foundation upon which to build with a positive meaning if we choose that, or we can simply see all life in pure honesty without any definitions.

We may have been taught to assign particular meanings to certain aspects of our lives but then when we step back and look at the 'big picture' of life we can see that those judgements were incorrect and that it is impossible to comprehend the true meaning of a situation, as we are unable to see the ultimate, 'bigger' picture of the universe.

I remember many times in the past (and you will be able to too in your own life experiences) where I believed that something that looked unpleasant on the surface, turned out to be the most beneficial thing possible in hindsight, and visor versa where something looked like the best thing ever, and then turned out to be not at all what it seemed. This happens to us all the time, we enter relationships that look and feel great initially but then later become a source of struggle and challenge, or we enter particular jobs believing that we are going to really enjoy the job and that the job will bring us all of the pleasant things we want, only to find out later that it has become a drudgery.

## The Secret Self

I remember of a couple of instances where pre-judgments turned out to not be what my mind was making of them. In my late teens and early twenties I was often moving from unemployment to one job to the next, a plumber to a decorator and then back to being 'on the dole' as the term often goes in England, and I just couldn't seem to find a job that appealed to me or that I wanted to stick to, my old mentality used to be to work as little as possible, this seemed to be due to the fact that I couldn't bring myself to stick to something that did not excite me. I can remember being at a friend's house, near his window and watching the postman as he delivered letters to the different households on the street with what looked like a near empty bag. My conditioned mind at the time thought, 'that looks easy,' and my eyes lit up like Christmas trees. So based on what little evidence I saw, I was convinced this was the dream job for me. Easy pickings I thought...

So I immediately applied and got the job. By day two I realised I had been fooled by my limited perception and had subjected myself to hard graft (hard work), for one year to be precise, let me tell you that the bags were not light at all, but extremely heavy, as heavy as my days in the army, but that wasn't all, you didn't have to deliver one full heavy bag onto one street, I had to deliver up to five heavy full bags of letters into a whole neighbourhood of dozens and dozens of streets. Me being the new employee got the worst possible delivery round, a round that all other postmen and women used to dread, I would often start work at 5am in the office gathering and collecting all of the letters, and then make my way out onto my round about 8 or 9am, and many times (especially in the winter) I would finish at 4 or 5pm when it was almost getting dark, no short 6 hour shift for me as I was initially told by others, it's not that the person who told me was lying, it's just that it didn't apply to those who get put on the longest rounds. So what I believed was to be my dream job actually turned into my worst nightmare, lesson learnt, what is it they always say 'don't judge a book by its cover,' good solid common wisdom if ever I heard some.

The second instance comes to mind in regards to meeting people. Once again in my early twenties I decided I was going to apply to do what is called an S.I.A badge course, the S.I.A badge allows a person to work in most forms of security, and to also work as a doorman or 'bouncer' as the term was more commonly known. I turned up to this course and remember being sat there in the study room as many of the other guys on the course were walking through the door in to the room to take their seats for the course, two guys who seemed to be friends walked through the door together laughing and joking loudly and play fighting with each other in the doorway, through the belief in my minds judgements I immediately took an instant dislike to one of the guys, thoughts like idiot, arrogant and many more explicit swear words came to mind. It turns out that the guy I instantly disliked happens to now be one of my most loyal and best friends who have shown his genuine friendship over time and still to this day. Oh how wrong my mind was, don't always believe the mind, and don't take everything the mind says literally, that is a daily practice for you right there. The next time your mind throws up judgements of people and situations, be sure to be aware of those judgements and to not buy into them so much, see if you can remain impartial and only see 'what is,' as opposed to the conditioned minds judgements and interpretations of 'what is'. Remember that we very rarely can see the whole picture of each situation and how it correlates to the whole tapestry of existence. Who knows what life may bring from one moment to the next; this is the beautiful mystery of life.

These simple grounded stories clearly show the wisdom of non-judgment, as it is impossible to know how one situation may affect the next. Often the things we initially label as bad turn out to be the most wonderful things possible ... or maybe not ... life ebbs and flows and all we know for sure is that one thing always flows into the next.

In other words, stop trying to understand and let life just be life, let 'what is be what is' without trying to understand or define it. When we relax, the need to judge or understand a great freedom may arise and we can find ourselves in the wisdom of the is-ness of existence without any explanation, lost in the beauty of the universe in its most basic form.

Life can be full of contradictions. Without deconstruction there is no opportunity for transformation and without the bust there is no boom. Without the British rule in India there would have been no rise of Gandhi to oppose it, without hot there could be no cold; each one depends on the other in a sense and so it is impossible to say that anything is ultimately positive or negative in this reality as both depend on each other for their existence. When we venture beyond the good and bad, beyond the appearance of duality, we arrive at the place of truth which neutralises and harmonises both. All becomes accepted as equal and valid, all just different aspects of the same one existence. We often waste so much time and energy on judging people, situations and circumstances and through our societal conditioning it is often negative judgements and definitions that are brought to bear and these negative judgements only serve to bring our state of energy down as our beliefs can easily translate into unpleasant emotions within the body.

Also when we are negatively judging situations and people we are causing segregation in various ways. Positivity is connection and negativity causes disconnection. Whenever we see lack, we send out the energy of separation and if we judge another negatively we are often reinforcing that belief within them as their ego will often fight back against that judgement and may continue with that behaviour in an attempt to negate what has been said about them. If we find and focus on the positive aspects of that person, then they will feel encouraged to become even more like that and we are creating the opportunity for more connection. When we do not judge a person in either a negative or positive way, we leave the door open for them to consciously or unconsciously step into the neutral truth of reality, we open the space for them to slip into the true self beyond the ego as we are not defining them in any way. Without judgement we are leaving the door of truth open for them but this occurs on a subtle level not detected by the mind. Our silent recognition of their true self invites them to also step into the silence that connects them to who they are. Often all we need is to not be judged or told what to do, as this allows us to relax and release the baggage of the mind and obviates the need for the ego mind to defend it.

> *"When you choose to see the good in others you end up finding the good in yourself"*

And when we know the truth of ourselves we see the truth in another and therefore that is what is best to focus upon. This will also help others recognise the truth within themselves.

# The Habit of Thinking

*"Over-thinking ruins friendships and relationships and creates problems you never had"*

When we examine how much we think on a daily basis, how many thoughts run through the mind, it is apparent that most of us seriously 'over-think.' Most of this mind activity is not we ourselves, we are just constantly replaying audio software programmes, and it is only because we believe those voices to be ourselves that we continue to do so. Thinking, for most of us, has become a habit, almost an unconscious compulsion or addiction. At any given moment most of us are thinking about something, trying to work something out, thinking about what he said and she said, thinking about next week, next month and next year. This compulsion to think can make life miserable and can create issues that do not really exist. We have had to endure much suffering and conflict because of this addiction to thinking.

When we have nothing to do and are able to enjoy a quiet moment to ourselves, we are constantly thinking and thereby creating restlessness. This is often the reason that we experience bouts of stress and depression; because we do not know how to disengage from the mind when it is not needed. And because of this constant, habitual thinking, we never really experience the present moment and what it contains and we never really experience our body and the five senses, fully. We also tend not to truly experience other people, only the impressions our mind is forming about people. And with our full attention being focussed on this thinking, we slowly forget who it is that is having the experience and how it looks and feels.

To move from illusion to truth we must go beyond the level of the mind and at the very end of this chapter is the second of three foundational meditations that will help us move to that level beyond the body and mind identification.

# The Peaceful, Tranquil Mind

*"When we stop fighting the ego mind, inner peace happens naturally"*

When we come to the experience of truth and see the mind and its thoughts as just another experience that is appearing and disappearing within the moment and not personal to us, then we will relax and become at peace with the mind.

Often (especially in the spiritual community) we may 'think' that what it means to be spiritual is to have a clear, calm and peaceful mind at all times, but this is not necessarily the case at all. As long as we are alive, the mind will have thoughts flitting through it. It is natural for those thoughts to be present but fighting and resisting them often creates an inner struggle which leads to an unhappy mind. Mediators will sometimes go through the process of reaching these beautiful states where the mind becomes completely still and empty but then once the random thoughts return they will worry that they have done something wrong. Remember that the moment we allow those thoughts to occur yet make peace with them, is the time when we can relax and become tranquil.

When we end the war within, peace and tranquillity is the common outcome. You see, it is not simply a case of whether thoughts are there or not, it is a case of whether we are fully engaged in them or just watching them passing through, as it were. Whenever we allow those thoughts to occur and allow them the space to be there, and grant them the permission to enter the mind at will, this will instigate your 'falling in love' with the mind. We may allow ourselves to love each thought that comes as if each thought is a beautiful experience occurring in consciousness. When we observe and note our thoughts in this way, nothing will ever trouble us, as we will now have 'made friends' with the mind and the mind will happily be our servant from then onwards. The moment we begin to observe the thoughts in the mind, and we observe our true nature as the 'observing' itself, we will become pure nondual consciousness.

All pain and internal strife is a result of a misalignment due to resistance against our mind and emotions but when the resistance ends, alignment is restored once again in an instant. It is important not to pursue any particular states of consciousness, or to try and repeat any state of experience you have had, as this can create more turbulence in our mind. We all want to 'feel good,' but this wanting is often a goal set by the mind in an attempt to create this effect at some future point in time. This may instigate a frantic scramble to try and chase impossible, unreachable pleasant states of being. It is best not allow this to happen. Instead we will do best not to do anything except to notice what happens when the mind is not actively pursuing another state of being.

This mental pursuit of a pleasant state is exactly what we should cast aside. When we detect this false 'move of the mind,' we will understand that doing nothing and chasing nothing is the best way for the mind to relax and for us to enter true inner peace. Tranquillity of mind will occur by doing absolutely nothing and instead allowing our minds to be whatever they are in that moment. In other words, we often get a taste of how pleasant and blissful it can feel when we enter into particular states of consciousness through meditation and a stillness of the mind, but the more we chase these states and try to repeat them, the more they will elude us. This is because it is the ego mind itself that is doing the chasing. It is the mind that has become addicted to feeling good and wishes to continue feeling good but this mental pursuit will only create restlessness and cause us to miss the target every time. All that is needed at this stage is to do nothing, just let whatever comes ... come, let whatever arises ... arise, and do not try to change, control, create or suppress anything, let it all happen freely, whilst 'you' watch it. When this happens we may be surprised to find that a deep inner peace will come, and from this deep peace, bliss and tranquillity will be the result. If this does not happen however, it does not really matter as we are now in the place where both pleasant and unpleasant states are witnessed, ultimately beyond all states.

Daily practice ...

Firstly, reflect on any illusions or misperceptions you may be holding. Take a moment to look deep into your mind and then when ready, repeat the declaration below with meaning. As you repeat it, relax and let the energy of illusions and misperceptions melt away. Trust that the declaration will do its work, as what you say, goes.

Repeat this Declaration daily—*'I let go of all illusions and misperceptions'*

## Foundational Meditation #2—'Natural Noticing'

This is the second of the three foundational meditation practices in this book. This meditation is best practiced once we have become comfortable with the first meditation (I watch the mind ... I watch the body, Chapter 2.) Working with the first meditation will create a significant 'gap' between us as the 'watching consciousness' and the body/mind organism, so that thoughts, emotions, feelings and sensations may be observed as they arise and pass. The first meditation is non-specific and its purpose is to enable us to become comfortable in the seat of the 'watching consciousness,' and to build an initial capacity to generally watch the body and mind activity, which prepares us for the second meditation.

What is Natural Noticing?

Natural Noticing is a meditation by which we may become specific in the thoughts, emotions, feelings and sensations we notice. 'Noticing' simply means being aware of something, an effortless observance of whatever phenomena arise in the body and mind. As soon as we begin to notice this phenomena, we automatically and instantaneously move to the position of the pure 'watching consciousness,' and the more specific we are regarding what we notice in the body and mind, the deeper the level of 'watching consciousness' we move into, and the more that thoughts and beliefs are transcended. As we move deeper into this consciousness, we begin to make everything that is unconscious, conscious, and by doing this transcend the body and mind whilst also significantly reducing the unwanted content of the mind over time.

This meditation will also help us greatly, in our daily life. When we are confronted with certain thoughts and feelings, it is through this practice that we will find it much easier to identify and deal with whatever arises and be able to move to a level of inner stillness whilst transcending the thoughts or emotions through pure thoughtless watching. This will become easier as we practice until eventually, all negative thoughts and emotions are caught instantly, by our awareness, before they have a chance to cause inner suffering, turmoil or distress. Through this meditation we will awaken beyond the identity with the body and mind and move into the liberated consciousness which is unbounded by physical limits.

Christopher J. Smith
# How to practice Natural Noticing Meditation

*Find a quiet place where you are unlikely to be disturbed. Sit in an upright position with your back straight and head looking forward at a 45 degree angle from the floor and choose a comfortable, upright position such as the cross-legged sitting position on a cushion or sat in a chair with your feet planted firmly on the ground and your knees at a 90 degree angle...*

*You can either place your hands one palm on top of the other on your lap, or you can turn the palms of your hands upwards and place them on your knees, whatever feels most comfortable...*

*Now close your eyes...*

*As you close your eyes, look towards where the tip of the nose would be if you had your eyes open and allow your gaze to focus on the blackness of the mind in that direction...*

*Now, when ready, take three medium-length breaths in through the nose and out through the nose...*

*Now breathe naturally. Do not force the breath, allow it to occur naturally and be aware of it for a minute or so...*

*Now just notice the breath and whenever it arises on its own, breathe, but do not force or suppress the breath... allow it to occur naturally, in its own time. Allow yourself to notice the body and mind and to notice whatever arises and whatever leaves.*

*Notice whatever thoughts, emotions, feeling and sensations make themselves known to the body and mind... and then 'label' it. For example, if worrying, fearful, happy, funny, angry, sad, loving, jealous, desiring or sexual thoughts occur, make a mental note and say... 'worrying... worrying... worrying,' 'happy... happy... happy,' 'angry... angry... angry,' or 'sad... sad... sad' and so on. Regard it for a short time in a non-judgemental way, and then notice as it leaves the mind and fades away under the light of your watching. Do not try to push it away, just allow it to do what it wants to do, and just notice it. If it appears to be a strong, persistent thought that does not seem to be passing, then gently let it go and return to noticing the breath, noticing the breathing occurring naturally as you inhale and exhale.*

*Then you may leave the breath whenever ready and begin to scan the body and mind again, noticing whatever arises. If nothing arises, then just remain silently watching. If an emotion such as fear, happiness, love, sadness and anger arises, notice it and then label it as you are watching it. Make a mental note and then say, 'fear...fear...fear,' 'happy...happy...happy,' 'love...love...love' or 'sadness...sadness...sadness' and so on. Watch it for awhile in a non-judgemental way, and notice as it leaves the body and fades away under the light of your watching. Do not try to push it away, just allow it to do what it wants to do, and just notice it. If it appears to be a strong, persistent emotion that does not seem to be passing, then gently let it go and return to noticing the breath, noticing the breathing occurring naturally as you inhale and exhale.*

*Then you can leave the breath when you are ready and begin to scan the body and mind again, noticing whatever arises. If the fearful emotion still persists, then notice it and explore how it feels in a non-judgemental way. If it is no longer there, then simply scan the body and mind and observe whatever makes itself known. If nothing is there, do not create anything, just remain silent, watching, or make a note and say 'silence...silence...silence' or just remain watching and listening to the silence itself, whatever is most comfortable. Maybe a feeling of restlessness, frustration, tiredness, wakefulness, weakness, strength, pleasantness or unpleasantness may arise. Notice it and then label it as you are watching it, you may make a note and say 'restless...restless...restless,' 'frustration...frustration...frustration,' 'tired...tired...tired' or 'awake...awake...awake' and so on. Watch it for awhile in a non-judgemental way, and watch it leave the body and fade away under the light of your watching. Do not try to push it away, just allow it to do what it wants to do, and just notice it. If it appears to be a strong, persistent emotion that does not seem to be passing, then gently let it go and return to noticing the breath, noticing the breathing occurring naturally as you inhale and exhale.*

*Then you may leave the breath whenever ready and begin to scan the body and mind again, noticing whatever arises. If sensations such as hot, cold, itching, pain, numbness, tingling or aching arises, notice it and then label it as you are watching it. You may make a note and say 'hot...hot...hot,' 'cold...cold...cold,' 'itching...itching...itching' or 'pain...pain...pain' and so on. Watch it for awhile in a non-judgemental way, and watch it leave the body and fade away under the light of your watching. Do not try to push it away, just allow it to do what it wants to do, and just notice it. If it appears to be a strong, persistent emotion that does not seem to be passing, then gently let it go and return to noticing the breath, noticing the breathing occurring naturally as you inhale and exhale.*

*Continue this pattern and allow whatever arises to be noticed in whatever order it arises. The above are just examples of how you would interact with each phenomenon that occurs. If you become distracted by something externally, then simply note that you have become distracted, let the distraction go and return to noticing the breath or once again continue to scan the body and mind.*

*As you become more comfortable with this practice, you may decide to pay more attention to each activity that arises and remain as a watcher of it until it fades away. You may find as your practice continues over a period of time, that you spend more time noticing what arises within the body and mind, until eventually you no longer need to revert back to the breath, but instead remain in the silent, watching consciousness, noticing whatever appears in the body and mind.*

*Allow this practice to transform you into a silent watcher of the body and mind's activities, watching and noticing the different movements of thoughts and the different sensations that arise in the body. Watch them impartially without judgement.*

*Continue with this practice for 15 to 30 minutes each day, build it up over a period of weeks from 15 minutes to 30 minutes, for at least a period of forty days and you will see powerful results.*

*After forty days consistently, of this practice, you will find it effortless. Once this is the case and it is very natural to slip into this meditation easily, then you may continue on to the next meditation practice—'Pure Meditation' (chapter 13.)*

*Remember that as with all practices and methods, patience and persistence is the key to success . . .*

# Chapter 10
## Dropping all Attachments

*"You can only lose what you cling to" Buddha*

We often suffer in so many ways throughout our life, and at the root of all of this suffering is attachment. The things that we hold and do not let go of from the past and the future expectations in our minds, binds and limits us; they become fears as we then fear losing them or not attaining them, and that then appears to block our natural peace and joyful state of being, preventing it from being felt and seen.

Our natural state of being is one of being undisturbed, a state of being that is happy to allow different experiences, people and possessions to come and go freely within our life without hoarding or creating ties. But the 'personal conditioned self' does not operate in this way, it likes to form attachments to boost its sense of personal identity.

## The Nature of Attachment

*"Mental clinging and grasping to what is ultimately not you, is attachment"*

Often we may say *'who would I be without this, without him or her, without my family, money or job?'* Or we may be heavily identified with the body, with our looks or talents. When our identity and energy becomes entangled with the material things of this world, we can call this attachment. The mind continues its identity by creating mental ties and associations with the various things around it, and uses these things as a reference point and orientation of its personal self, and so when something is taken away or eventually goes away, the mind feels a deep pain because it believes it has lost a part of itself.

When this happens it limits our peace and joyfulness, because with attachment comes the opposite energy of loss, the fear of losing those things we are identified with and attached to, and which we feel create our sense of joyfulness, wellbeing and completeness.

Our attachment to people, people's opinions, circumstances and possessions creates our suffering. Why? Because if we lose or do not gain the thing we are attached to, we feel pain, disappointment and suffering as a result. We will experience a sense of loss or failure which pains us, because we are heavily invested and dependant on that particular thing for our joy and sense of self. The moment that we become attached to something, we are saying, whether consciously or unconsciously, that we need that certain thing for our happiness, and that we will be unhappy until we get it.

This attached conditioned mentality to the happenings of the external world often leaves us in a place of inner suffering and disappointment, as it is impossible to have things the way we want them one hundred percent of the time as things are constantly changing, coming and going. In modern society we can see that things have been structured in such a way to try and achieve consistency, or at least a place where consistency is greater than unpredictability. But ultimately, life is one of constant flux and change as this story concludes below...

> *Everything changes*
>
> *"Suzuki Roshi, I've been listening to your lectures for years," a student said during the question and answer time following a lecture, 'but I just don't understand. Could you just please put it in a nutshell?*
>
> *Can you reduce Truth to one phrase?'*
>
> *Everyone laughed. Suzuki laughed.*
>
> *'Everything changes,' he said. Then he asked for another question."*

The quicker we can come to the realisation and acceptance that everything constantly changes and that to try and attach and hold onto things is ultimately futile, the sooner that a great peace will descend upon us and suddenly we may find that we cherish life like never before. Unfortunately most humans through their conditioned state of consciousness only come to appreciate those things that have either been taken away or are in the process of being taken away, maybe you have experienced this? Please realise that everything in this seemingly material world is in the process of being taken away, or more accurately transformed from one state to another. Nothing is in a fixed state, everything is changing and the more we can accept, let go and be at peace with the changing nature of life, the more we are able to 'roll with the punches' of life so to speak, the more flexible and fluid we become. Indeed we become adaptable and this guarantees that we align ourselves with the power and flow of existence, as from this place of acceptance and allowance comes the end of all internal struggle and suffering. The ability to roll with whatever life brings us within the present moment without inner resistance is pure freedom and the end of suffering.

## Happiness and Attachment

*"You keep insisting you feel good because the world is right! Wrong! The world is right because I feel good! That's what all the mystics are saying"* Anthony De Mello

One of the first things we are taught as we grow and develop, is that in order to be happy or fulfilled, we must be successful. The western interpretation of success is basically the acquiring of material possessions, status, admiration and achievements...the big pay-cheque at the end of the month, a large house, attention, the latest model car, holidays, marriage and 2.4 kids and so on.

We are basically taught that the determination of our happiness comes through the right external circumstances being in place and as soon as we learn this and believe it to be true, our joy and completeness is finished and it's done. But let us try to understand how this works by making a distinction between joy and happiness. The way that I would like to define happiness here is the following...*'That which pleases us from our external situations.'*

Whereas 'joy' is...'*...that which is naturally present within us when we are not blocking or hindering it, our natural state of being, Internal causeless joy.'*

The first is a feeling that appears to be triggered by the outside; the second is an internal state of consciousness that comes naturally when one is just being their true self without needing or attaching to anything. One is caused and one is causeless.

# Happiness

What we have mostly come to define as 'happiness' is when things are 'going our way,' and when we say this we mean when pleasant things are happening to us, more accurately what we define as pleasant, as what is pleasant for one person may be unpleasant for another. We develop these ideas of what is pleasant and what is not pleasant based on the beliefs we have about things and these beliefs then become the catalyst that triggers internal responses to the things we experience externally, thus determining whether we experience pleasant feelings or unpleasant feelings.

So it would be more accurate to say that we feel good or not good on 'behalf' of outside experiences as opposed to the actual experiences themselves causing us to feel a certain way. It is our inner responses (and mostly our conditioned responses from the ego) that determine how we feel.

Please contemplate this as it is very profound...

Of course we have been taught and have come to believe that life functions in a completely opposite way to this, that there are certain circumstances that automatically make us feel a particular way, but in truth how we feel comes down to how we respond to outside influences, whether consciously or unconsciously, not the other way around.

So because our conditioning has been one that places a great emphasis on being fulfilled and happy based on what happens outside of us, we have developed dependence on the outside to feel good and to bring us a sense of happiness, and it is because of this mentality that we have developed such strong attachments to things, but only to the things that we believe make us feel good. We may notice that we always attempt to move towards those things that appear to make us feel good. Even the things in our lives that do not appear to make us feel good on the surface, are serving us in some way otherwise we would not continue to engage with them. In other words, it must mean on some level that we have the belief that the alternative is worse than continuing in the same way, For example, we may continue to work in the same mundane, unfulfilling job, justified by the fact that it is better than having no money or any job at all.

Everything we experience outside of us is an endorsement or permission to feel good. These are 'things' or experiences that we constantly tell ourselves make us happy. One person may feel that they must go to the gym three times a week to feel happy, whilst to another the mere thought of going to a gym at all, is more like a nightmare. Another may believe that they need to travel to be happy, whilst someone else may be happy staying home because they believe travel is stressful. Some may believe that they need a loving relationship to be happy, while others may believe that being single is the way to happiness. This demonstrates that the outside world is simply neutral and that it is our ideas about the outside, and primarily our ideas about how the outside relates to us, that determines whether those things appear to make us feel pleasant or unpleasant. In other words, if we believe something will make us happy, then it probably will, and if you believe that not having something will make you unhappy, then your inner response will be unhappiness, when you do not have what you believe you need.

So this type of happiness is very much unstable, as this story points out below...

*Impermanence*

*There once was a young man who wanted to face real life. So he left home and travelled to seek the real world. During his travels he reached a village and met a certain young family, where the wife was pregnant and the husband was hard working. They welcomed him and invited him to stay with them. He was there for just one day and night. During that time, the husband suddenly died and his wife mourned so much that it affected her pregnancy and she gave birth prematurely. The young traveller saw death and birth in quick succession. He saw the impermanence that caused both grief and happiness. The wife grieved at the loss of her beloved husband and yet was happy to have a baby. He helped that family with the funeral service and then continued his travels.*

*He arrived at another village. Here he knew two brothers: one was successful in business and another one was not. He smiled at life and moved on to another village. A year went by and he returned to the same village and met the same two brothers. Then he discovered that the one who was successful had failed and the one who had not been successful was now doing well in his business. He saw how change happens in life; how success and failure had brought both fulfilment and disappointment.*

*Time passed by. After he had travelled for many years he realised that he was getting old. He thought that it was time for him to return to his home town. This period of travelling had let him come to know both departure and return. He felt that life offered no control, but impermanence and was just a series of changes. He realised that youth changed to old age, and impermanence meant that there was no guarantee that there would be a tomorrow. The here and now is the only time which everyone has. It took a life-time for this man to understand life as it was. At the end of his life, he rested in peace and joy.*

You see, life is in a constant state of flux and change, everything constantly coming and going, changing and transforming. A sense of sustainable good feeling is impossible to maintain within it, as one day something will go the way we would like it to go, and another day the opposite will happen. If our happiness is dependent upon the outside world and whether things happen or don't happen, then one moment we will feel great and yet the next minute we will feel sad (does this sound familiar?) This seems to be a normal life-experience for the majority of the population, to the point where people have come to believe that this is just a normal and natural by-product of life. However, this is not so. It is instead, a by-product of an attached and dependant mind. This type of happiness is always something that is pursued in the future, it is always a chasing and searching for the next fix or goal in an attempt to make us feel happy. This is what most of our modern consumer society has been based upon, the idea that true fulfilment is an outside phenomenon of accumulation and achievement.

Achievements, material possession and the various fruits of life are beautiful and should not be denied, they bring a great richness to the experience of life, but to be reliant upon these things for our ultimate joy and self-identity is not a wise choice on our part, as it will always lead to a 'roller-coaster ride' of high and lows within us that will cause us suffering. This is fine, in and of itself, but not wise if we have chosen the path of truth and most joy, because when given a choice . . . what would you choose...? Pain or pleasure, sadness or joy? Every sane person if honest, would choose joy, and the path of joy leads us closer to our full potential and to the essence of who we are; that core frequency within. What will we be 400 years from now, how silly to argue and fight and suffer, how much we should appreciate now and be happy to live life?

Being in a place of joy also creates a healthy atmosphere and quality of relationship with those around us. In other words, we affect our world in a positive way when we feel good and joyful as opposed to feeling unpleasant and in a place of inner suffering. But there is another way to exist that is one hundred percent viable, a way that is more natural and in alignment with our true nature. This is the way of causeless joy.

## Causeless Joy

Causeless joy is exactly what it sounds like, joy without a cause. This type of feeling is a natural feeling that occurs when we simply relax into the essence of who we are in this instant. It is the perfume that emits from our natural being in the moment, the same way that a beautiful flower emits its scent. It occurs when we are not in relentless pursuit of happiness from the external world and when we stop looking for something about which to be joyful, then suddenly, joy will happen naturally and spontaneously.

I am reminded of when a friend once came to visit me.

> *A friend came to me in order to try to understand a little about why they were so unhappy. He looked very miserable and mentioned that his relationship was not going well, that he was unhappy in his work and that there were some issues with an ex-partner. We spoke for a while about the nature of the mind and ego, and how our thoughts and beliefs make us unhappy. We then spoke about whether it is possible for us to be aware that a thought cannot be who we are, but is instead that we are the one that 'sees' the thought. I suggested to this person that he try a particular meditation practice and to work with a specific question. The question was, 'who is it that is aware of thinking as it happens?' I suggested that he work with this question and allow himself to be directed wherever it was pointing.*

## The Secret Self

*About a week later I saw my friend again. He approached me with a spring in his step and a huge grin. My eyebrows raised. I asked him how he was, and he immediately, enthusiastically proceeded to tell me how effective the meditation and question practice was, and how he had been able to detach from the mind and observe thoughts as they came. He also told me how good he felt and how joyful he now was. Then I asked about the situation with his job, his partner and ex-partner and whether or not anything had changed at all. He said 'no.' So, I said 'why are you so happy then?' He simply replied that he did not know, he just was and could not stop smiling. He also said that he now seemed to be free of his 'thinking' and had never felt better.*

*Nothing had changed in his external situation, but yet he was much happier. So what had changed?*

*The only thing that had changed was his identification and relationship with the mind and thought, and as a result he was experiencing the smell of the perfume of inner space and freedom . . . causeless joy.*

*In fact he was so joyful and could not stop smiling that people were asking him what had happened. I then asked him, 'so all your external situations are the same, but yet you have gone from unhappy to joyful. So what does that tell us about what you were feeling before?' He looked at me with a big grin and wide eyes and replied, 'I guess the outside was not as large a problem as I thought it was.' I said, 'the outside was never the problem, never has been and never will be, the problem was always about what you were thinking and believing about the outside and those particular situation. That is what made you unhappy.'*

*'So how do you feel about those situations now?' I asked him next. His reply was, 'to be honest, I don't mind too much anymore, I am just really happy.'*

When we are not dependant on the outside for our happiness and we understand our true relationship with the mind and thought, all 'causeless joy' occurs. Two months later I saw my friend again who was still smiling and joyful and asked how he was. I asked if anything had changed and he told me that all of his previous issues had now been resolved, and that his life was running far more smoothly than it had done for a long time. Suddenly he was now enjoying his job, his relationship and his ex-partner was no longer a problem. It was as if he had entered into alignment with who he is, which caused his outside circumstances to all of a sudden work out. This demonstrates the power of anyone experiencing causeless joy. The feeling of peacefulness and joy also brings more alignment to the external situations. This however, is just a 'bonus.' If outside alignment occurs, this is a positive, but if not, then it does not matter too much, because as my friend discovered for himself, his happiness was the end-result in any case.

Most of us, on a day-by-day basis, are constantly looking to the 'outside' in our search for happiness; the next achievement, activity or compliment. But if we could just end this relentless pursuit for a few moments, allowing everything to be just as it is without trying to change or add anything, then what would be revealed to us is a pure natural state of inner joy; a joy that cannot be contained, an ecstatic joy wanting to burst to the surface, a state that is revealed as we relax more and more into ourselves in the here and now.

I remember in the earlier days of this inner awakening, I was once in a nice restaurant with my partner at the time. We were engaged in conversation and I found myself experiencing an immense sense of causeless joy that deepened into a state of ecstatic bliss. My partner at the time was trying to continue the conversation with me, but I was just completely immersed in the bliss of self and she naturally became a little frustrated. What I later learned was how to control this bliss, so that one can pay attention to the external world fully whilst also feeling the beauty of causeless joy and bliss simultaneously.

This story below demonstrates the plight of humanity's search for happiness and joy...

> A fisherman was lying in the warm afternoon sun on a beautiful beach, with his pole propped up and his line cast out into the sea. An energetic businessman walked by.
>
> "You aren't going to catch many fish that way," said the businessman to the fisherman. "You should work harder."

*The fisherman looked up and good-naturedly asked, "And what would I get for that?"*

*The businessman replied that he would catch more fish, sell them for more money, save the surplus, and invest in a boat and nets, which would let him catch even more fish.*

*Again the fisherman asked, "And what would I get for that?"*

*Somewhat impatiently, the businessman explained that he could then reinvest the even greater surplus and buy more boats and hire staff, becoming a big business and catching ever more fish.*

*Again the fisherman asked, "And what would I get for that?"*

*Now the businessman lost it. "Don't you understand that you can become so rich that you never have to work for a living again? You could spend the rest of your days sitting on this beach, just enjoying this sunset!"*

*The fisherman's eyes lit up. "And what do you think I'm doing right now?"*

This story is a microcosmic example of what most people are doing on a daily basis; they are going the long way around for happiness, when joy is right here and right now if only we could realise this. The moment we end the relentless pursuit of happiness or even enlightenment, is the time that our joy and enlightenment will be awakened within us.

## Love and Attachment

*'Love without attachment is light'* Norman O. Brown

One of the biggest misconceptions that we have about 'love' is that love is attachment, that to love someone means to cling to them and to be with them all of the time. Our actions based on this one piece of conditioning is the cause of much suffering and conflict within relationships. When we attach to someone it is because deep down we feel some loneliness inside, a sense of incompleteness, and so we are looking for the other person to try and fill that loneliness. We then feel pleasure and 'completeness' when with that person, and we believe that this comes directly from that person. Our mind will then seek attachment to that which we believe is bringing us our fulfilment and good feelings.

In reality though, what is happening is that our lover is just bringing us temporary satisfaction. Through our concentration on them, we temporarily forget our sense of incompleteness and when we feel good in their presence, it appears to bring us a feeling of wholeness. But the reality is that it is actually our conditioned mind that creates this sense of wholeness on behalf of that person, not the other way around. In other words, it is our conditioned beliefs and ideas about what that person represents for us and gives us that triggers and engenders the effect we experience.

The more we believe that it is the person or relationship that is going to make us complete, the more we will grasp and cling-on to them for fear of losing that which we believe is making us a whole being. This mentality turns a relationship into being 'need-based' as opposed to true, unconditional love.

Love is not attachment, love is unconditional and it gives inner freedom to us and freedom to the other. When we become attached to someone we are imprisoning them with our chains of need, and not only them, we also imprison ourselves, because with this comes the fear of losing that which is being desperately sought, and so we become a prisoner to our own attachments. If I were to chain you to another person with one chain, and attach you to a car, a house and various other material objects to other chains, are you free or bound?

We are only free if you have the ability to move around freely, wherever and whenever we please, are we not? This is how love must be for it to be true love; it must have the quality and space of freedom. And by us having the freedom and ability to come and go as we please, we also give that same option of freedom to the other person, animal, experience or material item, we are not trying to trap anything and make it our own.

I remember reading about how the American Indians were baffled when the white men settlers came to try and make deals with them about possession of various parts of the land. The American Indians literally could not understand what the white settlers were trying to propose, it seemed completely alien to them the concept of trying to 'own' a piece of land. In their minds the land belonged to everyone and could not possibly be 'owned' by any individual. Nature will still be around long after any human lifetime, so how could one ever truly possess it in reality?

To think we can possess and hold onto anything demonstrates a total ignorance of how life really works. This ignorance contributes to our suffering and the suffering of those around us. Many horrific things have been done in the name of this ignorance, and so as soon as we see life for what it really is and how we can best relate to it, only then will we be free and free to love and be loved in its purest form.

# Detachment

*"Detachment is not that you should not have anything, but that nothing should own you"*

So, one of the ways we can break free from mental and emotional attachments is through the art of practicing detachment. On a daily basis the learnt ego mind is constantly trying to grasp at things. That is its primary nature. Fundamentally the mind bases its sense of identity on the accumulation of the past, the collecting and attachment to information, experiences, people and memories.

It is an inward action not an outward action and so in other words, detachment is about becoming aware of when the mind tries to wrap and coil itself around each and every person, object and experience as opposed to physically distancing ourselves from a person, circumstance or object. It is a reminder for us to remember our essential nature and not become 'lost' in the things that are not ultimately us, as many of us so often do. Most of us function like sponges, absorbing and taking everything very personally and identifying with most of the things that happen within our daily life experiences.

We often identify with our possessions, job, status or title but we can practice detaching from these things, and then we can go one step further and practice detachment from the body and mind. We can possess something and can say 'my' or 'mine,' but what is 'yours' or what you 'have' is ultimately not you and 'your' body, mind and possessions are ultimately not you in the same way as things being carried in a box, are not the box itself. Please contemplate this.

Christopher J. Smith

# Practicing Detachment

On a daily basis, the ego mind is constantly enmeshed and mentally invested in the material things of this world. We often take things very personally but in doing so, we tend to suffer as this makes an issue or 'thing' very personal and self-identified. In the practice of detachment we are simply reminding ourselves by becoming aware, that we are not the things that happen to us and that those things are not our true identity.

In the Ancient text of the Bhagadgita, chapter 18 verse 17, it reminds us of our true relationship to the nature of form and experience... *'One whose mentality never considers being the doer and whose spiritual intelligence is not attached to fruitiveness; such a person even if warring with the whole world; does not actually slay anyone nor become entangled by fruitiveness.'*

What is being referred to here is that we are not ultimately the things of this world or the results, nor are we (as the body) the doer of what is done; in fact we are that which is beyond the body and action. If we can just realize deeply this one sentence above, then we will be completely free of all attachments and therefore move into total inner freedom and a sense of boundlessness.

> Practice
>
> The next time a situation arises that is challenging or is not going the way you would prefer it to, say to yourself *'I am not this situation, and I am not the outcome of this situation.'*

As you repeat the above mantra, you may feel suddenly relaxed and notice a change in your level of awareness, whatever arises allow it to be there. Continue to remind yourself of this in each and every situation until it becomes completely natural for you to be aware of it and you will begin to feel a great inner freedom arising within you.

Our minds can often get entangled in the material possessions that we acquire throughout our life and may very easily form a sense of identity around material possessions. Just like a child can want to hold onto a toy and say 'it's mine!' so too can we adults. We often develop attachments with 'grown-up toys' such as cars, money and properties etc.

## The Secret Self

When you find yourself next using a material possession, or even when you are simply sat doing nothing, contemplate and remind yourself *'I am not this... ... (fill in the blank, a car or money as an example.)* Once again be open to what happens, you may once again notice a change in your awareness and a sense of inner freedom arising. Practice this as often as possible until it becomes natural for you to be aware of this in each and every moment.

The biggest identity and yet limitation we have, is our identification of ourselves as our bodies, minds and thought processes. When we believe the body, mind and thought to actually be what we are, we tend to suffer as a result and to take things very personally. We may often become lost in a false identity made up of untrue ideas and perceptions about ourselves and others and in addition we often have negative perceptions through our societal conditionings which then cause us inner-suffering and turmoil if we believe them to be real.

Firstly begin by repeating the following statement either when relaxing or engaged in some task or action, repeat... *'I am not the body.'* As you say this, notice any changes in your perception. You may find that you become a watcher of the body; you may feel as though the body is moving itself or is somehow separate from you, but just note non-judgementally whatever happens and continue the practice.

For the next practice, repeat the following statement when relaxing, engaged in something or when you find yourself judging or intellectualising something. Notice your 'thinking voice' in the head and repeat *'I am not the mind, I am not the thinking.'* As you say this, notice any changes in your perception and within the mind. You may find that you become a watcher of the mind and thoughts; you may feel as though the thinking is happening itself or is somehow separate from you, but just note whatever arises and continue the practice.

The practice of detachment is used to create some space and distance from the body and mind. What we essentially are, is something that is 'behind' the body and mind so to speak, and so the more we become a watcher or witness of the body and mind, the more we can create a gap between what is truly us and what is the body and mind experience.

The creation of this gap is not about retreating from the body or mind, it is simply about establishing our true identity beyond it so that we can then actually use the body and mind in a more effective way without being subjected to all the limitations and sufferings that belief in our 'being' the body and mind can bring.

As an example, let us imagine that you had a virtual reality computer game and that you could put on a headset and step into the game with your consciousness. Now tell me this, would you have better success and freedom in the game believing you are the character and believing you are subjected to all of the characters limitations, fears and sufferings, or would you be able to do and push yourself more if you recognised that the body was not you and you are actually a consciousness that is not 'trapped' within the game, or body itself?

Suddenly, with the realisation that you are neither the body nor mind, you could have unlimited potential as you would not be blocked by fear or suffering and you would be able to achieve new heights within the game, without limiting yourself in any way, and doing it all from a place of inner freedom as you are not attached to the material things of the world. Contemplate that possibility for a second ...

The plain truth is that most of the things that we have been led to believe are normal, such as suffering, physical and emotional pain, are simply warning signs that we are out of alignment from the true natural self. When we feel pain within the body, it is a warning signal that something is not right, that something is out of alignment and balance is it not?

The same is true with emotional pain, depression and other forms of internal suffering; these signals are here to tell us to move back into alignment. When we do so and are not being limited or slowed down by suffering, we can suddenly concentrate all of our unblocked, aligned energy on living-out our full potential from a place of total inner freedom and joy. With a small distance between ourselves and the body and mind, we can then push the boundaries of our experience.

The whole spiritual process is about 'coming out,' so that we can move back in. In other words coming out of the identity of illusion so that we can be 'in' the world but not 'of' the world and so that we can experience and move in the world from the position and freedom of the

'True Self.' Most of us are trapped in the belief that we *are* the experience, when essentially we can never be found in experience itself, and can only be found in the one who is having the experience and prior to all experience.

A contradiction then occurs and as the mind becomes detached, the experience and experiencer seem to become one, so there is no subject-object split, a non-duality results. From this place we become detached from the world whilst also being totally and completely involved within it, with full intensity.

# Intensity

It may seem from an inexperienced perspective that not having mental attachments or identification to the world of shape and form would somehow make us walk around in an ungrounded, spaced-out way with our 'head in the clouds,' but actually, quite the opposite can occur. When the border between the subject and object has dissipated, the capacity for total intensity and involvement can occur and whatever we fix our attention upon can become absorbed by us, and we by it.

When thought and mind is no longer having so much attention paid to it, more of our attention becomes available for every experience we have within the present moment. You see, when we are not identified with anything, then we are totally free to be involved with everything, in much the same way that a child plays in a playground.

Wherever we are and whatever we are doing, we are there one hundred percent without distraction. We have full intensity and involvement in creating a complete immersion and an alertness to whatever is happening. If we are having a conversation or business meeting with someone, our undivided attention is there, listening to every word and gesture and if we are engaged in physical activities like sport, exercise or work, we are there giving ourselves to it wholeheartedly and completely. This ability to pay attention and focus is one of the major keys of all success in any and all areas of life. It is almost as if reality bends to the will of the one who commits themselves to it fully, in much the same way as a magnifying glass can reflect the sun and concentrate its energy on one specific point to burn a leaf. It is the intensity and concentration of our energy that can determine whether something blooms or withers.

Christopher J. Smith

# How Awareness Flows

*'When awareness is unobstructed, it moves freely. You become a self-sustaining flow of energy. Like a water fountain you are an independent generator that is self-sufficient. An energy unto itself'*

We as awareness have a particular flow, and when the flow is natural and unobstructed, it becomes self-sustaining, self-healing and self-sufficient. In other words, no outside energy is needed to keep this light unto itself, shining strong.

Try this simple meditation as you relax...

> *Close your eyes and become aware of your breath, notice the breath coming in through the nostrils, and notice the breath as it passes your lips on the out breath.*
>
> *Now take three conscious breaths-in, holding each one for a moment before exhaling. After the three breaths relax.*
>
> *Now this time, as you breathe in through your nose, imagine and feel the breath moving up from the base of the spine all the way to the top of your head, and making its way out of the top and down the front of your body as you exhale.*
>
> *Do this slowly ten times, and notice any changes in how you feel.*

We need not 'steal' energy from somewhere and be owed a debt; we are our own energy-bank with continuous access to its funds. When this energy flow is natural and as it should be, we are in balance and harmony within ourselves and with life. There is no war within; therefore there is no war with others or with life. We will move into a place of total alignment with the stream and flow of existence in an effortless self-generating way.

For most of us, this self-sufficient flow of energy is not functioning. It appears to be blocked and stagnant and has been blocked by our conditioned programming, misidentification, false perceptions and most of all, fear. This fear that we carry comes from the fear of losing those things that we believe are a part of who we are. When all mental and emotional attachments to the things we are not, are let go and seen to be untrue, then fear will have no grip over us any longer. It is not that fear will never again be experienced, it is simply that without our identification of it, it has no hold over us any longer. It is simply watched and observed as a phenomenon that appears and disappears within us as pure, intelligent emptiness.

Daily practice...

Firstly, reflect on any mental and emotional attachments you may be holding. Take a moment to become still and look deeply into your mind and then when ready, repeat the declaration below. As you repeat it, relax and let all attachments melt away. Implicitly trust that the declaration will perform its own magic.

*'I let go of all mental and emotional attachments to this world'*

As you say the above, note any changes within you that may occur, and know that as you say this you are releasing any mental and emotional attachments you may have been holding. Continue with this daily practice consistently until you feel that your mind has become free of mental attachment. When the mind is free of this attachment it becomes unbounded, and when it becomes unbounded, Enlightenment is the result.

# Chapter 11
## The Three Guidance Systems

*"Every time you do not follow your inner guidance, you feel a loss of energy, loss of power, a sense of spiritual deadness." Shakti Gawain*

My question to you is . . . what is it that guides you?

Are you being led by your instincts, intellect, intuition or a combination of all three?

Do you guide yourself and make your own decisions or are your decisions being made for you?

Most people of course would say that they decide what they do and do not do, but is that really true?

Are they deciding or is the conditioned mind and instinctive body deciding?

There are three main guidance systems below, which are used separately, together and not at all by some people. These systems are Instinct, Intellect and Intuition, notice that they all have the word 'in' at the beginning of them implying that those systems operate from within us at some level, each displaying a certain level of intelligence, consciousness and functioning, like rungs of a ladder.

Each guidance system supersedes the one below it and can take-over it's functioning. As an example, what is instinctive in us can be overridden and controlled by the intellect through logic, and what is intellectual can be superseded by the intuition. I will give examples below.

As we move up through the guidance systems, the previous, lower one is used less and less, and the higher one becomes the most dominant means of guidance.

The order of intelligence is as follows . . . instinctive is the lower level, intellect comes next and finally intuition is the highest form of intelligence a person has at their disposal. I will speak about each guidance system in more detail below.

## Feeling Lost and Confused

In today's technological world we have the luxury of being able to use a GPS system (Global Positioning System) when we are travelling in a car, to prevent us from becoming lost and to guide us towards our chosen destination, but what about our own internal guidance system, who or what is helping us along our path, helping us take the right turn and avoid the dead end?

Our inner guidance is very important in our experience of life. Every day we have to make decisions, from the more mundane things to the more complex situations we encounter. Consistently feeling lost, confused or fearful is not something that we prefer to experience and not something that is going to serve us well, in directing our life experience. Being confused can create an inner suffering that misaligns our energies and this tends to happen when we are a 'personal self' identified with the body, mind and all the thoughts contained within it. When confusion occurs, suffering is optional. When we are lost and confused, that is, lost in the mind, we suffer, but if you remain merely as a 'witness' we do not suffer and simply become an unidentified 'watcher of thoughts.' This shift in consciousness beyond thought and brings with it a whole new kind of intelligence to which most of us rarely has conscious access. It is in our true position as the 'witness,' that we are in touch with the most intelligent of all our guidance systems, the intuition.

## Instinctual Guidance

Instinct operates from the level of the body and lower energy systems such as the adrenal glands and sexual organs as an example. 'Lower' has no negative connotations in this context but just means that it is not as 'intelligent' an operating system as the intellect or the intuition, but is nevertheless an extremely important component of the human system. For example, when we walk across a road and suddenly notice a car speeding towards us, we need instinct in order that our adrenaline will be stimulated and enable us to jump out of the way to avoid death. So our instinct is a last resort, fail-safe system which protects us when we have no time to make a rational decision, which under normal circumstances would be made through the intellect and logic, or for the more advanced stages of evolution... through intuition. We could refer to this operating system as the 'primal instinct,' as it is the same level from which most animals operate. It is an in-built mechanism for the survival of a species, and at the heart of our genetic code which is passed on from generation to generation. Unless of course, the programming is somehow altered or an organism becomes fully-conscious and knowingly changes it's behaviour. This instinct can be 'programmed,' for better or for worse, and this is one form of the 'conditioning' which has been discussed throughout this book.

Generally an organism becomes conditioned by its environment and surroundings, but this is not always the case as it depends on the level of Intelligence of that organism. The human species is quite unique on this planet in having self-awareness and an understanding of our biology and functioning. Unlike most of the animal kingdom we have the ability to make rational decisions based upon all of the information available to us. That being said however, unfortunately most human beings tend not to always operate in this logical way and only operate, for the most part, from their instinctual nature, a nature that has also been conditioned to function in a particular way. However, we have all been conditioned and programmed in many ways, even in some ways that dictate most of our life and the decisions we make on a daily basis.

A good example of this is the sexual instinct, which is perhaps our most primal instinct of all. When a human catches sight of another naked human, this can cause an over-riding compulsion to mate that they are unable to deny, but someone who is maybe a little more 'conscious' and has the intelligence to override this instinct, will be able to resist the extreme temptation. Many addictions become instinctual compulsions also, to the point where it rapidly moves beyond the level of conscious choice into a feeling of being 'out of control.' Repetition is often the key to conditioning and when an action is performed often enough, the body and mind may become programmed to automatically function a particular way without our full, conscious awareness.

The instinctive Guidance system, as with many other natural functions, is basically for the purpose of survival and procreation, and so it is not really a system upon which we can rely for guidance in our life. In fact, many of the world's troubles emanate from our more primal, instinctive and compulsive nature, and from our conditioning, conditioned reactions and conditioned beliefs that go unquestioned. Whether intentionally or unintentionally we have been programmed by our environment, society, media, and our education systems and so many other things to operate in a particular way and to view things in a certain light. This has ingrained itself within our biology, and so we must regain control of our instincts by becoming more intelligent and conscious beings. As Einstein said, *"...a problem cannot be solved from the same level of consciousness as it began,"* and so to remedy our instincts we must move to the next level of consciousness and beyond, intellect/logic and intuition.

## Intellectual Guidance

The main characteristic that separates man from the rest of the animal kingdom is our ability to think using logic and discernment. The intellect operates from the level of the mind, and manifests itself in the form of thought and the collection and processing of information which can be stored as memory. When discerning reality and making choices, the intellect uses logic to determine an answer. Also, the intellect will use any previous information gathered, to influence its logical decision making. Logic functions based on mathematics and probability; it makes decisions based on what choices seem more likely to create the desired outcome. It may for example, say 'if I go here... then this will probably happen, and this person will say this... and so then I will do this,' and it may also be influenced by previous experience and other known information in order to determine what choices to make.

The intellect is an upgraded form of guidance, from the instinct, as it does not simply react instantaneously or automatically in any given situation, but instead considers how best to approach the situation using information and discernment. Even though intellect is a very powerful form of guidance, it is still limited because it can only see certain elements of the complete picture and can only make choices on limited amounts of information or on logic and probability which may not always be correct. As an example, if we try to predict the outcome of a horse race for example, we may have lots of information about the individual horses, the trainers, the jockey's particular skills and ground conditions etc., but even with all that information, although it is possible to predict a 'likely' outcome, it is impossible to be sure of everything that will happen, down to the finest detail. Anything at all could happen, the horse may fall or be unwell and unable to run at its best, the jockey may be unseated or an 'outsider' in the betting may run the race of its life and so any bet on a horse can never be absolutely guaranteed to be successful. Intellectual guidance therefore, cannot always be relied upon as it may be wrong, incomplete or subject to unaccountable external influences.

Another example could be that in making a decision to go ahead with a particular project, we may have assessed all the various possibilities of whether the project is likely to be successful or not, but despite this, the project may still not be successful due to something completely unknown and unexpected preventing it from going to plan. This may be something that the intellect could not possibly have foreseen. The intellect is only able to make a decision on the limited information it has available at the time, whereas the intuition can point us in the direction best suited to who we are, and so any direction it may suggest, is always one which is intuitively the best for us. Intuition can read and work with the greater energies of ourselves and the universe, whilst intellect can only work with what is overtly apparent.

## Intuitive Guidance

As the instinct and intellect are of the body and mind, the intuition is of True Self and the unseen dimensions of existence. The Intuition is different from the body and mind as it cannot be conditioned or programmed to function in a set way or in a limited capacity and this ensures that intuitive guidance always comes from a 'pure' source as opposed to coming from the influence of conditionings. There is no logic behind intuition, and there is no rational explanation for it as it manifests itself in the form of 'sensing' and an internal 'direction' that makes itself known through thoughts and feelings. It appears as an inner knowing, whereby we just know and feel something to be true without explanation or understanding. It also makes itself known from within the present moment and at a time when we are in deeper contact with our true natures. One way to be true to our nature and access intuition is through 'pure meditation' which simply means being ourselves

## The Secret Self

fully as an observer of the mind, body and true self (for an explanation of pure meditation, see Chapter 13—Practices & Teachings for Deeper Awakening.) The deeper we go into our pure meditation, the more we begin to bypass the instinct and intellect and connect more tightly and closely with the intuitive abilities within. The more the volume of this subtle form of guidance can be turned-up and listened-to, the more internally 'quiet' we become and as we connect to the silence and stillness within, we become more receptive to the intuitions pointing and direction. It is similar to being an astronaut on a foreign world where we must be quiet so that we can hear and follow the commands from mission control. Mission control just like intuition can see the bigger picture, and it can instruct us as to where to go and what to do next, whereas the astronaut just like the body and mind can base his own decisions only upon small parts of the overall picture, based on the limited information available and its logical reasoning.

The mind, through its limited ability can only see a few steps ahead and cannot even be one hundred percent certain that what it believes will happen, will come true. To use an analogy, imagine a large maze where the mind is at ground level within the centre of the maze itself, and the intuition is looking down from above at the maze. The Intuition can see where all the routes lead and how to get to the exit, whereas the mind can only see the immediate path ahead and does not know what is around each corner and which is the best way to choose. Any one of a dozen paths could be the path to freedom or to a dead end.

When we relinquish the need to control and direct where we intend to go, the intelligence of intuition can then be our guiding force. Once we realise there is a decision to be made, we must metaphorically 'get out of the way' and allow our existence to guide us and live through us. Or when we surrender into our true nature, and let go of our intentions or desire to decide anything, then life will guide us and our intuition will automatically lead us towards the best options in our lives. Be in no doubt that life will always make the best possible use of us and place us wherever we are 'meant' to be. By being in alignment with who we are at the highest level, we become aligned with the greater existence of the universe and ensure that the universe will guide us in the best possible direction for ourselves and for the universes evolution as a whole.

# Ego vs. Intuition

So how can we be sure that it is the intuition that is guiding you and not the conditioned ego mind?

The first thing we must do is to stay completely empty, we must let go and surrender that which we are not, which is the ego (identity of being the body and mind, and the false 'persona.') We should relinquish the need for 'personal' control of our lives, and instead relax and allow things to happen in a more natural way. We should still continue with all that is necessary to function in our lives, but should not regard ourselves as the sole practitioner of these things. When we live in this way, then we will be 'empty vessels,' and only an empty vessel can be filled. The more we are filled with the pure 'life force' of existence, the more that intuition will be there, guiding us through every moment. We will not need to 'try' to do anything at all as it will just happen automatically and effortlessly. From time to time, thoughts from the ego will enter our minds to try and 'feed' us with doubts and fears, but we should just stay as the pure 'watching self' unaffected by the passing stream of thoughts, emotions and experiences, and these thoughts will dissipate quite effortlessly as they cannot influence our pure essence.

So, the more grounded we are as the 'true witnessing self' the more that intuition will be our guiding force.

We can tell the difference between whether it is the mind making a choice or being directed by intuition, by being aware of whether the choice is being mulled-over in the mind or not, where pros and cons are being considered and where there is excessive mental analysis of a decision. You see, the ego will look to intellectualise and create an inner conversation about a decision. An inner dialogue will be created which may say, 'if I do this, then that will happen,' and this is the intellectual ego mind, and it is often coming from a personal sense of identity (the false persona/mask.)

The intuition will be much simpler and may manifest as a brief, subtle thought-form without explanation or rationale, or a feeling may arise where we just know that we must do something in particular—with no questions asked. The intuition will often show itself as a strong, inner 'knowing' with a drive and conviction not initiated by the mind, not initiated by any belief, but yet seeming to emanate from an inspiration (in-spirit-ation, from pure spirit itself). The Intuition will never show itself as a fear, only the mind creates fear; instead intuition will always arise from a spontaneous, loving clarity, a love for life and existence itself. Pure love is guiding us along the way and moving life along in a way that is best for all concerned.

The most appropriate 'urge' will make itself known to us at just the right time and everything will happening in harmony with all else. When a response is needed, the correct response will come, often spontaneously, instantaneously and effortlessly from our deepest core. The core within that is one with the source of life itself.

## How to Make a Decision

Whilst intuition is the highest form of guidance, the intellect and logic can also combine with intuition to make a decision. You see, many sound decisions can be made with logic and intellect alone, but when they are combined with intuition, they become a 'powerhouse' of guidance. When presented with a decision, we should first use the intellect to weigh the options based on the knowledge we already have and also on previous experience. We can then use logic to assess the pros and cons involved in all the factors surrounding the decision at hand. The intellect engages the memory and the logic uses that memory to try and discern the best course of action. At this point, we can now use intuition for the final guidance.

Each of the three guidance systems requires a different length of time to activate. The instinct usually has a very quick response or reaction-time, whereas the intellect and logic will take longer to work-out a solution, whilst the intuition can often take an even longer time. It may sometimes be the case that we may not make a decision immediately, choosing to 'sleep on it,' or even wait a significant amount of time before our decision is finalised. As the intuition becomes stronger and more refined, it will become quicker in its decision-making. Intuition only really occurs when we discover who we are and move into full alignment with it, and hence into full alignment with the universe. At this time, we may have realised our ultimate path and have started-out in that direction, whereas in our mind we may only be considering the very basics of our direction in life, and this may even constantly change as the conditioned mind shifts its focus. This is similar to a boat that sets-out in one direction with the knowledge that it is on the correct course, just continuing along that same route until it arrives at its pre-determined destination. Whereas the mind will constantly change directions and destinations, often going around in circles and getting nowhere.

So, the best way that we can use inner guidance is with the intellect, logic and intuition all working together. In other words, once we have all of the facts, we can then allow the intuition to dominate by tapping into inner 'stillness.' We may contemplate, which means shifting between thought and stillness or no-mind, and the correct choice will arise from a deeper place within. Once we have considered all the information available and as many variables as possible, the intuition will now be in a strong position to make the correct decision and this intuition is accessed through inner stillness and quietness. People often report that insight and clarity of all kinds including decisions, is best achieved by meditation, stillness being a mini-meditation itself. Every time we become 'still' and connect with the deep, quiet place within, beyond the chatter of the mind, we access that intuitive ability, and a clarity that we otherwise would not achieve. Sometimes it is possible that we may become 'still' and consider possible options and yet experience unpleasant feelings arising from those options, whereas with other options we may experience pleasure. The key is to listen to what 'feels good,' and where there is an 'inner-pull' towards a certain direction, this will usually be the correct choice. The more 'still' we become, the stronger that the 'inner-pulls' of the intuition will become.

Also, we should always use logic in alignment with the true self for guidance and we do this by asking the question, *'is this decision for the betterment of all concerned, or is it just for self-gain?'* This is an important question to ask, as it enables us to understand whether our decision is in alignment with the universe and pure consciousness or if it is just emanating from the ego and a sense of separation and self-preservation. The ego always makes decisions based on what is good for only its own interest, whereas the pure consciousness that is aligned with the universe, always does what is best for all concerned, because it 'knows' that we are all 'one' and connected to all life, and always wishes to see the 'one-ness' flourish.

## Three Ways to Approach Life Situations

There are three ways to approach and deal with any situation. These are, to change something physically, to change something mentally, such as our beliefs or perceptions and finally if neither of these applies, for us to surrender, accept and trust life.

A large part of our inner guidance is learning how best to deal with various challenging life situations as they occur. I suggest that there are three main ways we can deal with any situation that involves the body, mind and pure consciousness levels. As above, one way to deal with a challenging situation is to either change it physically or to remove yourself from the situation physically. For example, assume you are suffering from financial problems. You should firstly become aware of the problem. Then, 'surrender' and accept the situation as it is. It is 'what it is,' at this moment in time. The more we accept what is within the now moment, the more we can come into alignment and ease with life as it stands right now.

Attempt to end the struggle or inner resistance against current circumstances, because the tendency of the conditioned ego is to struggle, and this struggle puts you at unease within yourself. So once we relax and end the struggle, we achieve alignment with the power of existence itself, and the force of life can move through us and endow your action or inaction, with potency. From this point we may now be able to change the situation physically or even remove ourselves from it. For example in this case, maybe we would put in place a plan in order to pay-off the debt, or if the debt is too bad to manage, maybe we would choose to become bankrupt. Whatever we are able to do physically is our first option for remedying the situation.

Once we have exhausted all physical options and yet the problem still remains, then we may move to the second option, that is changing how we view the situation. Maybe you can use your creativity to solve the problem, or maybe you can look at it from a different perspective or even detect a possible opportunity arising from it. If you can't change your perspective about it, then we must allow the situation to be just 'as it is,' without our struggling to change it or presenting an inner resistance to it. In this way, we remain in alignment with the universe and trust that it will eventually provide us with the appropriate solution, creativity or inspiration to transcend the situation.

This is often where patience and persistence is needed to transform a situation. Sometimes things may change quickly or take longer, but as long as we are aligned in the moment with life, and with no inner struggle causing us suffering, eventually life will find a way, through us, to transcend a situation that is no longer in alignment with who we are. This is why the absence of inner struggle is important, because the more we resist, the more it will likely persist. Why? Because our very resistance to a particular situation means that we have not overcome it within. Our resistance within is often similar to a mirror reflecting back at us, our mind and state of being and if we resist what is outside, it means that we have not learnt to transcend inside, and so this will most likely continue until we do so. How do we transcend it? Through surrendering and allowing it to be, and by surrendering the limiting belief and thought which is creating the inner struggle, we release our identity with the thoughts and beliefs about the situation, and so it will then fade-away, as it no longer has power over us. Then, with all inner resistance and struggle gone, the situation outside has space to change. All obstacles in life are first overcome and transformed within, and then they serve no purpose being outside of us any longer.

## Do not Compare Paths

A common trait of the learnt ego mind is to compare its path with the path of others, especially with those that seem to be on a similar path to ourselves. However, it should be noted that no two paths can ever be the same and so it is essentially a waste of time and energy to try to compare them. A huge part of our social conditioning has been to live by comparison, to judge our success and achievements with those around us or in the same field as us. But every path is different and therefore cannot be possibly compared.

Comparison only creates unhappiness and disingenuousness, because if we compare ourselves to others we may only feel bad about ourselves and this may affect our own uniqueness because we are too concerned with emulating others. Sometimes the conditioned self has its own ideas about how we should act or what we should be doing. Should I be doing what others are doing (this goes for those on the spiritual path especially)? Do not be fooled by the ego into believing that you should dress, act or behave in a certain way, just be you. You are unique! Just be true to following your own unique path and remain faithful to who you are naturally, within the moment.

## Trusting Intuition

*"The intuition is a sacred gift and the rational mind is a faithful servant. We have created a society that honours the servant and has forgotten the gift"* Albert Einstein

In the beginning, our minds may harbour doubts about the validity of intuitive guidance and if we are inclined to trust those thoughts, then we may become unsure about which path to take. These fears and doubts are of the ego mind and its conditioning and emanating from its need to retain control within the limits of its old safe programmed patterns. It 'forgets' that its logic and intellect is not fool-proof. We may even have family members and friends that question or even ridicule us about our intuitive decisions and direction, but we should not allow that to deflect us, as they are merely using their own common guidance of instinct, conditioning or intellect. Remember that it is not their path but ours, and only we can walk it. We are each on our own unique paths and we need not to answer to anyone but our own true self from within the heart. If we feel something to be true and right for us, then we must be true to ourselves and follow our inner guidance.

Trust and confidence will increase with experience and the depth of our own pure selves. As we follow our intuition and realise that in hindsight it has brought us positive experiences, people and places, our trust and reliance upon it will become more solid, we will develop a freedom to relax and trust intuition when we find ourselves in challenging situations and there are important decisions to be made. Life will create innumerable synchronicities that are inexplicable by normal rational means. For example, we may find that the 'right' person comes into our life at just the right time, or we discover numerous pieces of information that all correlate to just what you need at that time in order to guide us in the right direction. The more in alignment we are with our true selves and existence, the more synchronicities will occur, and we will be able to recognise this as a sign that we are moving along the right path in harmony with wherever existence is taking us. Life will then provide more and more opportunities for us to discover who we really are. Always remember that it is not about where we are going, but more about what we are discovering about who we are that is of extreme importance, as the limits of our capabilities and potential lie within our discovery of the True Self.

Synchronicities happen all the time, more often than people realise and it is simply a case that most people are not aware of them and do not see them, or often dismiss them as a coincidence or randomness. But as we become more attuned to them and move into greater alignment with the whole universe and our True Self, the synchronicities begin to be revealed and occur more often, sometimes happening in rapid succession.

Carl Jung who founded analytical psychology coined the term 'synchronicity.' Here is Jung's most famous synchronicity story about a scarab beetle, the Egyptian symbol of rebirth. This story is taken from: C. G. Jung, *'Synchronicity: An Acausal Connecting Principle,'* Trans., R. F. C. Hull, New York: Princeton University Press, 1973, pp: 109 -110.

> *"My example concerns a young woman patient who, in spite of efforts made on both sides, proved to be psychologically inaccessible. The difficulty lay in the fact that she always knew better about everything. Her excellent education had provided her with a weapon ideally suited to this purpose, namely a highly polished Cartesian rationalism with an impeccably 'geometrical' idea of reality. After several fruitless attempts to sweeten her rationalism with a somewhat more human understanding, I had to confine myself to the hope that something unexpected and irrational would turn up, something that would burst the intellectual retort into which she had sealed herself.*
>
> *Well I was sitting opposite her one day, with my back to the window, listening to her flow of rhetoric. She had had an impressive dream the night before, in which someone had given her a golden scarab—a costly piece of jewellery. While she was still telling me this dream, I heard something behind me gently tapping on the window. I turned around and saw that it was a fairly large flying insect that was knocking against the windowpane from outside in the obvious effort to get into*

*the dark room. This seemed to me very strange. I opened the window immediately and caught the insect in the air as it flew in. It was a scarab beetle, or common rose-chafer (Cetonia aurata), whose gold-green colour most nearly resembles that of the golden scarab. I handed the beetle to my patient with these words, 'Here is your scarab.' This experience punctured the desired hole in her rationalism and broke the ice of her intellectual resistance. The treatment could now continue with satisfactory results."*

Life and the True Self is always speaking to us, trying to guide and nudge us in the right direction and all we must do is pay attention and move to deeper levels of consciousness within ourselves for the path to open up and become apparent. The more relaxed and 'still' we become, the more intuition will find its way to our hearts. It will bring a deeper meaning to the phrase 'follow your heart' and we will find ourselves living from the heart, in each moment, fully present in the 'here and now' in our natural states, being led down a beautiful path, visibly lit for us. To others it may seem crazy, but our knowing will prevent any criticism from being heard. All synchronicities lead and merge into the road of your True Self and destiny.

## The Real Secret

Many of you reading this may have heard about or read the book, 'The Secret,' which is based on the idea that if you believe, think and feel what you want, that you can actually create it for yourself, and that this is the 'real' secret to life. It has been referred to as the 'law of attraction'. However, whilst many of these teachings have some truth, it is far from being the real secret to our existence, and neither is it the whole truth of the 'creation process.' The real secret is not so much what you do, but is rather 'who you are,' that is the real 'secret of secrets,' and who you are, is the 'secret self.'

Our path and direction in life is created by what we embody in each moment. For example, most people, as we have discussed, are not living as who they really are, but from conditioned, unoriginal beliefs, ideas and perceptions. These are traits that we have acquired as we have gone through life, and then embodied. Because of this, most of us follow a life path that resonates to the frequency of those conditionings and not to our own, unique prime frequency.

We all have a unique prime frequency that is inbuilt within particular themes of life we may experience, but for most of us this 'base frequency' is being obscured by conditioned surface frequencies, and so the surface frequencies begin to take precedence as we identify with them and are therefore embodying them. It is as though we are allowing a piece of virus-infested software to attack our computer. The sooner we can eradicate the virus and reboot the system, the sooner we can return the computer back to performing its original intended functions, in alignment with the creator's original design.

These falsely conditioned frequencies are in effect blocking our pure raw potential and the true identity of who we really are. It is not that we must 'try' to attract what we wish to be and experience, it is just that by discovering the Secret Self and releasing that which is not really us, that we 'clear the path' to ourselves, which was being blocked by who we 'thought' we were, based on our conditioning. As soon as we awaken to our true identity beyond the ego, we then in effect, 'reboot the system' and this allows access to all that is a match to whom we really are at the core of our being.

Then, from this place we have a clear path to allow our intuition to guide us in the best direction of that which is in alignment with who we really are. Does this not sound much easier than 'trying' to be whom we are and 'trying' to experience what we want to experience? All that is needed is for us to relax and release who we think we are, do the right things to discover who we are, and all will make itself apparent from there onwards. When we discover our source nature and dissolve the illusionary identities, what we do in the world will then become apparent and obvious. From there, we will no longer need to try to make things happen, it will all become spontaneous and effortless. Our path will be much clearer and smoother and by discovering who we are, we will gain access to the original source frequency from which all true potential is possible.

The real secret to life, that which the ancients and enlightened masters knew, is that it is 'who we are' that creates all our experience, and it is who we are, that opens all the doors to existence itself and thus allowing us to realise our true potential.

# Relax the Need to Know

*"Trust your intuition. You don't need to explain or justify your feelings to anyone, just trust your own inner guidance, it knows best."*

The ego mind's reality and identity is tied-up in a sense of past and future. It wants to know the future so badly because it will then feel that it has control, and it wants control because it fears the unpredictable, and it fears what might happen when things are out of its control. So whenever doubt or a need to know the future arises, we should just remain aware and comprehend that this is the fear of the mind itself... it is not who you are.

And so there is a tendency of the mind to attempt to understand why things are happening and where things are going, as if life is leading to some particular future event or outcome that is some kind of 'special completion.' And the way to avoid being caught in this trap is to never ask 'why something is happening' and 'where things are leading,' just simply stay aware of the unfolding of each experience within the present moment. There is no future, there is no special event where everything ends and is perfect as the mind perceives it and wishes it to be. No-one has ever seen the future. Please look.

So why would we say 'never ask why or where?' Quite simply because there is no answer to those questions and any answer would merely be an individual interpretation that could never be fully verified by anyone or by life itself, and so why even bother asking.

One person will interpret something as meaning one thing based on their belief system, whilst another will see it a different way based on theirs and neither can be known to be correct. Each is just an idea and a view of life from a limited vantage point. Life has never told anyone directly that certain events and experiences mean certain things, it is all down to individual interpretation.

Those types of unanswered questions will only serve to keep a person focussed on the future and therefore trapped as the ego identity, in a restless and agitated state, with no definite answers forthcoming.

So let go of trying to discover 'where and why' and simply allow yourself to trust and flow with and as the grand intelligence of life itself. When we discard the ego we allow the totality of the universe to shine forth through us. Many people live with a rigid plan in their mind of how they want everything to pan-out in life. A plan is no problem as long as we are prepared to be flexible as things naturally change and do not always work out as expected. If a plan is causing uncertainty and anxiety then let it go completely and enter the flow of life wholeheartedly in the present moment.

The deeper we relax into our natural essence and allow ourselves to 'let go' totally and completely, the more that intuition will be there with the volume turned up to maximum...

> *"Don't seek, don't search, don't ask, don't knock, don't demand... relax. If you relax... it comes.*
>
> *If you relax it is there. If you relax, you start vibrating with it"* ~ Osho

# Chapter 12
# Self Investigation and Transcending Limiting Beliefs

*"Knowing yourself is the beginning of all wisdom"* Aristotle

In this chapter, our aim is to discover and explore the True Self and to identify and transcend the limiting belief systems that are contained within the mind at the subconscious level.

I will guide you through the investigation with certain questions and pointers. These questions and pointers rely upon your contemplation of them and this process can only work through your willingness, persistence and introspection with continual investigation, until the beliefs are transcended. They are there simply to guide you in asking the questions that will take you deeper within and to enable the mind to unravel.

The cause of all of our troubles and suffering comes primarily from our misidentification of self, and the ultimate way to move beyond suffering is by locating and establishing the 'True Self,' which 'self-investigation' will aid us to do. Once we have established who we are, it will then be much easier to identify any limiting and negative belief systems we have which are also causing us suffering, torment and setting boundaries to our potential and range of consciousness. For this we will use the guided questions of 'transcending limiting beliefs.'

## Why Self-Investigation?

*"Who looks outside dreams, who looks within Awakens"* Carl Jung

It is only through introspection which is the act of looking within, that you will be discovered. You cannot be found outside and no issue of yours can be ultimately solved there, it is all finally resolved and found within.

As stated above, the only means to discover our true nature is by looking within. We cannot discover ourselves on the 'outside,' and so we need to shift our attention away from the outside to within, to who is actually having the experience which we call 'life.' You may have experienced that, in challenging times we tend to look within ourselves, but often when things on the outside are going as planned, we tend not to look within quite so much. It seems almost counter-intuitive to ask this question. What is the point at looking who is there? We know who is there, it is 'me' of course, but who or what is 'me' exactly? And how established and grounded are we, in who we really are at our core.

We often stop at the 'me' answer and never look more deeply for exactly who or what is there. But if we dared to look within and investigate further, we may find that the thing we took for granted, our very idea of our 'Self,' is not what we presumed it was, in fact we may realise that it was the presumptions that were the problem all along.

It is all too apparent that there is much suffering in this world, and here I am not speaking of actual physical suffering (although this is also related and caused by what we are speaking of,) I am primarily speaking of the internal suffering that largely goes unnoticed because most people keep it to themselves and have come to believe that this is normal, so many people simply continue to suffer in silence. This is in fact, the suffering of 'misidentification.'

When we misidentify who we are, we find ourselves trapped in a case of 'mistaken identity,' believing ourselves to be something that we are not, and when circumstances and changes affect those 'mistaken identities,' which they inevitably do in this world of constant change, we tend to suffer for that also. When we identify with the material objects of the world we become 'lost' and then often may be overwhelmed by fear, anxiety, grief, confusion restlessness and other negative states. Then we tend to make erroneous decisions based upon a distorted perception which has a severe negative impact on our life and the lives of those around us. Suffering ultimately equates to unhappiness, but when the suffering is gone, when unhappiness is no longer there, natural happiness and joy appears.

If we wish to truly be free from inner suffering and the distortions of misidentification, then Self-investigation is a 'direct route' towards this

Inner Freedom and true natural joy, which can only be realised upon the discovery of who you truly are.

## What is Self-Investigation?

Self-investigation is a means of discovery and the unveiling of our true nature, thereby freeing ourselves from misidentification. The result of this discovery is the end of suffering and the beginning of total inner-freedom. It is a logical, subtle, experiential and practical means of discerning what we are 'not' and a realisation of what we really are.

Self-investigation is also a logical process or tool of exploration and discernment. It is a means of establishing our one true identity through the questioning of our essential reality, asking and discovering who we are and who we *are not* with utmost honesty and precision.

This methodology was originally made popular by the great Indian sage Ramana Maharshi in the early decades of the 20th century. He was adamant, through his own Self Realisation and discovery process, that we could all come to know ourselves through this process of self-inquiry and that we could find the 'I' behind the 'I,' as he called it. Ramana said that in all of us there was a true 'I' that for most lay hidden behind the false 'I' that we believe ourselves to be, and that through self-inquiry we could establish our true identity beyond the false 'I' or ego self.

So this is what we will concern ourselves with in our own investigations and explorations, using the following questions as a guide. I will explain how to interpret each question and how you can best contemplate and meditate upon each one.

Once we have established who we are, the process of transcending limiting belief systems will be so much easier. This self-investigative method of discovering our own nature is a direct route to the acceleration of your awakening and self-realisation and should propel you quickly towards the end of your spiritual search.

## The Importance of Honesty

As we work through this process of self-investigation and the identification of limiting beliefs, we must be completely honest in our exploration, otherwise we will only end-up denying ourselves the huge potential benefits that are achievable through these inquiries.

Lying to ourselves has often been a massive part of the issue for so many of us and has actually led to much misidentification and to the limiting beliefs that we may have acquired. For example, instead of facing and confronting certain thoughts or judgements about people or a situation, we may often deny them and suppress them. This is gross dishonesty and self-deception.

As we become more aware and awakened, this process begins to work differently, in the sense that when certain thoughts arise we can just let them pass without acknowledging them. This does not therefore elicit any emotion within us, and we are able to simply allow them to pass without further analysis. However, our thoughts often generate an emotion within us and when this occurs and we don't confront these thoughts and emotions we are being untrue to ourselves and not admitting that something has affected us negatively. These thoughts, beliefs and emotions must then be made conscious and released.

Whenever we do not release them, they linger and create a dense energy field within the body and limit our range of perception and without realising it, we may become unhappy over time. As the unreleased emotions build, they only serve to block our true light and free nature and our expanded consciousness will become more constricted and limited.

So, as we are working with these questions we must be honest about the beliefs we hold and what the true identity is, at our core.

Be aware that with this type of inquiry, thoughts and emotions may arise from time to time that block or try to divert our discovery. Do not pay too much attention to the mind or your emotions when this happens, simply persist with the questions. Or if you feel particularly drained or uneasy, take a break and return to the investigation later. It is only through persistent awareness and asking of the right questions that we will break through the imaginary layers of the mind and recognise the pureness of our true reality.

# Self-Investigation (from Transient Nature to the Constant Self)

*"To know what you are, find out what you are not"* Sri Nisargadatta Maharaj

In the self-investigation process, we are essentially seeking the true self, but first we must discover what we are *not*. Once we establish what we are not, whatever remains will be what we actually are.

The way to see what we are *not* and eliminate that from our investigation is to search only for that which is constant within us and our life experience, and everything that is transitory and subject to change, may be disregarded. This is essentially *not* who we are, and that is the key to the process. We are looking for our essential and primary existence that has always been there and this is the one constant in all the experiences that you have ever had and will ever have. Absolute honesty must always prevail.

Regarding the actual investigation, we must take our time, be patient and thorough with our clarifications, and allow ourselves to really sit with what we discover and let it sink in. The purpose of self-investigation is not for the mind or intellect, the questions are not to be answered intellectually, they are there to draw your awareness in a certain direction towards that which is true, untrue and that which you really are. They are 'experiential' questions, which can be used time and time again for direct experience of the truth. We must always look with fresh eyes each time and not through past experiences, or what the conditioned mind believes to be the truth. Through the investigation we are attempting to reveal the 'self,' through whichever gap may appear and lead us to our core essence. It is important that we do not attempt to 'rush' it, as our investigation needs to strike at our very core. It must strike deeply within for us to make any significant progress. What we may find through our investigations is that we experience a number of epiphanies and realisations along the way that shifts our perception in subtle or even very profound ways.

> *We can ask the initial question, 'what is the one constant in my life that is not subject to any change?'*

The pertinent question is, in all of our life experiences, all the way from birth to now, what has been the one constant in our life and experience of life? This will enable us to eliminate those things that we are certain are not part of our true natures. For example, our clothes, money, car or property? We should firstly begin with the external attributes and slowly work inwards to the root and core of who we are. From external circumstances and possessions to relationships and family, and eventually to body, mind and belief systems etc., it is important that our investigation process is thorough and that we do not just short-circuit it and assume that we already know the answers.

Remember that the questions below are simply a guide for us to investigate life and our own nature and that they are not guaranteed to guide us to our true nature automatically. It is our curiosity, exploration, contemplation, Introspection and persistence that will do this. With each question we must become very still and quiet within and to this end it may help if we do it after meditation practice. This will help to settle the mind, make us more introspective and provide a greater capacity to investigate. As we become more naturally aware and relaxed and meditative more often, we will notice that self-investigation becomes easier and is something that can be practised anywhere, at any time. However, initially we may find it helpful to isolate ourselves for thirty or sixty minutes or so, as we would for our regular mediation practice.

## How to 'Self-Investigate'

Before I lead you through the self-investigation, I would remind you that this investigation and questions on the investigation are not for the mind to solve. Instead, the questions are for the purpose of directing your attention towards the place where the question is pointing to. We are looking for the experiential and not for an intellectual answer, so contemplate the question deeply. Contemplation simply involves moving between thoughts about it into an inner silence, and moving back and forth between mind and no mind. Allow the question to take you wherever it leads to, even if this requires several attempts to achieve.

I am about to lead you through the investigation and explain each question for clarity and afterwards there will be another set of questions to work with yourself. My explanation of the first investigation and set of questions arising is just an example of how to use the questions and what to look for. You may well experience a great inner 'shift,' just from this, but I would advise you to work with the rest, alone, in order to go through the process yourself.

# Preparation Meditation

So, before we begin it is important to relax and be calm. Let us work with the meditation that we are familiar with from chapter 2 (How to Awaken) of the book on meditation, and that is the 'I watch the mind... I watch the body,' meditation.

> *So find a quiet place where you will be more likely be undisturbed. Sit in an upright position with your back straight and head looking forward at a 45 degree angle from the floor and choose a comfortable, upright position such as the cross-legged sitting position on a cushion or sat in a chair with your feet planted firmly on the ground and your knees at a 90 degree angle...*
>
> *You can either place your hands one palm on top of the other on your lap, or you can turn the palms of your hands upwards and place them on your knees, whatever feels most comfortable...*
>
> *Now close your eyes...*
>
> *As you close your eyes, look towards where the tip of the nose would be if you had your eyes open and allow your gaze to focus on the blackness of the mind...*
>
> *Now when you are ready, take three medium length breaths in through the nose and out through the nose...*
>
> *Once you have inhaled and exhaled three times, repeat this internal mantra with the breath...*
>
> *Say, 'I watch the mind' on the inhale...*
>
> *And 'I watch the body' on the exhale...*
>
> *As you breathe in gently, say to yourself 'I watch the mind'*
>
> *As you breathe out gently, say to yourself 'I watch the body'*
>
> *As you say the mantra, allow it to gently direct your awareness towards both the body and mind as you breathe. Repeat each mantra at the same time as the inhalation and exhalation of the breath...*
>
> *If you find that you have become distracted by external noise, then just simply become aware and acknowledge whatever the distraction was*

*and gently return to the inhaling and exhaling of the breath with each internal mantra...*

*If you find that you becoming lost in thinking or distracted by bodily sensations, then simply acknowledge what you became lost in... Let it go... and return awareness back to the breath and mantras whilst watching the body and mind activity once again.*

*Each time you become unaware, make a conscious note of it but do not judge yourself or become angry. Simply return to the mantras and breathing...*

*Allow the practice to turn you into a silent watcher of the body and minds activities, watching and noticing the different movements of thoughts and the different sensations that arise in the body, watch them impartially without judgement.*

*Continue with this practice for 15 to 30 minutes before you begin the 'self-investigation' below. This meditation will also help you to achieve the most appropriate state of consciousness for the 'transcending limiting beliefs' method below...*

*Remember that with all practices and methods, patience and persistence is the key to success...*

## 'Who am I?' (Finding the Constant Self)

Firstly begin with the question, 'Who or what am I?'

Take a moment to become quiet within and contemplate these questions with honesty in order to discover your Constant True Nature as you are led through the Self-investigation.

*Are you the objects of the world?*

Often when we engage with material objects such as cars, properties, money, clothes and other material possessions, there can be a conscious or unconscious tendency for us to identify with these things. The language we use commonly indicates clearly where our identities lie. For example, most people say 'I'm going to drive 'my' car, or I am going to withdraw 'my' money from the bank. This 'my' that we use refers to the sense of personal/ego identity that we mistake ourselves to be. It is almost as though we have a 'shopping cart' of identities and those things that we see as being a part of us or our personal sense of 'me,' are added to this cart.

Most people carry and attach to so many objects of the external world, that they come to have their identity invested within these objects, as if it is a part of who they are. This is where the word 'possession' in 'material possessions' becomes quite literal. It is as if the 'entity' of our 'identity' possesses these objects and where we cannot make a clear distinction from what is us and ultimately not us, the lines of our identity seem to become blurred and when this happens, we are often setting-up ourselves for inner suffering. What can also often happen is that what we 'own' or possess often ends up owning or possessing us. For example, if we identify strongly with money and how much money we have, then when some of this money is taken away, we will feel a sense of sadness and lack of energy, as if we are losing a part of ourselves. This feeling of loss only ever occurs when we are closely attached-to and identified with an object.

## Am I the Body?

We now need to become quiet and still in order to investigate whether or not this body is really us. Ask the question, 'am I this body?' Please contemplate all these questions and suggestions below but also remember that they are just guides and you may well have your own examples of the changing forms of the body. Remember also that we are trying to recognise that which is constant and changeless within us . . .

Are we our names, John . . . Chris . . . Nicky . . . Laura . . . ?

Does a name, a group of letters, really explain who we are . . . ?

Can our name come and go . . . can it be changed or modified . . . ?

If the name is changed, then surely that name could have never truly been you . . . ?

So let us look at other, smaller aspects of the body. Our finger and toe nails and hair are part of our bodies, but when we cut the nails or hair and those pieces become detached, we soon realise that they cannot be us because we are still here in our entirety...

As the hair and nails grow we trim them and eventually what was once their roots, will eventually rise to the surface and be cut-off. So, we ultimately cannot be our hair or nails. When they have been trimmed and discarded, we can be sure that is not us in the waste bin...

Our body is made of seventy percent water, and as we take-in new fluids our body pushes out the old fluids through urine and sweat to be replaced by brand new fluids until eventually all old fluids are replaced with new fluids. So we cannot be the fluids as they are something that comes and goes while we still remain. When sweat drips from the forehead onto the floor and the urine is expelled, we can certainly say that we are not the water, which makes up more than two thirds of the body. If we say that we were the fluids of the body, then how can that be us when they are gone and yet we still remain...?

Can you be your finger? I had a friend who lost a finger and he seemed no less conscious or complete a person after losing the finger and I am sure that he became aware that he was not that finger when it was no longer attached to his body and disposed of. So, are we our fingers, or are fingers things that may come and go, while we remain...?

If we can agree that one finger is not us, then the same rule must apply to however many fingers are detached from the body. Even if all our fingers are gone 'we' were still there to witness their going... and even their returning—if a finger should be stitched back...

And what if a whole hand, arm or leg was removed? Does who we are, essentially still remain...?

When a limb is lost, what is it that still remains and who is aware of its coming and going...?

If we are still there to observe the loss of a body part, then whether it is one limb we lose, or all of them, what is it that remains to observe this loss...?

When we see someone with no limbs, essentially who they are, still remains...

## The Secret Self

As we spoke about in detail in chapter 2, the whole body and all of its cells are completely replaced within each seven year period. All tissue, cartilage, bones, blood and organs are completely replaced within not simply somewhat changed, or even transformed, but literally, completely replaced. It is similar to getting out of an old car and stepping into a brand new one, so what is it that always remains the same as bodies are constantly replaced...?

If we say we are the body, the body that we now inhabit, then in seven years we would completely disappear as the old body is totally replaced. Who bears witness to the constant changing of the body and what remains the same, as one body is replaced with a whole new body...?

Where did the seven year-old body or the fourteen year-old body go, or the twenty one-year old body go that we believed was us? It completely disappeared, but a 'constant' must have remained while the body changed, so what exactly remained? Look and see...

Within the body, we experience sensations and emotions...

When we experience a sensation we call pain, who is there before it occurs and to notice it as it arises...?

Who is there during the pain and after it fades away and disappears...?

Who watches the coming and going of all various sensations...?

Are sensations transitory and what is it in the experience of noticing these sensations that remains constant, before it occurs, as it is present, and when it leaves...?

Sensations arise, but you do not arise. You are always there...

Do emotions come and go? Take anger for instance. During the onset of anger, who observes its growth and who watches the rising intensity of this emotion as it intensifies, remains and eventually dissipates...?

Who watches the ascent and decent of all emotions...?

Who is there long after anger is forgotten...?

If this anger or emotion is you, then should you not be able to find it within you at any and every moment...?

If it is you, then why when you remain, does it not remain always...?

Who remains, prior, during and after all emotions...?

So are you the body? Do not simply look within the mind for an answer, but instead look within your own experience, within this moment. Now, contemplate that question and examine it within your own experience...

## Am I the Mind?

Let us look at each aspect of the mind. Have you ever caught yourself day dreaming, been lost in thought, and then suddenly snapped-out of it...?

What does it mean to 'catch' yourself daydreaming? It means that you suddenly become aware that you have been deeply engrossed in thinking...

So who is it that catches you thinking, that catches thinking occurring, that is aware of thinking occurring, and can snap-out of thinking...?

Thinking means thoughts, a mental conversation, internal audio and dialogue, a mental commentary of momentarily real external events, remembered or imagined events...

Who witnesses this audio, this mental conversation and who catches the inner dialogue in action as it is occurring...?

Who hears the noisiness of this inner conversation...?

To whom is this inner conversation talking...?

Who sees the images and pictures of the mental movie being played in the mind...?

Who is there still watching after the day dreaming has stopped, who was there before it began and who was observing and involved in the day dreaming while it was happening...?

Can a thought be aware of itself...?

Can a thought notice a thought...?

If a thought did notice a thought, how would it see itself...?

When a memory is being played in the mind, what is it that is watching the playing of memory...?

When the thinking of memory ceases to be played, who remains there noticing the absence of memory and what is it that observes the appearance and disappearance of all memories...?

Who watches the remembering...?

Who is there watching imagination as it is occurring...?

Who watches the mental display of pictures and images...?

So many different thoughts run through the mind each day, each hour and each minute so who watches the passing of all these thoughts? If you are a particular thought, then why do you not come and go when the thought comes and goes...?

What remains as thoughts change...?

If you are not the thinker of thoughts, who watches the thinker and the thoughts...?

If the thinker and thoughts are not you, then what takes place in the space and gaps in-between thoughts and thinking...?

Who is there, watching as the gaps appear in between sequences of thought...?

If gaps and spaces can occur in the mind, then the thinking mind cannot be constant and if the mind is not constant, then what is constant in observing both thought and gaps between thoughts...?

Those that have meditated will know that absence of thought does not mean absence of awareness and that in meditation, as thoughts occur, who is it that perceives these various thoughts...?

## Who is Aware of the Mind?

Who bears witness to imagination, memory-pictures and colours in the mind, to ideas, judgements, negative thoughts, mental commentaries or to the noisy mental voice, the constant mental chatter, negative thoughts, positive thoughts and who remains, constantly watching and experiencing all of this mental phenomena...?

What is there to witness fast mind activity, slow mind activity and no-mind at all...?

What resides underneath the mind and what is behind the mind, watching it, peering-in at it...?

Who is it that is aware of dreaming?

When we fall asleep at night, we seem to drift from being conscious into unconsciousness...

But who is it that observes the slipping from consciousness into unconsciousness...?

When we begin dreaming, who is it that notices the dream taking place and who is watching the detail of the dream as it unfolds...?

# Where am I?

As you notice a sensation like pain, where are *you* in relation to this sensation and where do you observe it from...?

Whilst noticing an emotion such as anger, who is it that is aware of anger as it happens...?

Where is the anger observed from...?

When thoughts are witnessed passing through the mind, what sees these thoughts, and where are these thoughts being seen from...?

As imagination, memories, pictures, colours and thoughts are observed, from what location is the observing happening...?

What is the position of the observing...?

When the observing of thought occurs, from what distance is this happening and what is the distance between thought and the watching of thought...?

How many feet, inches or centimetres away is the watching of thought...?

If mind and thought can be observed, then that must mean that thoughts happen in front of us and we are *behind them,* peering in at them ...

Can the one who is aware be aware of itself?

Can the witnessing of thoughts and mind be witnessed itself ...?

Can watching itself be watched ...?

When silent watching is observed and thinking is observed, what watches both of these ...?

Can the one who is having the experience be experienced ...?

Can the perceiving of what is perceived, also itself be perceived ...?

## When am I?

When we notice our own true nature, when does this noticing take place ...?

In what moment does observing the observer occur? Check within your own experience ...

When we become aware that we are aware, when does this occur ...?

Now rest and relax, this is the end of the Investigation.

The above are examples and hints on each question to help you form an idea of how you can contemplate and introspect on these questions. Please continue as often as possible, to work with the guidelines above, to increase your powers of investigation. This will prove very useful in your self-investigation.

Below are the same questions without any external guidance, hints or examples. You should meditate and contemplate on each question thoroughly and as often as possible. Remember that the initial key to discovering your real nature is 'persistence,' and do not be disheartened if it seems that your investigation is unfruitful, just continue to ask and investigate whilst remembering that it is not the answers themselves which are important, or at least not in intellectual form, it is the experience and discovery to which it will lead you to with each asking of the questions.

To perform the investigation below, sit somewhere quietly where you will be undisturbed. You may read directly from the book or simply wish to write the questions down on paper and work from there, whichever feels most comfortable for you.

'Am I this body?'

'Am I the mind?'

'Who is aware of the mind?'

'Who is it that is aware of dreaming?'

'Where am I?'

'Can the one who is aware be aware of itself?'

'When am I?'

# Transcending Limiting Beliefs

*"Unless you learn to face your own shadows, you will continue to see them in others. Because the world outside you is only a reflection of the world inside you"*

The greatest mistake we can ever make, concerning our true nature and happiness, is to search outside ourselves for it. We try to find ourselves in the things we do, have and achieve, and we look for our sense of happiness and satisfaction in the same places, but it always appears just to be out of reach. It is never something that can be held for long, as it is constantly moving, just like chasing a carrot on a stick. We are constantly searching for the next thing, as the ego mind can never be satisfied.

It is because we perceive ourselves and our happiness as being *outside* that we suffer the opposite effect, the effect of becoming mentally disturbed by what takes place outside. When the mind does not get what it wants, it becomes disturbed and attempts to apportion blame or resolve it from the outside. This makes as much sense as trying to change your reflection in water by splashing it around. Instead we should change what is being reflected in our mind and then the reflection will change and the issue will be permanently resolved, as all problems and issues only exist within our mind and thoughts, and are never 'woven into the fabric' of life situations themselves.

Most of our minds are racing, with hundreds of thoughts per minute and sixty plus thousand every day, and many of these thoughts have beliefs attached which derive from a Root belief foundation. The mind, being structured in this way is very much like a house of cards. When we pull a card out from the very foundations (Root belief), the whole house will collapse and when a limiting Root belief is exposed in the light of our consciousness, the various beliefs and thoughts that were existing on the surface, collapse and fall away as they no longer have a platform upon which to sit. It is similar to a single tree rooted in the ground with many branches and twigs emanating from the initial base and if the tree is diseased from the twigs to the base, the question is do we try to heal the twigs to end the disease or do we take care of the problem from the roots upwards to achieve a lasting cure for the entire tree?

A belief is a very powerful entity, it can engender many conflicts and issues and it can be like a virus that spreads, infecting the whole mind with one idea, an idea that can spill over into everything you do and see, into our whole way of life. We have seen this with certain extreme religions or radical groups and cults; one strong belief can poison the mind so that we see this belief in everything and everything is then filtered through it. Then the only true way to cure the mind and eliminate this virus is to direct awareness towards it and question its validity, to transfer it from the unconscious to the conscious, and decide whether or not it is true.

## Identify the Thought or Belief

*"Underneath each consistent negative thought is hidden a belief, and behind each belief there is a Root limiting belief supporting it. Find the Root belief, question it and watch the foundation collapse in to the Freedom of your Awareness"*

Not all thoughts have a belief attached to them, some are just fleeting, and others are a little more consistent and recurring. A thought on its own has no power or potency, yet a thought with belief is extremely powerful and potentially dangerous, it can start a war or destroy a race or nation. But no belief is a match for our awareness, and no belief or thought can stand up to the light of pure consciousness. This is how powerful we all are, essentially. Just simply identifying a belief or thought is the end of its power over us, because as soon as we place it under the bright light of our awareness, it cannot last for long. So many people are almost completely unaware of all of the thoughts, beliefs and stored emotions that they are carrying, the thoughts and chatter that are constantly repeating in the mind, narrating everything that they or others do, the judgements, complaints and inner arguments with what the 'here and now' contains. By becoming more introspective, we move to a deeper state of consciousness where the core of our being can be felt, and where all thoughts and beliefs can be recognised. It is only at this deeper level that we have the power to heal, to heal through awareness and the questioning of what we believe to be the truth.

> We have all been 'belief thieves' at one time or another, because nearly all of the beliefs that most of us carry in the subconscious mind are other people's ideas or beliefs, societies beliefs or the collective unconsciousness's beliefs. These also may be the result of lifetimes of conditioning passed on from generation to generation, through culture and also through our very DNA, built into the fabric of how our body functions. But luckily we have the ability to change this within our own lifetime and set ourselves free and also to change the direction for the next generation as a by-product.

To question a belief is also very powerful, as by questioning it we can come to undermine its authority and structure, pulling out the foundation from underneath it. A thought only turns into a belief when we accept it as true and many people when exploring the subconscious mind are completely surprised by what they find. They may be carrying beliefs that they were not even consciously aware they had, and yet while they are not consciously aware of them, they still have the power to cause a person to automatically and instinctively react in a certain way. As soon as we identify and question our beliefs, we are giving ourselves the opportunity to review and clear-out that which may have been causing us and others much distress and which may have been limiting our progress in life's pursuits.

Below is a list of the most common and limiting belief systems that most of us will have held at one time, or indeed may still do to this day. Look with honesty to see if any of these beliefs below have been yours at some time or another, or maybe even now.

Common limiting beliefs...

- 'I cannot tell the truth because I may be judged'
- 'I do not want to get close to this person lest my heart is broken'
- 'I do not want to ask for what I want, because what if I am rejected?'
- 'I cannot trust people because I have been betrayed before'
- 'I cannot pursue my dreams because I do not know what I would do if I fail'
- 'I cannot do X because of Y'
- 'I am not lovable'
- 'Nothing I do ever works out'
- 'I am always unlucky'
- 'I am not good enough'
- 'It's better to blend in than standout'
- 'I am not happy until I have reached my end goal'
- 'This is too difficult'
- 'I do not need help from anyone'
- 'It is too late'
- 'To suffer is human, it is normal'
- 'People think I am unattractive'
- 'I never seem to have enough money'
- 'I am a failure'
- 'People do not like me'
- 'I am so disorganised and have no discipline'
- 'I am no good at... (*fill in the blank*)'
- 'I cannot lose weight'
- 'I am disconnected from life'
- 'I am not safe'
- 'I am not worthy'
- 'I am unimportant'

- 'I have a boring life'
- 'If someone reassures me, then I will do it'
- 'My life is harder than that of others'
- 'I have a right to suffer and be unhappy'
- 'I have nothing to be thankful for'
- 'I do not have enough opportunities'
- 'Others are better than me'
- 'I will not be happy until I get what I want'
- 'I am all alone'
- 'I cannot do it'
- 'Making money is a struggle'
- 'I do not deserve it'
- 'I am a bad person'

Seeing these common beliefs may give you some relief, as if you have experienced these thoughts and beliefs at any time, you may have thought that is was only you that has them. The whole collective unconsciousness of humanity has had these thoughts and beliefs at some time or another throughout their life, and some people will still be carrying many of these limiting beliefs and thoughts to this day.

> So, what we are now going to do now is to take one of those common beliefs and subject it to a series of questions in order to unearth its 'root' origin so that we may question and ultimately transcend that belief.

> Questions 1 and 2 are more logical in nature; we are simply asking if the belief is true or not, and we do this through contemplation and providing a 'yes or no' answer. Logic is very clear cut, and that is why logic is used in these first two questions, because either the belief is true or it is not. It is either fact or fiction.

A person may say, *"It's not true but that's how I feel."* It may seem harsh, but quietly frankly it does not matter how they feel. They feel the way that they feel because of a belief they hold, and so we need to question that belief and ask if it is true or not, and this can only be achieved through clear cut logic, as emotion and feelings are a more primitive state of consciousness than logic. Obviously emotion and feeling serve their own purposes but derive more from instinct, whereas logic is an unbiased way of arriving at the truth. We may all feel differently about some things, but our feelings do not always represent the actual truth of a situation, in reality.

Question number 3 requires a great degree of stillness and introspection; because we are attempting to drill-down to the root belief underneath. I have provided examples below, but when investigating for yourself, you must look within the mind, be honest and see what transpires. Be patient and allow the question to take you further within.

Question 4 and onwards are beyond logic, they are questions to guide your awareness into that which is deeper and pure, and to establish your identity in the face of any thought or belief. Do not force anything; instead take your time and let the questions work naturally, let them point you to that which is being spoken of.

Firstly make yourself aware of a disturbing thought or surface belief that continues to recur. This is a 'persistent thought or belief', for example, *'Things never work out for me.'*

## Example #1—*'Things never work out for me'*

We must answer yes or no, so firstly ask the question, 'Is it true?'

## #1 *'Is it true?'*

When we ask the question 'Is it true?' we are questioning the very foundation of the belief that we hold. This belief supports all other streams and persistent patterns of thought related to it.

For example, thoughts of pessimism about a situation or circumstance will stem from this belief that 'things never work out for me,' and once these subsidiary thoughts are also believed, they will create an emotional response in the body, one of hopelessness or frustration and this can lead to our body becoming limp and our giving way to a situation or challenge, or pursuing a goal. The thought itself can create a debilitating effect on the body. For example, a weight lifter that believes he cannot lift a certain weight, will probably fail because his body will respond to what the mind says. As Confucius said, *"he who believes he can and he who believes he cannot, are both usually right."*

So by asking, 'is it true?' we are challenging the assumption that it is true, and questioning its validity. We do this because if we discover that it is not true, it will collapse all of the other disturbing thought patterns that cause us suffering and limitation—in just the same way as pulling-out a support in a house of cards. Pull the lower one out and the whole structure will crumble.

When we believe something to be true and leave it unquestioned, it causes disturbance and limitation.

> Is it true that 'things never work out for me?'

Often, the mind is focussing upon specific instances where things did not go the way we wanted them to, but does that justify stating that 'things never work out for me?' 'Never,' would mean that nothing at all ever has or ever will work out for us and that is obviously untrue because 'some' things have worked out for us all at one time or another.

Think of a time when things have worked out for you. It does not have to be something major, it could be a small thing or many small things.

And so we should become very quiet and contemplate what instances demonstrate to us that the statement 'things never work out for me,' is untrue.

For example, 'I remember when I passed my driving test or an exam, or when I won that money or was praised and successful in the job I do,' etc.

Often, the mind is focussing on a certain negative examples and therefore 'forgets' all of the other successes.

But if you still come to the conclusion that, yes, 'things never work out for me,' then please move onto the second question below but if you reach the conclusion that, actually the belief 'things never work out for me,' is false, then you can drop this belief, and move straight to question 4, below.

## #2 *'Am I one hundred percent certain it is true that things never work out for me?'*

If you have answered 'yes' to question number 1, then we ask question 2 to make absolutely certain and contemplate, with stillness, whether the belief that 'things never work out for me' is true or not.

So we should take into consideration the possibility that we have actually had things go our way in life before, and then once again become still and contemplate. Then we can answer yes or no but the key to these first two questions is to use straight logic, is it a yes or no to the question 'do things never work out for me,' because when we are logical about it, either it is a true statement and literally nothing works out for us, or some things work out the way we want and others do not, in which case the answer to the question would be 'no.'

If the answer is still 'yes,' however, then we move onto question 3 below. If the answer is now 'no' then we move onto question 4.

## #3 Ask the question, 'If 'yes'—why would that be bad?'

So if we have answered 'yes' to question 2 above, then we must use question 3 to get closer to the root belief supporting the belief that 'things never work out for me.'

We do this by asking, 'if things never work out for me, then why would that be bad?'

So if we ask that question we may say, 'it would be bad because, I would feel like I have no control of my life.' In which case we would need to go further and ask, 'and why would that be bad?' We may then say, 'because I would feel powerless'

> *So, your root belief is actually 'I am powerless,' and we therefore now need to question that root belief with question number 1, once again.*
>
> *Ask, 'is it true that you are powerless?' Yes or no?*
>
> *In answering, try to give examples of being in power and in control, something you have had control over now or before?*

You may say, 'well I have control over myself and the decisions I make, or I had control in this situation at work where I completed a job successfully, or I have control over my reactions to things that happen or I have control over my finances etc.' There may be many examples but what we are doing is placing the root belief under scrutiny and determining whether or not it is true that you are powerless. In other words, are you completely powerless? Yes or no? You either are or you are not.

If you say yes or no to this question, then continue to question 4.

## #4 'Who is it that is speaking this. Which identity?'

So if you said 'no' to any of the above questions you will arrive at this question, and if you have said 'yes' to the last question, then you will also have arrived at this point.

> This is where the deep self-investigation will really pay off. With this question we are now asking, 'who is it that is actually saying I am powerless or that things never work out for me?'
>
> Is it the pure-self speaking, or the ego-mind identity? Are these limiting beliefs and thoughts a product of mind or pure consciousness, of the ego or the awakened one?

With this question we are pointing even more deeply to the root of the issue, and that is not the thought itself, but the identity of the thought. It is the identity of these thoughts that turns them into a belief, and this is the crux of the issue, at the heart of our suffering is identity.

The question is about becoming a little more introspective, and determining who is creating these beliefs, the mind or the awakened Self. Do these beliefs happen on the level of the ego-mind or pure consciousness? Become quiet and still and look within.

Then when you feel able to, you can answer, 'who is it that is speaking this (belief/thought)? Which identity?' Your answer will be either the ego mind or the pure self.

Whatever your answer is, move to question 5 below.

## #5 'Can you watch this thought?'

> Is it possible to watch and observe this thought and as this thought arises, can you be aware of it?
>
> Who is there to watch it come and go?

Become very quiet and still within, stop and become introspective, look inside the mind and notice whether or not we can watch thoughts as they occur and as they pass.

If we can, then we know that it is possible to be aware of all thoughts when they arrive in the mind.

> Would you agree that the fact you know of a particular disturbing and recurring thought you have, is evidence that you are and have been able to watch and be aware of this thought?

If you can identify it, that must mean you can be aware of it, which is the same as saying you notice and watch it.

So now you may have noticed you have the power to be a watcher of this thought or any thought and even of thinking itself.

Now move on to question 6 below. If you are unsure of being able to watch thoughts, then continue to become quiet and still and try to observe thinking as it occurs and also work with the meditations and practices in this book to help you move to this level of being able to observe thought. As soon as you become aware that you can observe thoughts and thinking, imagination and memory etc., then you can move onto question 6 below.

## #6 *'And who are you?'*

Now that you are aware that you can observe thoughts and thinking, the question, 'and who are you?' is pertinent.

> So what we are asking is, 'if you can observe the thoughts and beliefs above, that have been causing you disturbance, then who are you? Are you the thoughts or are you the observer of these thoughts? Which comes first?

> To find an answer to this question, we must really become introspective, quiet and still, and look to see 'if I can observe and watch thought, then am I the thought or the watcher of it? Am I the thoughts themselves or am I separate from thought and is there distance between I and thought?'

The next questions are a form of meditation. We must be extremely patient and persistent with our looking and observation.

Are you the thought, or is the thought appearing within conscious observation?

> Be quiet and still and ask, 'and who am I?'

We are not looking for a quick answer from the mind, we are looking for the direct seeing and experiencing of the question, and to where the question points.

Once we have taken sufficient time to peruse it, and all becomes clear, we may move to the next question, below.

If clarity is not forthcoming, and there is still some confusion, and you still cannot say what you are (thought or the one who observes thought), then simply rest and come back to this question at a later time, and in the meantime continue with the meditations and practices in this book.

## #7 'And can you watch the watching of the mind?'

Arriving at this question means that you have now come to the conclusion that you are the watcher and observer of thought and not thought itself and that thought is a 'coming and going appearance' in the watching consciousness.

> We now need to take things one large step further, and ask the question, 'and can you watch the watching of the mind?'
>
> Another way of saying this would be, 'can you watch the watching itself?'

So here we are concerned with looking beyond thought altogether and attempting to determine whether or not the 'watching,' the watching of thought, can itself be watched.

This, like pure meditation, requires a great degree of awareness, effortlessness, quietness and stillness.

Completely relax all bodily and mind activity and look to observe the watching itself that stands before thought and mind. Silently watch the silent watching.

This is where all roads of 'form' end.

No answer is needed here, only the persistent watching of watching is required.

Remain watching the watching.

If this is a struggle at first, please just practice until this watching of watching becomes possible at any moment. Continue to spend some time there and enjoy it.

It is Pure Meditation...

Now let us go through some more examples, but this time we are only going to work through the first three questions, as these are the only questions that differ with different beliefs. Questions four to seven remain the same but of course, when you work with these questions for transcending your own limiting beliefs, you will usually work with all seven questions together in order to complete the whole process. Below are four more examples to work with, so feel free to add the remaining questions at the end.

## *Example #2—'I'm not loveable'*

We must answer yes or no to the first two questions and to question 3 when the belief has been taken back to its root and put back through question 1 (is it true).

## *#1 'Is it true?'*

> So once again, with this belief we are going to ask the question, 'Is it true that I am not loveable?'

We are not looking to our feelings to give us the answer. As our feelings are only a response to what we believe, so we must go to the source, which is the belief itself and question it. It must be questioned with straight logic, otherwise the feelings and the mind will say, 'er, well...um...I'm not sure...maybe sometimes' etc. In other words, there is confusion with the mind and feelings without logic because one moment the mind can think one thing and the next, another thing. And the same is true of the body; one moment it may feel one thing and the next, another. If we are relying solely on feelings then our investigation will never be able to give us a clear, precise and honest answer.

There is only one answer, either it is true or it is not true, there is no in-between. This cannot be based upon what you may think or feel; it is only by looking factually that we can arrive at the pure and precise truth. You are either unlovable or loveable. If even one being finds you loveable or we see one reason that you are, then you are loveable.

> If ten people are not in love with you, does that make you unlovable...?

Have you met everyone in the world or universe to determine whether they all find you loveable . . . ?

In other words, the belief that says 'I am not loveable,' is saying that nobody ever has or ever can love me. How can that ever be known to be one hundred percent true and accurate . . . ?

If it cannot be known, then the belief cannot be true.

So become really still and contemplate . . . Is it true . . . yes or no?

Remember that honesty is the key to all these questions. Either you are loveable or you are not at all. Which is it . . . ?

If you still come to the conclusions that, 'I am not loveable,' then you can move onto the second question below.

If you come to the conclusion that, actually the belief that 'I'm not loveable,' is false, then you can drop this belief, and move straight to question 4.

## #2 'Am I one hundred percent certain it is true that I'm not loveable?'

If you have answered 'yes' to question number 1, then we ask question 2 to one hundred percent make certain and contemplate, with absolute stillness, if the belief, 'I am not loveable,' is true.

So maybe we have a strong feeling that is convincing us that the belief that 'I am not loveable,' is true. This is fine if we come to the conclusion 'yes,' but question number 2 gives us an opportunity to look again even more closely . . .

So we ask question number 2 and look even more closely with contemplation and stillness, 'am I one hundred percent certain it is true that I am not loveable?' We should take our time with the question and give the option of 'no, it is not true' a chance, through our contemplation of it.

Maybe we can remember some occasions where we have been loveable, or qualities we have that are loveable etc.

If the answer is still 'yes' then we should move onto question 3 below. If the answer is 'no' then we move onto question 4, as above in the very first example...

## #3 'Why would that be bad?'

So if we have answered 'yes' to question 2 above, then we must use question 3 to get closer to the root of the belief that 'I am not loveable.'

We do this by asking, 'if you are not loveable, why would that be bad?'

So in answer to that question we may say, 'it would be bad because, I would never have a romantic relationship.'

Then we may ask in order to qualify it further, 'why would that be bad?'

You may say, 'because I would be alone.'

So the root belief is therefore 'if someone does not love me I will be all alone.' So now we question that root belief with question number one again.

> Now ask... 'Is it true that if someone does not love me, I will be alone?' Yes or no?

Give examples of not being alone such as... I would not be alone because I have my family around me, friends, pets, work colleagues, opportunities to meet people and I have the whole of life all around me... or you may say, I do not feel alone when I am enjoying myself.

If you answer either yes or no to this question, then continue to question 4 previously in the very first example.

## Example #3—'I never have enough money'

We must answer yes or no.

## #1 'Is this true?'

> So once again with this belief we are going to ask the question, 'Is it true that I never have enough money?'
>
> Become very quiet and still and contemplate the question...

So often the mind focuses on not having enough money, and it does this because it maybe has certain expectations of how much money for other things you should have. In other words, the mind often focuses on thoughts of 'lack' and what we do not have, and neglects what we do have.

> Would you say that most of the time the basic things you need to pay are paid for ... ?

Sometimes everything is paid that needs to be, but still the mind tends to ignore that and focuses on ... 'I should have more than that, or I do not have enough.'

> If you had to put it in percentage terms, what would be the percentage of your basic needs being paid for, compared to those not being paid ... ?

> As an example, do all your basic needs get paid for one hundred percent of the time? Or eighty percent of the time?

> So again we should be specific with the question, 'Is it true that you never have enough money?'

> Do you 'never' have enough money ... ? Or do you sometimes have enough money ... or even most times have enough money ... ?

If either of the above is true, then saying you 'never' having enough money is inaccurate ...

> Become still and contemplate honestly ...

If you still come to the conclusion that, 'yes, I never have enough money,' then you can move onto the second question below.

If you come to the conclusion that, 'no, actually the belief that I never have enough money is false,' then you can drop this belief, and move straight to question 4 in the very first example ...

## #2 *'Am I one hundred percent certain it is true that I never have enough money?'*

If you have answered 'yes' to question number 1, then we ask question 2 in order to make certain and contemplate with stillness as to whether or not the belief 'I never have enough money' is true.

Maybe we have a strong feeling that is convincing us that the belief 'I never have enough money,' is true, and we reach the conclusion 'yes,' but question number 2 gives us an opportunity to look again, even more closely...

So we ask question number 2 and look even more closely with contemplation and stillness, 'am I one hundred percent certain that it is true that I never have enough money?' We should take time with the question and give the option of it not being true, a chance through our contemplation.

Maybe we can remember some occasions where we have had enough money, where our basics have been paid for, or when we have had more than enough money left over afterwards...?

If the answer is still 'yes,' then we move onto question 3, if the answer is 'no,' then we move onto question 4 in the very first example...

### #3 'If yes, why would that be bad?'

So if we have answered 'yes' to question 2 above, then we must use question 3 to get closer to the root belief supporting the assertion that 'I never have enough money.'

> We do this by asking 'if I never have enough money why would that be bad?'

We may say in reply that, 'it would be bad because, I would get into debt or lose my home.'

> Then we may ask again to narrow it down further, 'and why would that be bad?'

You may reply, 'because it would make me a failure.'

> So your root belief is 'not having enough money makes me a failure.' Let us now question that root belief with question number one again.
>
> 'Is it true that not having enough money makes you a failure?' Yes or no?

We often believe due to our conditioning that money defines success, and so because of that belief, when we do not have as much money we then believe that we are unsuccessful. But we can be successful in many different ways than ones which solely depend on money.

Are you a failure if you are happy, or you have good relationships, skills, kindness, compassion or does the determination of success or failure depend only upon how much money you have...?

Continue to contemplate and investigate all the different angles...

If you say yes or no to this question, then continue to question 4 in the very first example...

## Example #4—'People don't like me'

Answer yes or no.

### #1 'Is it true?'

So once again with this belief we are going to ask the question, 'Is it true that people do not like me?'

Become very quiet and still and contemplate the question...

Sometimes what can happen is that we focus on certain situations or incidents where people or a person showed their dislike of us. Maybe it was subtle and maybe it was extreme, but these occasions may stand-out in our mind and give us the impression that all people dislike us rather than it being just certain individuals.

So again we need to be specific with the question, 'Is it true that people do not like me?

'Is it true that 'all' people do not like me?'

The belief is referring to the idea that 'people,' which is a very general term, do not like me, that *all* people do not like me.

'Is it true that 'all' people do not like me?'

Become still and contemplate honestly...

If you still come to the conclusion that, yes, 'people do not like me,' then you can move onto the second question.

If you come to the conclusion that, no, actually the belief that 'people do not like me,' is false, then you can drop this belief, and move straight to question 4 in the very first example...

### #2 'Am I one hundred percent certain it is true that people do not like me?'

If you have answered 'yes' to question number 1, then we ask question 2 to make absolutely certain and contemplate with stillness whether or not the belief that 'people do not like me,' is true.

> So maybe we have a strong feeling that is convincing us that the belief that 'people do not like me' is true. This is fine if we reach the conclusion 'yes,' but question number 2 gives us an opportunity to look again even more closely...

So we ask question number 2 and look even more closely with contemplation and stillness, 'am I one hundred percent certain that it is true that people do not like me?' We should take time with the question and give the option of 'no it is not true,' a chance, through our contemplation.

> So once again this belief can come from our own experiences of when someone showed their dislike for us, or where maybe we misinterpreted their actions or words as them disliking us. Does that mean that 'all' people dislike us or will dislike us...?

With introspection and contemplation ask the question, 'Am I one hundred percent certain that people do not like me?'

If the answer is still 'yes' then we move onto question 3 and if the answer is 'no' then we move onto question 4 in the very first example.

### #3 If 'yes, why would that be bad?'

So if we have answered 'yes' to question 2 above, then we must use question 3 to get closer to the root belief supporting the premise that, 'people do not like me.'

We do this by asking, 'if people do not like me, why would that be bad?'

So if we ask that question, we may say, 'it would be bad because, I would not feel very good.' And what is another word for not feeling very good... 'Unhappiness.'

So this time we do not need to ask the question again to narrow it down further, we have found the root belief.

So the root belief is, 'I need people to like me in order to be happy.' So now we question that root belief with question number 1 again.

We ask... 'Is it true that I need people to like me to be happy?' Yes or no?

As an example, you may feel happy when you achieve certain things in life, or when your chosen career is going well. You may be happy when you go on a vacation or holiday. You may be happy when you meditate or engage in a certain hobby, or when you exercise. You may be happy simply just relaxing and spending time on your own.

Continue to contemplate and see different angles...

So once again we ask, 'is it true that I need other people to like me in order to be happy?'

Or is it possible that you can have moments of happiness when engaged in other things or even being happy just being yourself...?

Become silent and contemplate...

If you say yes or no to this question, then continue on to question 4 in the very first example...

## Example #5—'People think I am unattractive.'

Answer, yes or no.

## #1 'Is it true?'

So once again with this belief we are going to ask the question, 'Is it true that people think I am unattractive?'

Become very quiet and still and contemplate the question...

Sometimes what can happen is that we focus on certain situations or incidents where people or a person showed their dislike of us. Maybe it was subtle and maybe it was extreme, but these occasions may stand-out in our mind and give us the impression that all people find us unattractive rather than it being just certain individuals.

> So again we need to be specific with the question, 'Is it true that people find me unattractive?
>
> 'Is it true that 'all' people find me unattractive?'

The belief is referring to the idea that 'people,' which is a very general term, find me unattractive, that *all* people find me unattractive.

> *'Is it true that 'all' people find me unattractive?'*
>
> *Become still and contemplate honestly...*

If you still come to the conclusion that, yes, 'people find me unattractive,' then you can move onto the second question.

If you come to the conclusion that, no, actually the belief that 'people find me unattractive,' is false, then you can drop this belief, and move straight to question 4 in the very first example...

## #2 'Am I one hundred percent certain it is true that people find me unattractive?'

If you have answered 'yes' to question number 1, then we ask question 2 to make absolutely certain and contemplate with stillness whether or not the belief that 'people find me unattractive,' is true.

> So maybe we have a strong feeling that is convincing us that the belief that 'people find me unattractive' is true. This is fine if we reach the conclusion 'yes,' but question number 2 gives us an opportunity to look again even more closely...

So we ask question number 2 and look even more closely with contemplation and stillness, 'am I one hundred percent certain that it is true that people find me unattractive?' We should take time with the question and give the option of 'no it is not true,' a chance, through our contemplation.

So once again this belief can come from our own experiences where we believed that someone found us unattractive, or where maybe we misinterpreted their actions or words as them finding us unattractive. Does that mean that 'all' people find us unattractive ...?

With introspection and contemplation ask the question, 'Am I one hundred percent certain that people find me unattractive?'

If the answer is still 'yes' then we move onto question 3 and if the answer is 'no' then we move onto question 4 in the very first example.

### #3 If 'yes, why would that be bad?'

So if we have answered 'yes' to question 2 above, then we must use question 3 to get closer to the root belief supporting the premise that, 'people find me unattractive.'

We do this by asking, 'if people find me unattractive, why would that be bad?'

So if we ask that question, we may say, 'it would be bad because, I would feel that people do not like me.'

And why would it be bad if people did not like you? Because, 'I would feel unloved.'

Therefore the root belief is 'I need people to like me to feel loved.' And now we question that root belief with question number 1 again.

We ask, 'is it true that I need people to like me to feel loved?' Yes or no?

As an example, you may feel loved when you are with your family and friends, or when you get praise for an achievement, or when you are appreciated by others for what you do and who you are. You may feel loved by simply loving who you are, and you may feel loved when you are supported by life itself.

Continue to contemplate and look for different angles.

So once again we ask, 'is it true that I need other people to like me to feel loved?'

Or is it possible that you can have moments of love when you are just being yourself and appreciating what you have...

Become quiet and contemplate...

If you say either yes or no to this question, then continue to question 4 in the very first example...

# Conclusion

*"The discovery of your true nature is beyond suffering and in the heart of freedom"*

The above methods, along with meditation as a foundation, constitute a very powerful and practical way of entering into and connecting deep within your essential reality and in ending the suffering and internal limitations you may have been experiencing on numerous different levels.

I would strongly encourage you to work with 'self-investigation' and 'transcending limiting beliefs' as much as possible until it becomes very natural to investigate and become aware in your everyday life experience, as I know that your consciousness, peace and joy will only continue to deepen with persistence, until one day you may find that neither become necessary anymore.

Each question above is pure 'gold dust' and is extremely powerful. They all have the ability to cut through illusions like a sword of truth. I would strongly recommend that you do not overlook any of these questions and work with them, knowing how much power they contain, to awaken you beyond all falsehoods to the very core of your true nature.

The destiny of a truly awakened being is not to be in 'practice' their whole life, because 'who' is practicing anyway... and who needs to practice to be themselves? The only reason practice and persistence is needed in the beginning is because the pure self has become entangled with its misidentification, and so a reorientation must occur in order to unravel itself.

As we have spoken about before, the real key to all of our suffering and to inner freedom... is identity. When we exist within a false personal identity we suffer, and take things personally as if we are separate from everyone and everything, from life itself. It is almost as if life is happening *to* us and not *as* us, but when we become our true identity, which is a point of reference not of the world, yet still in the world, then can we live in total freedom and peace.

What more can truly satisfy us in life than the realisation that you are life itself, that you are forever loved and cared for. That peace is available at anytime and anyplace to any one of us, and we can experience all life has to offer, intensely and without ever being marred by it. What tremendous freedom that represents.

When you discover who you are, you will realise that this is the greatest gift you could ever have, that it is and was everything you ever wanted and more, and that you are living consciously as you experience the world in a completely new way. It is a whole different dimension of consciousness and way of living and experiencing.

*"Pain is inevitable. Suffering is optional."*

One of the greatest things we will learn from the methods within these pages, is that suffering is optional and not inbuilt within the fabric of external reality and feelings. When pain arises, it itself is not what causes our suffering and when an external situation is unpleasant it does not cause suffering in itself. What causes the suffering are the mental fantasies we create regarding our pain, feelings and situations.

As we work with the above methods and become ever more conscious, we will begin to recognise and experience the above more frequently. We will notice that when we just observe pain, feelings and situations without mentally interpreting them in a certain way, that internal suffering ceases to exist for us. We will also begin to realise that it is a self-created illusion that occurs because of our ignorance of the truth—the truth being that we are ultimately not the thoughts, feelings and pain, but are simply watching it all, in a detached way.

Each time we experience suffering, it is an opportunity to look within and recognise with what we are incorrectly identifying with and then realign ourselves with our true nature through pure observation and awareness. Thoughts, feelings, pain and all situations are fine and exist to be experienced, and they all actually serve to make us aware of exactly where we are, within ourselves, at any given moment. Therefore suffering and challenges are always a catalyst for our deeper awakening if we recognise them to be so and surrender our identity of them. When we relinquish our identity with them, our own true identity becomes greater.

# The Birth of Wisdom

*"The end of sorrow is the beginning of wisdom. Knowledge is always within the shadow of ignorance. Meditation is freedom from thought and a movement in the ecstasy of truth. Meditation is explosion of intelligence."*
*Jiddu Krishnamurti*

To know thyself is the birth of all wisdom, as to know yourself is to know another, to know another is to know the world and to know the world is to know the entire cosmos. As above so below. To know the microcosm is to know the macrocosm and by understanding your own true nature and the pitfalls of misidentification, it gives one the wisdom to understand everyone and everything around them. Nothing remains confusing anymore, but yet contradictorily, you know nothing at all. This is also true of the emergence of wisdom, only by first seeing that you actually know nothing do you begin to know everything, not intellectually, but experientially and by peeking at the reality behind the reality, the essential reality behind all things.

Mind intelligence no matter how brilliant it may be, will always be secondary to the true intelligence that comes from the source of all existence, which itself gave birth to all conceptual abilities. By knowing ourselves, which means to know the source of existence, we tap into a whole new level of intelligence, a cosmic data base of pure wisdom. Also the wisdom arises from entering into the larger perspective of pure consciousness. If conceptual and intellectual intelligence is the base of a mountain, then pure consciousness is at the very peak and beyond, and because of its unique position it develops more wisdom by being able to see beyond the valley and trees to see the horizon in every direction. It is also able to see where the valley and trees themselves fit into the whole landscape. In other words, the mind may only see what is in front of it with the information it has, but pure consciousness sees all things and where all things fit together.

It is the birth of this wisdom that is a gift to the whole world, because real wisdom is rare—like platinum, and at this time maybe more than ever, real wisdom would serve better than ten thousand, mere pieces of information. We are swimming in information, more information than ever before, but yet information without wisdom can be both dangerous and redundant. One piece of real wisdom will make a huge difference in how that information is used and how we ourselves operate in this world. Intelligent, harmonious change derives from real wisdom, and real wisdom can only come from the deeper self.

Use the above methods to explore the depths of your nature and be abundant with pearls of wisdom.

# Chapter 13
## Practices and Teachings for Deeper Awakening

*"No one succeeds without initial effort, those who succeed owe their success to perseverance"* Ramana Maharshi

As the Spiritual process and our own self-discovery unfolds, we will realise that we are 'Awareness' moving in and out from the 'Awakened Awareness' to the conditioned ego state of thought and mind. What is happening here is that we seem to move in and out of focus like the lens of a camera, sometimes habitually focusing and paying attention to the antics of the thinking mind in a more contracted state, and then sometimes retracting into a more expansive silent Awareness. In other words, when Awareness is aware of itself it is Awake and when Awareness becomes lost in identifying itself as the thinking mind; we fall back into a place of unawareness. This unawareness is a more limited and contracted state in which we have less Alertness and Wakefulness, and where we have less conscious control and choice making abilities. When we are in the unconscious ego mind, our life becomes one of predetermination, where the outside conditioning leads us and takes us over and when we step into the truth of our Awakened Awareness, we gain inner freedom and freewill decision making. We also resume our life and direction, and can then be guided from a true inner place of intuition.

When we are in a state of unawareness we have less ability to choose, and frequent in a hazy dream-like state. This is normal in the beginning as there is a kind of untangling process that often occurs where certain thoughts and belief structures must rise to the surface to be transcended by the spotlight of the Awakened Awareness. In other words these false mental structures of the mind must rise to the surface to be transcended so that we may awaken more fully into the Enlightened Self.

The more and more frequently we remain Aware of the thinking mind and of Awareness itself, the busy thinking mind tends to slow down and become more refined. There may appear to be more space and peace within the mind and as the turbulence of the mind lessens, the Awareness of Self then seems to shine through and become more apparent. It is almost as if the constant chatter and our focus on the chatter, seems to hide Awareness from being Aware of itself. Awareness was always there just as the sun is always in the sky, but when behind the clouds it seems to disappear and this is the illusion that our attention on the thinking mind can create.

As we focus less on the mind and more on Awareness the ego begins to die, almost as if it is being starved of the oxygen of our attention. It is the attention and identification on the mind that keeps it alive and strong in us. As the ego begins to die through our retraction of it, the Awakened Self begins to go through subtler and subtler levels of Awareness, Insight and Realisation.

For this reason, this chapter and the practices and pointers within it are there for the more advanced stages of subtler and deeper Awareness that must unfold for the crystallisation of our 'True Nature.' It would be wise to work with these practices consistently until they become natural and therefore no longer needed. Also this chapter and the practices within it, may be read and contemplated randomly, as needed. Each individual practice, if undertaken with full Awareness and wholeheartedness will be invaluable in the Awakening process.

This story below will help you to understand this point clearly...

*The Great Crossing*

*A Great Spiritual Master said... "A man beginning a long journey sees ahead a vast body of water. There is neither boat nor bridge. To escape the dangers of his present location, he constructs a raft of grass and branches. When he reaches the other side he realises how useful the raft was and wonders if he should hoist it on his back and carry it with him forever.*

*Now if he did this, would he be wise? Or, having crossed to safety, should he place the raft in a high, dry location for someone else to use? This is the way I have taught the dharma, the doctrine—for crossing, not for keeping. Cast aside every proper state of mind, oh monks—much less wrong ones—and remember well to leave the raft behind!"*

So the point here is not to become attached to any specific practice, teaching or method, simply allow them to do their work until what they are teaching becomes natural within us. Then we may leave the practice behind and maybe share it with others so that they too may benefit from it.

## The Art of Letting Go

*"I let go. I accept my life as it is in this moment. I do not judge, I do not dramatise. I let life's events come freely and I welcome the lessons they convey. I stop struggling now. I let go and know that the universe always gives me that which is most appropriate for my Self-discovery"*

Why should we 'let go?'

Whether on the Spiritual Path or simply within our regular life experiences, certain negative thoughts, feelings and emotions will arise, which if believed and identified-with will cause us inner pain and suffering. This suffering when identified-with and held onto can create a kind of dense, hazy and dreamlike contracted state of consciousness.

These thoughts, feelings and emotions are a chain of internal events that can each be caused by another. For example, a belief will create a response in the body, and this response is an emotion or feeling. Conversely if we awake in the morning with a certain feeling or emotion, it can trigger a particular inner conversation and a mental picture which can in turn create thoughts with which we may identify. We may awake in a 'low' mood and then engage in a mental conversation about how bad it is and how disconcerting it is to experience this feeling or emotion. This is the ego mind creating a drama about the emotion or sensation which only serves to create even more suffering within us, because the more we judge it negatively, the more these unpleasant emotional responses will increase within the body. It is a vicious cycle within which, thought leads to emotion and emotion can lead to more negative thought and to more intense emotion and so on. This can be the cause of extreme rage, sadness and suffering. The more we engage in the ego mind's ponderings, the more the emotion and unpleasant feelings within the body become apparent, and if we identify with the body, mind and emotions as who we are, then we are more likely to act out this emotion in a physical way, which can create unpleasant consequences for us and those around us.

Letting-go of thoughts, feeling and emotions may seem like a very complex thing to do, something that means the retrieving of sometimes painful memories of the past, from childhood or previous lives, but actually the process is very simple, and the power of our Awareness is such that nothing can actually resist it.

The first thing of which we must convince ourselves, is that we do not wish to suffer anymore. This may seem like a 'given' as who among us actually chooses to suffer? Well actually, the conditioned ego-self does. The mind will often thrive on suffering and this in one way it strengthens it sense of identity. It may claim to 'hate it' but yet it continues to feed the suffering with negativity, saying one thing but often doing the complete opposite and this is why we must firstly make very clear that we have had enough of suffering and that it no longer serves us to identify with that. Once this is achieved we may now proceed ... The ability to 'let go' can often seem like something that is out of our control. How can we possibly let go of these thoughts, feelings and emotions in response to the things happening outside of us? But we should always know that we have the power within to set ourselves free.

## How to 'Let Go'

The first thing we must understand is that 'letting go' is not so much a process, but a realisation that we are essentially not the body/mind organism and the thoughts, beliefs, emotions and feelings that accompany it.

The beliefs, thoughts and emotions only cause us issue because we identify with them as being a reflection of us and who we are. If we can overcome this, then thoughts and emotions have no power to affect us, and have no ability to perpetuate themselves. Without a personal sense of identity (the ego) there is nothing for the incoming thoughts and emotions to create suffering with, nothing to push or bump-up against, no personal self ... no problem, simply phenomena, just passing like 'ships in the night,' coming and going quietly. No phenomenon can last or stay forever; every feeling, mood, emotion or thought will eventually dissipate and we can help this process by releasing them and letting them pass straight through.

So the fact that we are able to let go, means that we are holding onto something, and by holding onto something also means that we have the power to let it go...

Please try this...

> *Hold one of your hands in front of you and slowly make a tight fist.*
>
> *As you are tightening your fist you are creating a contracted state, in fact your whole arm, wrist and hand is tightly contracted.*
>
> *Now how do you release this grip?*
>
> *You just simply let go. Release it now.*
>
> *How does your arm feel and how did you release it...?*
>
> *You simply relaxed did you not?*

This is exactly the same with emotions or feelings. We tend to hold and focus on them and become tense and struggle against them, resisting them. But if we just simply relax and quit struggling, the emotion or thought is naturally released and as we relax and let go of that which is not us, a great peace and 'expansion' will come upon us.

> As you relax, release and let go, you can even say softly... 'I let go, I let go, I let go.'
>
> Cease all resistance, cease all struggle and relax, let everything be as it is...
>
> If tension returns... then let go and relax, if negative emotion comes then let go, totally let go...

The more we live like this and become accustomed to this way of being, the more lighter-hearted we become and the more enlightened we become. Light-heartedness is a crucial part of enlightenment.

# Notice the 'no–Space'

When we observe our environment, we often only focus on the objects we see, rarely paying attention to the massive amounts of space around and in-between objects.

We have been accustomed to only give credence to objects and not to the empty space in which all objects exist.

> So I now invite you to explore that empty space between objects and recognise that it is actually no different from who you are. In other words, as you observe the empty space between an object and your body, you will see that the empty space in you and in front of you is connected as one...

When we look deeply into our mind, behind the thought processes, we will see nothing but a vast emptiness, an intelligent emptiness, pure space. As we observe the space, become aware of how actually that space and our inner space is connected. Please look and see.

As we observe the space on the outside (in a room for example) we can also see 0ur inner space, at the same time, watching it.

# Non-Identification

Our mind has been conditioned to identify with the things that it experiences. This identity is a personal sense of self, the ego. So, for example, when we are faced with an injustice which goes against our belief system, it will often be taken very personally.

When we are told that we are either 'good looking' or 'ugly' we will take both personally, although one will usually inflate the ego self and the other will naturally deflate it. However, either one of them creates a personal response if there is a personal sense of self there.

The ego strongly identifies with the 'personality' and the personality is a combination of habits, tendencies, beliefs, opinions, likes and dislikes, and so where there is a strong personal sense of self, it identifies with those personality traits. It may say, 'I am an energetic person,' or 'I am a calm person,' or 'I am an intellectual person,' or 'I am an Aries, Pisces or Scorpio,' or 'a critical person.' In fact it will identify with any of these.

## The Secret Self

The personal sense of self may also look to identify with the 'looks' of the body, whether the body is tall, small, thin or large, the personal self will often find anything it can to associate itself with. It will identify with hobbies, talents, skills and status, and with occupation or achievements. Also the 'person' may have a position of self, invested in family and friends, with its roles of for example, a husband, wife, son, mother, father, sister or brother etc., in fact anything that the mind regards itself as being is an identification and all of the above are either ideas or objects. And so, practice enables us to drop identification with external objects, body and ideas.

> The next practice is to simply note what your mind is identified with at this moment and to be aware of when these identities arise and also to note exactly when you react to these identities throughout the day...

Also note and be aware of how the mind identifies with new situations and experiences that arise, how it personalises future achievements and goals and also how it personalises new skills that are learnt and acquired.

Practice disassociating yourself from the thinking mind and the thoughts arising from it. It is the mind that is the root, and so by not applying your sense of self to the mind, you will also cease identifying with external objects.

This disassociation will not affect how you perform or interact with people and situations in any way. In fact it will actually enhance your intelligence as you will be less susceptible to control by any reactive, instinctive forces as the personal self often reacts and responds very quickly. You may also find that you no longer take things quite so personally and will become more neutral; a more impartial observer of situations, people and events. Simply cease allowing a personal sense of self to manifest and just stay as the true unaffected One, the one that is unaffected yet still totally and intensely immersed in the world of experience.

This will provide you with a great sense of energy and freedom, as so much energy is drained when things are taken so personally all the time. As the grip of false identification is loosened, your true self will shine-through in a more vibrant and light-hearted way.

When the false identities fall away, the Pure Self is revealed.

## Sensing 'I AM' Presence

> How often do you recall hearing the words 'I AM' on their own without other words attached to them?

For example, I am good or bad, or I am sad, or I am a man or woman, or I am black or white, or I am straight or gay. When we refer to 'I am this' or 'I am that,' it is often just another form of identification. We are associating ourselves as some idea or object.

So the next practice is to enable us to reach our true self without involving any outside idea or concept; without adding anything, simply being 'I AM,' not I am this or I am that, just I am.

It is the most basic and fundamental sense of self, the primal sense of existence, just to sense ourselves as 'I AM' without attaching to anything.

Do not entertain any thoughts or ideas of yourself, just remain in the sense of 'I AM.' Feel it, feel your most basic sense of existence . . . It is often so basic that we forget this because the mind simply overlooks it—the mind is too busy attaching itself and its sense of identity to other ideas and objects. Just be 'with' and 'in' the most basic sense of self as 'I am,' and see if you can sense that right now.

Look to insulate yourself within your 'I AM' presence. Just notice, sense and stay as the 'I am,' nothing more, nothing less. Do not touch anything else, do not think and simply be the 'I am' itself. Just be aware of your most basic existence, the most basic sense of self prior to any conditioning, ideas or notions being applied to the mind. It is so simple that the mind will try and resist, but nevertheless just become immersed in your fundamental sense of 'I Am-ness.'

## To whom is the Voice Talking?

> This 'pointing' is to be aware of the mental conversation taking place in your head. For most people there is a constant noise and chatter taking place in the mind. This never ending dialogue can be irritating and tiring, and most people become immersed in the

mental conversation. But have you ever wondered exactly, 'who is it talking to...?'

Let me ask you a question, how many of 'you' is there?

You would no doubt reply that there is just one you.

But yet, if we examine the chatter closely, it appears to be talking to someone else... and if it is talking to someone else, that must mean there are two entities and not one. True?

For a conversation to happen there must be two entities involved...

So again the question remains, to whom is the voice in the head talking?

You may say 'it is talking to me,' but who is 'me' exactly? And can you identify where this 'me' is?

If the mind *is* talking to you, then you cannot be the chatter itself, so who is the chatter talking to?

You see, if you can observe and be aware of mental chatter taking place, then that must mean that you cannot ultimately be the chatter, you must be the one who is watching it, listening and being aware of the chatter. So who is this 'one' who is a 'witness' to the chatter? Contemplate this regularly.

Continue to ask the question frequently and let the question direct you to what you experientially discover.

## Do not Mind

Often, in our culture we use words and maybe forget the meaning behind those words. For example, 'mind where you are going,' or 'please mind your own business.' We use the word 'mind' quite a lot yet maybe forget what it truly means not to 'mind.'

When we say, 'mind where you are going,' it means 'think' about where you are going. So, often to 'mind' something means to 'think' about something.

So here is a beautiful yet powerful practice. 'Do not 'mind' what happens.' Often people 'mind' so many things that when a person says something about them, they 'mind' what is said. In other words, they ruminate, think and have an inner mental conversation about what has been said.

When a bill or payment demand is expected, they 'mind' it. They think, worry or have certain mental ideas about it, instead do not 'mind' it so much.

To not 'mind' something does not mean that you do not do anything about it, it simply means that you do not 'over-think' it and thereby create a problem. Often the conditioned mind will find or create a problem. That is just the way it works, because one of its primary functions is problem solving, but many times there is no problem to be solved. If anything, it is the 'minding' of something that actually creates a problem where none exists.

When your 'date' does not arrive, do not 'mind' this. Do not turn it into a problem by thinking about it or by regarding it as some reflection of your identity. It is not.

If you truly wish to be at peace, then stop 'minding' what happens. What a release and relief that would be. With all the experiences and situations you face in your life, do not 'mind' what happens, stop 'over-thinking' it and making it into a problem. Instead, be neutral to it, and let your actions arise from this peaceful neutrality instead of the reactivity of the ego-mind which is always looking to make things personal—and therefore a problem.

So the practice is . . . Do not mind what happens.

Begin with smaller things; note how the conditioned mind creates a conversation and problem out of the tiniest thing. Note how when you are looking for a car parking space the mind will make a problem out of it. 'Oh, what an inconvenience,' it may say, or even 'I can never find a \*\*\*\*\*\*\* parking space.'

Just be aware of this and do not fall into its trap. Be neutral and do not 'mind' what happens. What beautiful freedom this is, to go through life unaffected yet still able to enjoy the world completely without 'minding.' What strength, being outside of the mind's problem-creating nature, imbues.

## No Watcher, only Watching

The 'Watcher' along with other terms, has been used throughout this book. Words cannot describe our true nature, but they can act as pointers towards it.

> The word is one of these pointers, however it is not as accurate as it could be. The word 'watcher' implies that there is someone there, but we are not some 'thing' nor even some 'one.' There is actually no-'thing' there. Please note...

There is no 'watcher'...just 'watching' taking place.
It would be more accurate to say that 'watching' is happening.

> There is some intelligence watching, look and see for yourself...

> The question is, 'can you watch this watching...?'

If you watch this watching, beautiful things will happen.

This watching is the pure 'source' of life itself, and so the watching of the watching leads to a wonderful recharging effect. It is similar to a phone being connected to its charger. We may often feel refreshed, energised, peaceful, relaxed and acquire an extreme clarity of mind, taking us into deeper dimensions within our own essential nature which is not separate from what has been called 'god.' It is the creator and creation together as one in union. It is awareness, awake and aware of itself.

All beautiful qualities and states can arise within the connection to the prime consciousness within, that watching presence within.

So simply notice and pay attention to watching happening within your experience. Another way of saying this is... 'Can you experience what is experiencing?' Do not make these questions mental or intellectual, because if you do, you will miss the point. Instead look within and observe...

## Drop All Future Ideas

The mind thrives on thinking about the perceived future. It does this because it feels that the future will add something more to its identity; that it will bring happiness, fulfilment and success. It is an attempt to expand itself, but ultimately we cannot become more than we are already as we are already whole, complete and a perfect part of the whole of existence.

When we seek to become more expanded, happy and fulfilled, we overlook the most obvious truth within us, and that is the truth of our already wholesome and divine nature. To experience more is one thing, but to try and become more is entirely another, it is an impossible task. The body and mind may become 'more' or 'different,' but the true self will always remain infinitely unblemished and complete.

> Our conditioning tends to focus upon tomorrow as it says that tomorrow will be our liberation, our happiness, our enlightenment and fulfilment, but yet tomorrow never comes. If we look closely at what we may have thought in the past about the future, we will see that the mind has convinced us many times that this is 'it,' this is the very thing that will complete us or make us happy, that will add true value to our existence. The next achievement will do it, or the next possession, relationship, or pay cheque. Or maybe 'fame' will do it, or a promotion, but is it not the case that completion and fulfilment never comes, that it never lasts, and that the mind is constantly trying to get us to chase after the next thing? Has it not happened to you yet, as it has happened to all of us?

This is the nature of the conditioned ego mind, it always wants more and is never satisfied with what it gets, and so a person will often be left feeling unhappy and unfulfilled until they get the 'next thing' they believe will make them happy. Look at people's lives and you will see that this is the way that most people live. How frustrating and unfulfilling it is to live this way. What unhappiness and pain it brings, yet underneath this, we are always complete, and if we can only discover this completeness, we will be forever happy and fulfilled. If we just drop the idea that the future and the 'next thing' will make us happy, we will all suddenly be happy, peaceful and recognise our completeness.

> When we chase we are restless and unhappy, but if we relax and quit the chase, suddenly a great peace will come, as we will then experience what is beneath the restless mind. Our unhappiness is always a result of an attached, restless and unsatisfied mind but when we drop the future we drop the restless goal-oriented mind.

And when restlessness is dropped what remains...? Peace. And from peace, joy and bliss can build and our nature will prevail and become pleasantly dominant within us. What we seek is profoundly so close to home that it is actually 'hidden in plain sight' and is not external at all, it is not the money, fame, relationship or success, but our true nature, our wholesomeness. It is just that we have all been taught and conditioned to search for it out there in the world of experience, when all along it has been right here within us. It has always been here and will always be here... Can you see this...?

So then someone may say, but we must think about the future because our way of life depends on it. This is true to an extent, but we must remember and realise that the future in actual reality, does not exist. No-one has ever seen or experienced the future, they have only ever experienced their current experience within the present moment, and their whole life has been one continuous current experience, one continuous present moment experience. All life as we know it unfolds within the 'now' moment.

We can only ever think about the future in the present moment, and when the perceived future arrives, it is once again just the present moment.

Secondly we can still plan for the next sequence in the present moment, or what most people would call the future, but we can only plan and strategise right here and now. So this is the difference... we can plan whilst being fully present in the moment, and that way we do not lose our grounding by allowing the perceived future more significance than the here and now, whereas the mind usually reverses this. The mind is usually so fixated on the idea of the future and what it could bring, that it loses its grounding in the reality of the here and now.

So the practice here is to drop the idea that the future is real, and that it is more significant than the reality of the present moment, and also that the future will bring us true happiness and fulfilment.

Now try to become aware as the mind sends thoughts and imaginations about the future, and how the mind tries to get us to accept the idea that the future will bring lasting happiness, fulfilment and satisfaction. Observe how the mind will try to convince us that the next relationship, car, holiday, pay cheque, material possession or achievement will make us happy, and instead notice who you are within this moment and be aware of your true nature right here and now.

Drop all hope that the future holds the key to your happiness and fulfilment, because I say to you that it is a complete lie. You can use this phrase to remind yourself... 'All I ever truly want is more of myself right here and now.'

> Continue to remind yourself of this until this is a natural realisation within you and until you need not remind yourself anymore...

## Foundational Meditation #3—'Pure Meditation'

The real meaning of the word meditation is 'beyond body and mind.' This is what pure meditation is.

The essence of pure meditation is to simply 'be' and rest within our true natures. Some other practices that are labelled meditation are just concentration. They are exercises that have an object point of focus, the breath, body and mantra as examples but pure meditation is different as it has no objective point of focus.

Pure meditation is the pure self, resting as itself and being aware of itself, noticing itself. The pure self is the non-physical and non-objective Self, it is the point of vast nothingness within and it is the no-body. There is nothing there that we could observe and say, 'that is it.' It is the vast, intelligent, empty space from which all objects arise and are contained within.

So pure meditation is the process of placing awareness on awareness itself, watching the watching taking place, just as the sun illuminates itself by its very nature, so does awareness have the ability to be aware of itself. It is a light unto itself and when light is aware of light, this is pure meditation.

Certain directional questions may be asked to determine whether awareness is aware of itself. We can say 'can the watching be watched..?' Or 'can I watch the watching itself' and allow the question to direct us within to look towards the looking itself.

## Pure Meditation Sitting practice

This may be done with eyes open or closed, although at first, more depth can often be achieved with eyes closed. You can sit in the lotus position or sitting in a chair or eventually lying down, but I recommend only to lay down once you are easily able to slip into this at will, otherwise remain in an upright position to begin with.

Breathe naturally with your eyes closed... gently roll your eyes to the back of the head and inside the darkness of the mind, but only do it to the point of feeling comfortable, do not strain, and ensure you are comfortable and relaxed.

As you look inside your mind, become aware of the 'you' that is aware of everything that takes place within your experience, the one who is aware of thoughts, feelings, emotions and the experiences and objects of the external world.

Simply notice and watch the 'watching presence' within, that you are. If thoughts, feelings, emotions or outside incidents distract you, then simply become aware that you have become distracted and return your awareness to the 'watching presence' within. Continue to watch and observe and remain in that awareness.

> Do this 15 to 60 minutes every day. If you feel able to do it for longer then please do so. You may find it extremely pleasurable and restful and feel very refreshed afterwards.
>
> As a regular daily occurrence...

After some time this will all become natural and may be undertaken at any place or any time. You may find it so pleasurable and restful that you naturally feel drawn to do it several times throughout the day. A good time may well be during periods of waiting or travelling, such as waiting for an appointment, sitting on a park bench, relaxing in the garden, or on public transport whilst travelling. The effect is similar to a phone being plugged into its charger every so often, for recharging and re-energising. The more you connect the more you want to connect, and the longer you connect, the longer you are able to connect. It is almost like having your own sacred sanctuary within; one that stays with you wherever you go.

## Meditate whilst Travelling

Another simple way to speed-up awakening, is to meditate and connect with ourselves more deeply whilst travelling. One thing that can be very beneficial is to use the time of travelling wisely and sink into meditation whilst journeying somewhere. If you are a passenger in a car, for example, relax with eyes closed, and you can connect with the body. Allow your eyes to soften in the blackness of the mind and if there is music on the radio, then begin to meditate upon that music. Follow each sound and beat with full attention ... just purely listening and follow each sound, without consciously thinking about it or judging what you hear. Give it no thought whatsoever ... just listen and just meditate upon it.

Once the destination is reached, open your eyes and you will feel refreshed, relaxed, centred, peaceful, joyful, alert and grounded. With eyes now open, everything will appear more bright, vibrant, colourful and vivid. If your journey was thirty minutes then that is thirty minutes of meditation and connection time that you have gained, but if the journey was a long voyage by air then this would allow you even more meditation time. In this way you are using the time you allocate for inner awakening, very economically. The more you connect with yourself and slip into meditation, the more you will come to appreciate it, and the more you appreciate it, the more you will grasp each opportunity that is available to you to awaken. This will allow your awakening to experience the 'snowball effect.' In other words, it will gather pace exponentially.

## Shavasana Surrender

When it comes to the spiritual path and aligning ourselves with our true nature, 'surrender' is a word that you may hear a lot. In the West, 'surrender' is often regarded as a negative word as it implies giving up. However in this case it is not true that 'we' are giving up but that we are giving up and dropping what is not us ... the ego mind.

We are not surrendering to a person or even a circumstance, but what we *are* surrendering is simply the ego mind and it's resistance to 'what is.' 'What is,' referring to how the here and now appears and what is contained within it. For example if we are faced with certain external

## The Secret Self

challenges, difficult people and circumstances, then the ego mind will moan, complain and resist these, and this resistance is the cause of inner suffering and strife. So when we surrender, we do not surrender to anything external, we should simply drop the nagging ego mind that is not you, that is causing you so much suffering.

A beautiful way to surrender is through Shavasana, which is a yogic term for a laying-down posture. This posture allows us to really surrender, as it allows us to 'let go' and relax completely.

Relaxing the body is very useful, as when the body is relaxed the mind tends to slow down and become more relaxed also, this makes letting go of the ego mind much easier. Shavasana is important because laying down on ones back can be a reminder of death, and acceptance and preparation for death can be a great doorway to Spiritual Awakening. This therefore serves very well as a means of surrender, as true death simply means death of only that which is not ultimately you, and this is what surrender is about, dying to yourself, allowing a death of an ego to happen in order that the true self can emerge and shine through. And as the ego dies, the true self comes to life, or resurrects.

I would recommend this position when you are undergoing an unpleasant experience or possibly even extreme suffering or purging. Often on the spiritual path many darker aspects of the mind will rise up to the surface to be transmuted and released. This can often be unpleasant or challenging as the remaining parts of the ego will struggle against it and will fight to try and regain control. It is at this time that surrender is required, because through surrender, which is an absence of ego control, we do not feed the mind anymore, we starve the ego in order to diminish its power and therefore allow more of our true awakened nature to step forth.

We may need to go on 'surrender strike' many times over until the ego mind diminishes and is dissolved within us, in the same way that a tablet eventually dissolves in water and becomes the water itself. This is very similar to how the ego diminishes within us and how it becomes transmuted and transformed by the divine self.

So, find somewhere comfortable to lie, allow your hands to lie naturally by your side, and allow your legs to be shoulder width apart and both feet to fall naturally to an outward angle, simply relax and let go.

Sometimes there is a suffering and inner turmoil so strong within us that no form of practice or method is effective and this is a situation where pure surrender is called-for. We must let go and 'die' into the surrender of the mind. Die into the suffering and in doing so we will transmute the suffering from pain, to peace.

The more we relax and surrender the deeper we move into the depths of our inner being and consciousness. Surrendering to suffering can work as a catalyst to deeper spiritual expansion and inner peace and each time a surrender of the mind occurs, transcendence to a deeper level of consciousness will also occur. The more of the ego mind that is 'let go,' the more free and awakened we become.

## Drop Your Personal Self

The cause of all suffering derives from having a personal sense of 'self.' Hurt can only occur when there is some 'one' there to be hurt. Where there is a person... there is the potential for a problem to occur and when there is no person, there will be no problem.

Anyone that has conditioned reactions and takes things personally ultimately suffers. This occurs through the internal mental commentary of events, and inner conversation taking place, always identifying and relating an event to itself and therefore making it personal. We tend to filter and judge each event through a conditioned personal identity but as soon as the personal self is dropped, the conditioned reactions will also be dropped, and what is left is the silent watching space in which everything is seen and occurs. Thoughts may still occur, but they are not reporting to a personal sense of self anymore and not being personalised. These thoughts are not connected to anything but are assisting the 'pure life' itself, within us. Through awakening, an alignment of mind, body and source occurs and these will all work together in the right perspective.

Drop any personal sense of self completely, be nothing and see what happens. Be the being with no formal identity, without someone being able to say 'this is you' or without you saying 'I am this, or that.' Simply be 'no-thing,' be a 'no-body,' be a non-entity, be without any mental position or belief. Please look behind the mind and recognise that you have no solid form, that you are 'no-thing...'

*Vast emptiness*

*The emperor, who was a devout Buddhist, invited a great Zen master to the Palace in order to ask him questions about Buddhism.*

*"What is the highest truth of the holy Buddhist doctrine?" The emperor inquired.*

*"Vast emptiness... and not a trace of holiness," the master replied.*

*"If there is no holiness," the emperor said, "then who or what are you?"*

*"I do not know," the master replied.*

The more we become no-thing the more we will expand into that which all things are seen and experienced within. Experientially we will move into a sense of boundlessness and total inner freedom.

> Let go of the personal self completely and be nothing, live like you are invisible, live like you do not exist, and experience the magic that happens...

## It Takes Nothing to be Yourself

Many times the mind will create the idea that we have to do something to be or stay awakened, but to be awakened simply means to be just 'us', the natural Self.

> Does it take any effort to be the natural self... do you need to create anything or act a certain way to be yourself?

Do not 'try' to be natural... you are natural, you cannot 'act' natural otherwise you become very unnatural, you just are natural, it requires no effort, it is your effortless nature.

What takes effort is to try and create something about yourself that is not there, that is unnatural. To try and be and act a certain way, takes tremendous effort. To keep-up a false façade day in and day out, can be extremely tiring and yet all the while, beneath that façade, you are just naturally 'there,' which takes no effort at all.

Whilst experiencing the journey along the path of awakening, you may feel as though you fall from it, from time to time, as though you move from conscious to unconsciousness. But even in unconsciousness you are still there, in the same way that the sun and moon are always there although they are not always visible. It is impossible to lose oneself, we can never lose the 'awakened one,' you are always there, just keep reminding yourself to notice.

The mind may try to convince you that you must practice or that you must learn more to be or stay awakened, this is not so, as the 'natural self' is before and beyond all learning and practice, nothing else is needed in order for you to be yourself.

The mind may make you feel that you must make some effort, but I say make no effort. Just keep quiet and be natural.

> The mind will often try to draw you into a mental conversation and debate about how you need to do or be more, or how you need to return to awareness and how you have become unconscious. Do not worry, as these are just the last ramblings of the ego mind in its desperate attempt to hold you in bondage. Just remain silent, do not respond, and see what happens...
>
> Be nothing, do nothing and expect nothing...
>
> What remains?

## The Secret Self

*"You are pure spacious intelligence without form"*

What remains is the 'Secret Self', it's a secret because it appears hidden from most, unrecognised yet always in plain sight. It can only be accessed as we turn and place our awareness upon it, it is so obvious that most never consider to look, it almost seems counter intuitive to look back at who is looking, but when we do, the secret of who we are is revealed and opens up to blossom and flourish.

The first step is to recognise that there is a watching and witnessing taking place of thoughts, emotions and bodily sensations, what is it that is aware of these things? Who is watching? And can this 'watching' itself be seen?

Please look and see...

Secondly, as you become a witness to this witnessing of thoughts, feelings and emotions, look deeper and see you're witnessing of the witnessing itself...

As you look at this looking taking place... what do you find there?

Is there some intelligence there?

Is this intelligence solid in any way... does it have form or shape...?

Continue to look and investigate...

Is there some-thing there?

Or would it be more accurate to say that there is no-thing there? Please continue to look...

Is there some-body there... or would it be more accurate to say there is no-body there...?

Please look and see...

What you are cannot be told, but it can be pointed to for you to look yourself, only you can explore that which you are, no one can give it to you, they can only give you the methods and pointers, but without your use and curiosity of them it will never be discovered. Only you can experience it and bear witness to it, to your very self as it...

Don't just look back one time and dismiss, continue to look time and time again until it becomes more familiar and easy to access, until it becomes your nature and a constant living experience. It is a shift in consciousness and perception, a shift in perception from being condensed into the world and moving to a point of reference out of the world.

Don't just look, hang out in this place, in the place of your own being-ness and inner spaciousness...

Spend time wrapped up in the timelessness of your own true self.

# Chapter 14
## Enlightenment and Liberation

If we had to assign a meaning to life, we could say that it is to know oneself deeply and intimately, and to become aware of life itself in all aspects and on all levels. Also that we are here to bring everything into the illumination of consciousness.

Imagine a room that is in total darkness except for one tiny light shining in the centre; we would be able to see only a very small area of the room. Now imagine that your awareness is a bright light, that when turned to maximum brightness, can light up the whole room so that everything in it may be seen clearly. Even in darkness, the contents of the room are still there, but were hidden because of the dim light, but as soon as illumination through Enlightenment occurs, we become aware of everything that is there, and are now able to see into all the dark corners.

In this way it is possible to experience the entire universe and pure consciousness will know itself more intimately through what we term 'the human experience.' When Enlightenment occurs it is in fact the universe awakening to all the dimensions of existence. At present too few people have awakened to their true nature and the sad consequence of this is ignorance and conflict on many levels, throughout the world. Only when the consciousness of humanity has been raised enough, will we see a significant shift in the way we experience life and therefore in the way we interact with life on this planet.

Enlightenment and Liberation are the missing links, and also the key to happiness, health, freedom and the end of conflict and suffering.

## Enlightenment

*"Enlightenment is not a change into something better, but a simple recognition of who we truly are already, within the moment"*

## The Secret Self

For true Enlightenment to occur, we must look past information, stories and words, and instead look at what is behind them, as this Zen story below, points out.

Zen Story—The Pointer

> *"The Zen teacher's dog loved his evening romp with his master. The dog would run ahead to fetch a stick, then run back, wag his tail, and wait for the next game. On this particular evening, the teacher invited one of his brightest students to join him—a boy so intelligent that he became troubled by the contradictions in Zen teaching.*
>
> *'You must understand,' said the teacher, 'that words are only guideposts. Never let the words or symbols get in the way of truth. Here, I'll show you.'*
>
> *With that the teacher called his happy dog.*
>
> *'Fetch me the moon,' he said to his dog and pointed to the full moon.*
>
> *'Where is my dog looking?' asked the teacher of the bright pupil.*
>
> *'He's looking at your finger.'*
>
> *'Exactly. Don't be like my dog. Don't confuse the pointing finger with the thing that is being pointed at. All our words are only guideposts. Every man fights his way through other men's words to find his own truth.'"*

Truth, when expressed in words will contradict itself many times for the spiritual seeker until all words are dissolved and all that remains is just the pure view of truth. What can appear as a contradiction to the mind is complementary to the no-mind. When the intellect attempts to understand the words it will falter, if however the words are only regarded as a guide then we will stumble upon who we really are. Each 'pointing' has its appropriate moment to be a returning within, and our task is to simply be receptive enough to allow each 'turning' and 'looking within,' to happen.

As the story above relates, never confuse enlightenment with the words being presented and never try to gather information to reach enlightenment. This is impossible and will only create more blockages and obstructions. Instead, simply realise that the words spoken in this book or by any true guide, teacher or guru are only ever *pointers* towards your true nature. Allow yourself to be led to wherever the words are signposted.

The word and idea of Enlightenment has often gathered many different connotations, ones attributed to superhuman abilities and godlike prowess and whilst these things are in some sense true, or can be true, essentially Enlightenment is a lot simpler than anything the mind can envision. In fact, even though Enlightenment is such a simple phenomenon, at the same time it is truly profound, and much more profound than anything that the mind could ever dream of, so we must discard any preconceived notions of what we think of as enlightenment, otherwise these ideas will prevent us from ever awakening to it. For most it may never be seen, as it is so simple that the mind will overlook it every time. The mind is too busy chasing after what it imagines that it misses, and all the while what is forever obvious under its nose, that 'right here and now' goes unrecognised. Be guided by the story below . . .

*When Tired*

*A student once asked his teacher, "Master, what is enlightenment?"*

*The master replied, "When hungry, eat. When tired, sleep."*

When identity in thought ceases, Enlightenment just is.

When we stop chasing things in life, including enlightenment, enlightenment comes. Enlightenment happens when we rest in our natural state of being within the present moment and realise that 'this is it,' and when we accept what is here fully without wanting to be anywhere else, this is when it appears. Enlightenment is not a goal to be attained, it is a truth to be realised within the here and now. Our conditioned minds only ever take us into a sense of time through past and future memories and projections and this takes our awareness away from ourselves within the moment, and into the illusions of a time-filled existence. When we stop paying 'thought' so much attention, we are just simply 'here.'

When the mind no longer receives 'VIP' treatment from us, *we* appear, and Enlightenment just is.

## The Secret Self

Enlightenment appears only within the timelessness of the *Now* moment and it appears because *we* appear, as we can only be positioned and located in the heart of the timeless now moment.

For most of us, enlightenment is never realised because we have either a conscious or subconscious undercurrent of restlessness. Through the conditioned state of consciousness we are always seeking something other than what is right here and now and this creates a disconnect from life and within ourselves as our mind is attempting to place us within 'time' instead of remaining in the 'timeless.' As a result of this, all our energy is segregated and drained and our awareness becomes scattered. It is extremely tiring, trying to constantly project into the future all the time, looking to achieve this or that goal, trying to be somewhere different or feel something different. But most of us have gotten so used to it that we do not really notice how tiring it is, because it has become normal for us to function in that way. It is only when we stop that relentless pursuit that we will notice the massive difference in our energetic states and levels of consciousness, that we will suddenly regain and regroup all of our energy.

Imagine feeling more alive than you have ever felt before, having more vibrant energy than ever before, whilst also being fully alert and awake and also being completely relaxed at the same time. Can you imagine that? It almost sounds contradictory, but yet that is a tiny insight into how it could be for you. Also imagine having *all* intelligence and insight available to you in an instant, for whatever situation the present moment brings and without having to consciously retain any of it within the mind beforehand. It would just occur naturally when needed, as you would be connected to the pure intelligence of life so to speak. You would be fully aligned with life itself and therefore supported in every way.

It is truly impossible to describe what you are, but as you move into self-enlightenment you will realise that you are simply a vast nothingness, that nobody is there just emptiness. Please look.

The deeper we look within, the more we will see that there is nothing but empty space, but within it is an all-pervading intelligence beyond the bounds of body or mind. Our minds may find it very uncomfortable, but yet you as your 'true self' will regard it as a 'homecoming,' and a sanctuary of inner wonder and beauty, filled with peace, joy, ecstasy and deep rest.

Enlightenment is our home and freedom our nature. Enlightenment is life itself and the more that we connect with ourselves, the more that the events of the outside world seem less significant compared with the true beauty and bliss that is within, and that colours what we see in the world, because we are living in the truth of who we are, in pure joyfulness. We begin to see the world in that way also, the joy and beauty in life in all places. Suddenly life becomes a sheer joy, a beautiful mystery to be loved and enjoyed, and from this comes an amazing gratitude, thankfulness and appreciation for life. The more we begin to feel and perceive this way the more we radiate that energy out into the world and those around us. We become a beacon of brightness and warmth.

And suddenly we are free to be ourselves, like a playful child lost in the moment. We unburden ourselves and become light of heart (light hearted) and carefree ready to dance with the beat of existence. In Enlightenment we *are* life, internally and externally, and because we are no longer identified with being the body, mind or thought, we therefore become free from the sufferings and limitations of the body/mind. It is a beautiful liberation that truly sets us free.

*"What a liberation to realize that the voice inside my head is not who I am. Who am I then? The one who sees that"* Eckhart Tolle

## Freedom and Liberation of the Mind

*"Just as the great ocean has one taste, the taste of salt, so also this teaching and discipline has one taste, the taste of liberation."* The Buddha

As a consequence of de-identifying with the body and mind, and the dropping of all mental attachments from the world of flux and form, liberation and freedom is the end result. The moment we take that leap into the great ocean of our own true beings, we instantaneously move into a sense of total inner freedom from the form of the ever-changing world, which includes the body, mind and thought, or the body/mind organism. Without the mind being fixed and hooked on anything, including trying to get somewhere other than where we are, in the 'now,' a total and complete collapse of limited perception occurs which in turn frees the 'you' and renders our awareness unbounded and fluid. When the attention on mind and thought is lost, boundlessness occurs; suddenly there is so much inner and outer space, and thoughts and life challenges no longer feel so 'claustrophobic.'

In addition a complete freedom from thought and therefore a freedom from inner suffering is the result. The mind will feel more clear and peaceful than ever before and an intense beautiful silence will ensue. Everything will become so quiet that at first it may feel somewhat strange, but the more its influence is felt, the more it will be appreciated. It may seem very odd initially because all our lives we have been used to a loud, incessant chatter in the mind which acts as an interpreting overlay of the external world reminding us constantly that life is one of busy-ness and noise. But in reality it was always only our minds creating a smoke screen behind which the 'silence' could not be appreciated. As the mind breaks loose and becomes unbounded and free, a non-duality will occur and this non-duality removes the sense of a subject-object split, whereby there is a 'someone' observing a something, that then collapses and we are left in a place where the inside and the outside never meet. Please contemplate this.

## The Taste and Aroma of Liberation

While the true self is beyond the world of the ever changing, beyond both good and bad, and beyond pain and pleasure, liberation can emit a particular fragrance and flavour. This is because as the mind becomes unbounded it can cause certain things to happen within the body as a side effect.

When the mind is entangled with false and limiting belief systems, it directly affects our whole biological, chemical and energetic system, often creating many imbalances within the body. This means that our bodies can often feel unpleasant, lethargic and in a state of dis-ease. Most people have come to experience this as a normal state of human functioning, and this is often why alcohol and various types of drug are used by so many people to alleviate their feelings of ill ease and in an attempt to experience the more pleasant bodily sensations. Certain drugs release temporary feel-good chemicals and alcohol often pacifies the mind and reduces the amount of thinking, often acting as a relaxant. In the world of today, people do so many things in the pursuit of feeling-good and trying to reduce feelings of unpleasantness, but these means can only ever be temporary. In fact they usually create a pendulum effect. Alcohol and drugs may bring short term relief and pleasure for example, but yet the flip side is always the opposite feeling of unpleasantness as the effects wear off. A drug may get you 'high,' but this is invariably followed by a 'low' once the effects wear-off afterwards. This is the result of cause and effect, and balance. The body must balance itself out.

Inner freedom and liberation of the mind are two vastly different outcomes. There is no opposite effect, as it is beyond all effects and no effects, it is beyond pleasantness and unpleasantness, yet by the grace of its effect on the body, more often than not the body is left in a state of mild to extreme pleasantness, all the way from peace, joy and bliss to ecstasy. All of these effects and states fluctuate and happen within the consciousness of the unchanging self, both feeling pleasant and feeling unpleasant is simply a constantly changing effect within awareness. The true self is a pure witness and experiencer of both without showing preference to either, it is only the mind that exhibits a preference.

So, we are left with the best of both worlds and in the unchanging, timeless self we are always unaffected and unidentified with the pleasantness or unpleasantness of all experiences. But because the effect of liberation causes the body to experience pleasantness most of the time, we are free to enjoy it fully without attachment or clinging, and conversely, when we experience some periods of unpleasantness, we are also 'above' this and can move beyond the suffering or discomfort it may bring and all is witnessed as the pure self. This liberation of the mind only occurs when the minds knots and tangles come undone and the right relationship between thought and pure consciousness is established.

So in this sense, liberation of the mind turns the table of our experiences. Most people naturally feel maybe 70% of the time, unpleasantness and 30% pleasantness, whereas after liberation it can flip to the other extreme where we may experience pleasantness more than 90% of the time and the 5 to 10% of unpleasantness that might be left is neutralised by our occupation of the place of the true self and the liberation of the mind. Therefore we become free from inner suffering, as suffering only occurs when in the mind. In other words our experience of life either becomes one of extreme pleasure and joy, or we remain in peace as the true self when any form of unpleasantness occurs. With liberation we can become joyous, peaceful, and ecstatic and move with such ease and grace, our experiences become so effortless and we experience pure stillness of motion.

The only exception of this occurring is when the body is suffering from a debilitating condition or disability. If a body for example has chronic pain, then that body may not be able to experience pleasure for much of the time, and unpleasantness may be the dominant condition. Even so, this will not matter and ultimately not affect the one who has awakened to their true nature beyond the body and mind. For such a person it will be much easier to cope with this condition, as this being will remain a 'watcher' of the sensations of unpleasantness as opposed to becoming lost in the identity of 'I am hurting, or I am in pain.' Instead it will be perceived and experienced as 'pain is there, pain is happening,' in other words the lack of identity in it reduces the suffering of it because it is not made personal, it is not being perceived as happening to 'me' anymore, because for the awakened one there is no 'me,' no person, but simply just life itself, which also includes the sensations of pain. When the pain arises, there is just only empty space in which it occurs and in which it will eventually dissipate. If it does not dissipate, then it can be used and transmuted by focussing upon it.

As an example, in Shaolin monk traditions, the sensation of pain or discomfort is often used as a point of focus and concentration. They will often allow themselves to be consumed by the pain, allowing themselves to experience it fully. This then gives them a great ability to overcome pain as they learn to go beyond it with the power of their attention. When the sensation of pain is focussed-upon (and I invite you to try this) something amazing often happens, the pain begins to ease and diminish, as if the attention itself somehow dissolves it. You see, mostly in the Western world we have been taught to try and get away from pain at all costs, to take pills to numb it, or to try and focus upon absolutely anything else, believing that if we do focus upon the pain itself, it will maybe make it worse. This attempt to 'get away' from the pain actually creates more pain, and the extra pain and suffering that comes is a direct result of resisting or struggling against the pain.

Trying to run away from the pain in effect means that we are not accepting it, and therefore that we are struggling against it. This struggle then leads to suffering, whilst true acceptance leads to peace. The monks who focus on the pain first accept it and do not make it a personal problem or indeed a problem of any kind; they make peace with it and relax into it, allowing it to be there and for it to be experienced. This acceptance actually transmutes the pain, bringing peace and has even been shown to alleviate it; while on the other hand, struggle and trying to get away from it only brings you more turmoil and pain, as what you resist, persists. This truth does not just apply to pain, but to all things in our life experience. When we accept the things that have already happened and are happening in the present moment, it brings us the peace and strength to move forward, but when we resist and struggle it only brings more strife and pain.

## Trusting Life

*"Mind says 'show me and I'll trust you, universe says 'trust me and I'll show you'*

As we move along the spiritual path towards our self-realisation and liberation of the mind, or from the head into the heart, many fears and doubts may arise, such as, *'what if things don't work out' or 'what if I lose myself and can't function.'* These fears are normal and are generated by the mind in an attempt to keep its ego-identity intact and regain a sense of 'personal' control. Just the same way as a nervous passenger trying to take hold of the steering wheel of a moving car, as life moves along and unfolds, the mind may become scared and wish to interject for fear of what may or may not happen. This is fine and as long as we recognise that it is the last 'gasps of breath' of the ego, we can surrender those thoughts and allow them to dissolve in their own time, and leave them to preach to themselves.

Allow yourself to surrender and trust the unfolding that is taking place both externally and internally in your life and through the spiritual process.

## The Secret Self

The mind may say 'but I cannot trust,' but the real issue is not whether we can trust or not. We are always trusting something; we trust that when we board a plane it will arrive at its destination without incident, or that when you order a bowl of soup in a restaurant that it hasn't been tampered with by an unclean chef. So the question is not can we trust, but in what do we put our trust?

There are two main ways that trust happens in a spiritual sense.

Firstly that we trust what someone such as a teacher says, because we see in them the example of what we wish to be, or we trust what he/she says because we have resonance or some experience of that which he speaks.

Secondly we may have had an experience where life circumstances helped, interjected or supported us in some way (possibly many times) that left us beyond any doubt that life is intelligent and can be trusted, and that in hindsight life always seemed to work out for the best, providing us with situations from which we may learn and expand our horizons.

But something else may occur which requires no trust whatsoever and where trust is completely abandoned. This could be for example, a situation where we have so little regard for our personal safety that we would take a complete plunge into the unknown without any guarantee of what the consequences may be. Anyone who would jump off a cliff without first checking the height and what lies at the bottom is so fearless that death holds no worries for them and they must feel that they have nothing to lose. This type of person is certainly a candidate for liberation. Sometimes for liberation, you have to be a little bit crazy to say the least, as you have to be willing to let everything go.

*"Whether or not it is clear to you, no doubt the universe is unfolding as it should"* Max Ehrmann

We may arrive at a place where trust is not needed, as trust can soon dissolve into just pure being and existence itself. Trust is optional and whether we trust or not, life is still intelligent enough to allow creation to unfold naturally and in harmony. Life is always unfolding with perfect timing and only the human mind can disrupt that pure harmony for itself a little, from time to time, but even so, if this does occur then the universe will soon correct this imbalance to restore the natural order of things. Look around at the universe and nature and confirm to yourself that it is in perfect balance and harmony. It is only the human mind which has attempted to interfere with nature's balance. Existence is resilient enough to support us whether we trust life or not, but please examine your own life and you will realise that creation has always supported you and guided your life, but maybe in ways that you have not necessarily recognised.

When challenging situations occur in our life experiences, we can often feel like a victim—as though we are at the mercy of life and other people. We only feel this way when operating through the ego identity as the separate self; we may feel we are alone and maybe even that we are being punished in some way, but this is not so. I do not feel this to be the case at all. I have come to understand that the universe is benevolent and is corrective, whilst also providing opportunities for expansion and wisdom.

The universe is an aligning energy that works by gently easing the whole of creation into greater balance and harmony and part of that evolutionary process is the compression and challenging and dismantling process. From a scientific point of view we now know that on the surface that evolution is the opposite process to entropy. Entropy is the natural breaking-down of any system or entity which causes a slow dismantling to occur in order that a reconstruction can take place. Entropy happens to all matter, animate or inanimate. The process of aging and dying is entropy as is the rusting of iron, as it slowly crumbles to nothingness and as also it is the slow decomposition of dead flesh and even the gradual process of erosion of rock to become dust once again. It is the tendency of matter to return its original basic state.

But reconstruction is the way that life re-forms itself into a higher more evolved state. So in this sense the breaking-down process, which to us is reflected as life challenges, is the universe's way of providing an opportunity for us to correct something, bring it back into alignment and then evolve and expand it to a new level of being.

In other words, our challenges are opportunities that can actually be a blessing if we choose to let it be so. We can then correct and align what needs to be remedied and then by doing so, evolve to another level of being. The spiritual path is really all about this evolutionary movement, aligning mind, body and pure Self together in union and this can only occur as we connect to the deeper self within, which instigates a process of readjusting and integration. The Pure Self being the master and the body and mind being the master's vehicle to experience this reality.

# The Energy of Thankfulness

*"If the only prayer you said in your life was 'Thank you' that would suffice"*
*Meister Eckhart*

Say 'thank you' and be grateful for every experience in your life. Often, through the conditioned mind we say 'thank you' for all of the pleasant things that happen in our life, but rarely are we thankful for the challenges with which we are faced. Whenever a challenge is presented, most people do not feel thankful but rather, often feel that life is somehow 'against' them. This is understandable because the mind naturally inclines towards pleasantness and tends to reject unpleasantness. But the true Self does not 'favour' any particular experience and perceives them as all the same, and recognises that wisdom can be derived from all experiences, whether perceived as good or bad. In hindsight, we will often reflect and recognise that those challenges have made us stronger in some way and haven given us the gift of wisdom and insight, which in turn provides us with a greater depth of 'being.'

So if you cannot be thankful in the moment of receiving a challenge, at least see if you can reflect on all your experiences with gratitude and bless yourself for all you have experienced and learnt. To say thank you is a beautiful thing, it cleanses our being through its vibratory energy, because essentially thanking the whole of existence is also paying homage to our own self. The more wisdom we gain from our experiences, the more thankfulness we will feel and the more we will enjoy the growth and expansion of our enlightenment. No matter what, always say 'thank you.' Do not try to understand it or explain it and do not complain, just say 'thank you' and be grateful—and note what happens.

*Thank you, thank you, thank you ...*

Christopher J. Smith
# The End of the Spiritual Search

The spiritual seeker is the ego mind, and it is a 'cocktail' of the true self and ego mind that searches for enlightenment and freedom. It can either see a way out of its suffering or it sees the potential of what it could be, and so searches hard for the truth, to attain enlightenment. The contradiction is however, that with the end of the search comes enlightenment. It is the one who is searching, that is the very obstacle to the enlightened realisation of the true self and only when the seeker becomes tired and fades, does the beauty of enlightenment shine through. Only when the seeker gives up the search and searches no longer, does enlightenment make itself known. The purpose of all spiritual practice, is to burn itself out by wearing out the seeker, its purpose is to eventually fail, to encounter a barrier, at which point we are unable to go any further. When this happens and the practices begin to fail, our surrender will suffice.

The more the seeker relaxes, and relinquishes the idea of being a 'seeker of enlightenment,' contrarily, the more quickly awakening will occur. The idea of being a spiritual seeker is often the final chapter in the personal story of the ego. The ego turns awakening into a 'spiritual quest' whereby 'one day' we hope to succeed and the end-product will have been worth our long struggle. It tends to create a fairy-tale out of its pursuit of awakening, and this fairy-tale is exactly that, a fantasy story of the ego mind. Similarly, avid mediators may feel as though they are on a 'journey' and believe that when they 'clock-up' enough hours of meditation, that a sudden, profound explosion of enlightenment will occur. But enlightenment will only occur when we cease entertaining all thoughts of hope and the future. Whilst we still have an idea that we are moving towards some achievement, it will always elude us because there is no future, and you can never be found there. The future does not exist, only 'right now.' Enlightenment and awakening is right now and when we relax into 'right now,' fully, and completely, all else is relinquished as merely a mental idea and what will be left is the ultimate reality.

Meditation, spiritual practice and insight will bring us to the door of awakening and enlightenment, and this is all it *can* do. Then we must pass through that door and leave behind us all practice, knowledge, ideas and expectations. The threshold may only be crossed by accepting complete and total surrender and by giving up all else, including the idea of the spiritual path and its meaning. Let go of the spiritual search now, this moment and observe what remains.

## End of the Story

The awakening into enlightenment occurs with the ending of the mental story that most of us tell ourselves on a daily basis. We all have a story of who we are, where we have been, where we are going or what we are becoming. But with enlightenment, this all ends. We will simply feel vibrant and alive within the present moment, aware of the 'is-ness' of life and existence. We will experience all the vibrant colours, smells, sounds and feelings, and we will be completely immersed in it all, yet at the same time, totally free from it all, free to enjoy and participate in the world. Alongside the mental story, there is always suffering, because it tends to create a separate sense of self within the mind, whereby everything is highly personalised and appears to be 'happening' to us. This will create suffering as we will be affected negatively by even insignificant incidents.

This personalised sense of self, has the potential to become scarred by these events, and is easily changed by them and also by the many differing aspects of existence. Its identity has no real solidity to it. But when the personal story is discarded, freedom will occur in the 'now' moment. Discard your story now and observe what remains ...

## Non-dual Consciousness and Boundlessness

Enlightenment is like a cloud that dissolves and evaporates into the vast, clear blue sky. It moves from a limited and contracted state to the expansiveness of all existence. In this expansiveness a non-duality occurs similar to how there is no distinction between a wave in the ocean and the ocean itself. It recognises and senses that it is one with the totality, that there is no separation or boundaries, there is no distinction between the subject and object, they are one and the same. As the personalised sense of self and the personalised thought stream collapses, a merging and 'falling into place' of the subject and object occurs and it becomes apparent that only the identity and belief in thought was causing a mirage of separation, a separation that was never there in the first place. As this realisation deepens, a sense of spacious boundlessness becomes apparent and there will be a classical sense of oneness and connection to all things. Suddenly life and others are us, there is no distinction anymore and there is no personhood making that distinction. Yet at the same time, in stark contrast and in what appears to be a contradiction, a sense of individuality still exists at the same time as the sense of boundlessness with all things. Experientially both are there and neither compete with each other, they are complementary. This sense is beyond all mental levels, it is a deeper underlying knowing and truth that is a lasting, living, daily experience.

As we disregard the noise of the mind and become deeply aware of our own selves, the awareness of awareness becomes one, and a beautiful merging of subject and object happens. Simply remain quiet and still and be aware of yourself as the vast emptiness and space within and all around. The more we observe the observer, the more our perception expands. The seemingly external and internal worlds merge into one connected non-dual experience. It is similar to a wave on an ocean realising that it is the ocean itself, enabling a beautiful and flowing sensation to ensue.

## Loneliness or Aloneness?

As the blossoming of the enlightenment and awakening deepens, a sense of 'aloneness' may be experienced, which is not the same as loneliness which only happens to the personal ego self as it is cut off from life, others and existence. That loneliness may happen even when we are in large groups of people, because we are fragmented in our own personal sense of self and so lost in the mind that we isolate ourselves from the basic experience of life. We may also isolate ourselves from our true nature, and that is the real loneliness that we feel. If we are lonely, then we must be in bad company, that is, the personal ego self. When we are in the company of pure consciousness, we are in the presence of God, the best company possible.

Aloneness occurs when the awakening deepens to a certain level and we discover a sense of total quietness within. Because we have disconnected from the collective, conditioned thought-stream of the ego mind and the majority of humanity, quietude becomes apparent. A movement to a different level and to the pure collective consciousness of where everyone's true nature exists, has occurred. This movement transports us beyond the collective noisiness of thought and beyond space and time. The ego mind will very often become entangled with the minds of other egos, tuning into the same frequency so to speak, thinking about what others are doing and thinking, completely enmeshed in the tangles of the collective conditioned hive mind. Aloneness unlike loneliness has no negative qualities because there is no personal mind there to create a problem. Instead, there is a beauty and joy to this aloneness because we feel connected on a much deeper level, to all else, to life itself, and to the pure consciousness within. Only beauty, joy, peace and connection are experienced in this place.

## No-one there to Attain Enlightenment

*"The obstacle is the path" Zen proverb*

There is no spiritual path and there is no journey to who we are; we are the one that is before all paths and journeys. The ego believes that Enlightenment is in the future and can be reached by striving to attain it, but the belief that we are on a journey along a specific path is an obstacle in itself. Where will that journey take us? Enlightenment is an awakening to who we are within the present moment, and so any movement towards the future time will cause us to miss what is already here, now, in this moment. What is here and now in this moment is ourselves, so where else would we need to travel to meet ourselves? How far and for how long must we travel to meet ourselves? Enlightenment is not something that we achieve, as there is no-one there to achieve it. Enlightenment never happens to anyone, because enlightenment is the recognition of the absence of anyone. No-one becomes enlightened, as the very death of someone (ego) takes place in order that awakening and enlightenment may occur. Enlightenment does not simply happen to someone, Enlightenment 'just is,' right now, within your experience if you will only recognise it.

Enlightenment is simply the identity of being the ego undoing itself and when experientially, the idea of being a body and mind unravels, enlightenment is there, and there is no-one left. Only pure, empty space remains, intelligent space...pure consciousness. It was a façade all along, the ego never existed, and it was an illusion, a trick of the mind. There was never any personal identity there, it only seemed that way because the pure intelligence believed in the thoughts that were drifting in and out of the mind. The ego does not exist, it is an invented concept to help us understand the body/mind identity. It is a complete fiction. There is only absence, and the truth is that we do not exist...there is just existence...nothing more, nothing less. Look deeply enough within yourself, beyond thought and observe who resides there.

## No-one there to Suffer

When we discover our original natures, we will see that there is no-one there to suffer and when the personal 'me' is gone, and the relationship with the voice in the head no longer exists, all suffering will cease. Enlightenment is the end of suffering and a step into the freedom of the boundless consciousness of all existence, and it allows us to enter the emptiness of perception. Just as there is no-one there to be enlightened, there is also no-one there to suffer. Attaining Enlightenment means the end of the illusion of a personal thought-based idea of self and the end of an inner dialogue of thoughts reporting to anyone or anything. Suddenly there is no personal relationship in the head, there is no dialogue between the different voices of the ego. In addition, the thinking mind no longer receives attention, it is consigned to the background and the pure consciousness assumes prime position. For inner suffering to occur, there has to be someone there, someone to take it personally, but when we settle upon our true nature we will discover only beautiful, intelligent, nothingness. All our usual sensations, thoughts, feeling and emotions will arise, but there will be no ego present to take any of it on a personal level, it will all be simply another form of experience, taking place in the pure, vast, emptiness within. When there is no-one there but pure empty space, then everything passes straight through, there is nothing solid to be struck or chipped away and we will remain unblemished at the core of our beings.

This is a pure, empty intelligence, all-pervading and all-conscious. It has no shape or form, it cannot be weighed or measured and is beyond all physical forms and concepts. Yet this nothingness is so powerful and intelligent that it was the cause of everything that we see in the phenomenal world of constantly changing and fluctuating forms.

# Surrender

*"Surrender simply means to surrender the illusion of that which is not you, the ego"*

For the learned ego-mind, the word 'surrender' can be quite scary, as it is often seen as giving-up or quitting something, something that our Western culture tends to pride itself in 'not doing.' But essentially, surrender has nothing to do with giving-up something externally but rather has everything to do with handing-over that which is not you. If there is a giving-up of anything, it is a giving-up of the illusion that we are a separate ego-self, a mind/body identity made up of thought. The ego that believes it is a separate self will often jockey for control in many of life's situations, and as a result we often suffer unnecessarily for this need to control life and life situations through the fears of the ego.

You may have read about many NDEs (Near Death Experiences) where people have experienced a strong sense of fear at the point of leaving the body, but then have surrendered and through that submission, they were suddenly overwhelmed by an immense feeling of love and joy and their out-of-body experience then switched from an unpleasant experience to one of immeasurable love and happiness. Surrender is the transmutation of a separate fear-based struggle to that of complete connection and loving flow with all things. If we truly surrender whilst in the body, we will experience this beauty and connection here also. So do not wait to leave the body to experience heaven, instead realise that heaven and hell is simply a choice and a state of being, right here and now on earth.

You see, our true nature is that of being 'one' with the whole of existence and how can we be 'one' and flow with all of creation if we insist that we are a separate entity with our own ego-agenda?

We are all certainly a unique expression and flavour of the one totality of existence with an original body and flavour of being and at the same time our true nature is that of being the one existence itself. The ego however is not a part of this natural, unique expression of consciousness, it is simply a mis-perception of self. When the ego is dissolved, the unique self that we are, remains and shines-through brighter than ever, whilst also being in full alignment with the completeness of existence.

And how can we flow and merge in union with the totality of life if we are always trying to control life and people for individualist ego gain and 'personal' benefit?

How can we be available to receive what the supreme intelligence wishes to give us through its grace and support, if we allow the ego to dictate what is best for us?

The ego-mind is always looking to control people and situations because it has its own agenda in place; an agenda to feed itself and thereby to grow. Every time the ego gets its own way it receives a little more energy, and so it boosts the personal identity, giving a false sense of power and a larger sense of ego-self. The ego mind desperately wants to become greater and more powerful, but when really growing in an authentic way means giving-up its personal sense of self, it does not want any of this as it ultimately fears a loss in 'personal' identity. In other words it fears its own impending end.

What is being asked in surrender is the surrender of the 'person' and not the true Self, the surrender of the illusion and not the reality. The more illusions that are surrendered, the more truth becomes available one portion at a time, and as we move deeper into this truth our true identity as being 'one' with the whole of creation is revealed.

# Total Surrender

*"There are no levels of surrender, either we surrender or we do not"*

Someone may say, as people often do, through the mind, *'how will I surrender? How can I surrender, can you give me a technique to surrender?'*

I say, 'no!'

No technique can or will do it. It is not something that is done, it is simply a truth to be realised and acknowledged. Surrender is the realisation that we are not the mind and its wants, needs and sufferings, so we should simply just discard it.

## The Secret Self

When we are exhausted and tired of battling-with and engaging in the ego-mind's antics, we will soon discard and be done with it.

When suffering seems too unbearable and illusions dominate us, use this as the moment to quit fighting and surrender. Let go. The shell of the ego is like walking around with a heavy armoured suit on, just take off the damn suit and drop it, cut it loose and be done with it.

The more and more we 'let go,' the more and more we will effortlessly flow. To let go means to simply realise the truth, relax and surrender and just be yourself.

Do not try to surrender or pretend to surrender, or even surrender just a little. We either surrender or we do not, we either resist or we flow, we either struggle or we cease to struggle. We cannot be half within a sense of ego identity and half within the true Self at the same time. This cannot happen.

Either we realise the truth and are free, or we continue believing ourselves to be the illusion and continue to suffer it.

So, surrender to the truth of which you are and merge yourself into an embrace of the whole divine existence.

Do nothing … expect nothing and be nothing …

Relax and surrender into the arms of the divine intelligence. Allow yourself to float in the water of the universe and your own being. The wave remembering and recognising itself as the entire ocean …

# Chapter 15
## Awakened Purpose

*"As a being awakens to their ultimate nature, a beautiful mystery unfolds"*

As you awaken to your ultimate nature and move into a full realisation and liberation of Self, your life shifts in a big way, not necessarily in the sense that your external life situation changes (although it can), but in the sense that your whole experience and way of living and way of 'being' changes. You will find yourself in a harmonious flow with existence and when the 'wave merges into the ocean,' there will be an effortless movement that occurs. You will be completely free and awake to experience all of life's wonder and mystery, like a child exploring a beautiful garden, and while this beautiful mystery is there to be lived through, the ego mind will try to intervene and ask 'but what now, what is my purpose?', and this question may well spoil all the fun of life's effortless flow, because the mind would like to take you off into the future again, meaning that you would miss the beauty and enormity of this moment, which is the only life and reality there is.

The mind will say 'there must be a purpose, what is my purpose?', so let us explore this idea of a purpose . . .

## Who Asks the Question of Purpose?

Only the ego mind could make something as simple as life should be, into something as complex as we see today in modern society. Only the forward thinking intellectual mind could overlook what is in plain sight in front of us right now, and ask the question, 'what next?' It says, 'this cannot be it, there must be something more.'

When 'we,' through the ego mind is not obsessed with the idea of being somewhere else other than the present moment, and not dissatisfied with this moment, will we realise that our purpose is obvious and that it is what is happening right now. Why? Because that is all there is, and all that there is for us, is just what is happening in each moment right now in our current experience. What more could there be? Only what the mind creates or imagines, which is not the existential true reality, it is just pictures, images, thoughts and ideas in the mind, nothing more. Those contents of the mind can certainly be used to help create the next moment, but we should not do so at the expense of and by overlooking this moment, the true moment. One is true and the other is not yet in existence, and we are only able to think in the present moment anyway, so the idea of a purpose is very much the same thing. What most people, through the mind, think of as a purpose is something that only exists in the future, but any future idea can never be the purpose, simply because the future does not exist. No-one has ever seen it, only the continuation of the present moment's existence is real and all life is only experienced within the here and now, and so our so-called 'purpose' is obvious. Our purpose is what is here, and being done right now.

The intellectual mind is always in the past or future and never in the moment. In fact, the moment cannot be experienced through simply thinking about it, because the minute we think about it, and become absorbed in the thought, we are already in the past and have lost the experience of the 'Now.' Whilst this happens we actually move nowhere, we are always physically in the 'now' and can only think in the 'now,' but if we attempt to think about now, then experientially we lose the present moment.

The mind seems to always wish to complicate that which is so natural and simple and the story below is a good example of this...

## The Philosophical Frog and the Centipede

*A centipede is just going for a morning walk. Now, a centipede has one hundred legs.*

*A frog looks at him, and cannot believe his eyes. He blinks his eyes, looks again and thinks... a hundred legs!*

*How does he manage? Which one to raise first, then the second, then the third, then the fourth...? One hundred legs!*

*He thinks... If you forget the number, you will be caught in your own legs and fall down!*

*He rushes up to him, jumps, stops the centipede and asks him, "Uncle, I should not stop you on your morning walk, but a very philosophical question has arisen in my mind, which I cannot solve. I am just a frog, you know. Only you can help."*

*The centipede says, "What is the problem?"*

*The frog explains to him, "This is the problem: I saw your hundred legs, I counted them, and the problem is, how do you manage?"*

*The centipede replied, "I had never thought about it."*

*"I will try and see how I have been managing. I have never thought about it. I really have never looked down and counted the legs."*

*"You are great; you are a mathematician and a philosopher," said the centipede.*

*So the centipede tried, and he fell immediately, all his one hundred legs entangled in each other. He was very angry at the frog and said, "Never again ask anybody such questions. Keep your philosophy to yourself, you idiot! I have been managing my whole life, and not only I, but millions of centipedes are managing perfectly well. Nobody has fallen like me but now I am afraid. You have created such a question in my mind that if I don't get rid of this question, I may not be able to walk at all. Tell me how to get rid of this question."*

*The frog said, "I don't know. I am myself puzzled. I asked you because you are an experienced person, an old centipede, and you go every day for a morning walk; if you cannot solve it, how can I? I am just a poor frog."*

I do not know what happened to that centipede afterwards, but I can imagine that his whole life must have become a mess. Again and again the question would have haunted him, *"one hundred legs. Am I putting the right leg in the right place at the right time?"*

Life has its own ways. The moment we start trying to manage everything, we disrupt the natural way of things. Allow life its freedoms and do not be guided by fixed ideas. Experience! Experience and you will know what life is.

So forget any ideas of a future purpose and exist in the present reality. See the purpose as 'what is' right now and in what you are engaged within the moment. In that way we will always experience the beauty of this living reality.

## The Primary Purpose

Life is not about having 'a' purpose, it is about living 'on purpose,' there is a huge difference. To have a life purpose implies that there is something towards which we are moving in the future, as if it is something to live for in itself. Whereas living 'on purpose' is about living this moment totally and fully with vigour and attentive consciousness at all times. To live this moment on purpose means to live the whole of our existence intensely and completely, as all life happens within the here and now. It is to live mindfully within the present moment and to give everything our complete attention and care in the moment. It is all about waking-up to the reality of the moment in front and all around us. Life is a totally different experience when we live in the moment.

It is very difficult for the ego mind to understand that there actually is no ultimate purpose or 'goal' in life. When the mind tells us that we must have a purpose what it is really saying is that life must have certain goals and achievements that we must strive for, and that these goals make life worth living, thereby giving us a sense of destiny, meaning and accomplishment. But the truth is that only the human conditioned mind has goals referring to purpose, all other life and even existence itself has no goals. The whole of existence just unfolds naturally, going through many processes of change within the now moment with no concept of goals or destiny, it just simply flows and evolves, effortlessly changing and modifying as and when needed. Life is not moving from the imperfect to the perfect, it is moving from perfection to perfection, as you are yourself at the core of your being. It is only the misidentification of the ego mind that would work against life and when the ego dissolves, all that is left is just the pure perfect life moving from perfection to perfection. If there is any goal at all, it is that life itself is the goal.

The idea of a purpose is actually a little short sighted, because if we say for example that our purpose is to become the greatest singer in the world or even the greatest humanitarian, then what happens when this goal is achieved...?

Then the mind will have to find another, new purpose, and once that purpose is completed then another... and so on, there is no end to it. Also the mind ignores something very crucial when focusing on the idea or pursuit of a goal or purpose, and that is the reality of the present moment, and the fact that only the present moment exists, and everything can only be done within that moment. There is nothing else, there is no other time.

So if we are going to speak of purposes at all, then let me suggest what the primary purpose is of all beings...

## To be Here, Now

There is no future purpose. Why...? Because there is no future, there is only NOW.

Our primary purpose is to awaken to the reality of 'what is' and 'what is' is the present moment, it is the here and now and all it holds within it. There can be no kind of purpose without the grounding of reality first, by knowing, living and fully experiencing the present moment. It is impossible to have any kind of fundamental basis for a purpose without a greater awareness of life, self and truth. We are small slices of existence, and existence can only become the best it can be, when it awakens to itself, otherwise its capacity is limited when it is unconscious. When it is unawake it is only the 'tip of the iceberg' of what it could be and when we awaken to ourselves 'now,' we open the door to our full flowering and potential.

When our awareness is focussed on the idea of the future, it misses the reality of now, and by missing 'now' it neglects life, by not paying it the full attention needed to actually be a better and more conscious contribution to the world, and more importantly missing the joy of this moment. How can we say that to be joyful is more important than contributing to the world? Quite simply because a contribution may only be external, whilst being joyful encompasses both the external and internal ... in other words contributing to the world can be achieved in a high quality or low quality fashion. A person may help someone with unhappiness and frustration in their heart, which would determine that their quality of consciousness and action was lower, whilst one who is joyful increases the quality of everything they do, because then they are more likely to leave others joyful.

We could feed one thousand people and yet still make them feel miserable, or we could feed ten people and give them great joy. Which is the greater? It is our state of being that makes the difference in what we do and determines how deeply we touch another and add joy to this world. When we discover ourselves within the moment, we become effortlessly joyful, and when we become joyful we give others permission to be their joyful selves. What could be better than living like that everywhere we go, being a nurturer of souls, and a gardener of hearts, allowing people to blossom and flower into their true, joyful selves?

When we are able to be fully awake and aware of the here and now, the quality of everything we do and every interaction we make becomes magnified a thousand fold. Then we will really have the foundation to be a powerful element of life, and life will move through us and fill us with the vital force and inspiration. If we are not really here and are instead enveloped in some dreamy imaginary world, constantly thinking of the future, then we are lessening our ability to influence the world in a positive way. This will also limit our own capacity for joyfulness. If we constantly focus on the future, we will experience more anxiety than joy. Joy only becomes apparent when we settle and relax into the here and now.

> *"I need no future purpose, now is the purpose"*
>
> *"Life has no meaning, life itself is the meaning"*

To be of any real use to the world and to be joyful we must have access to the present moment, as this brings access to our true selves and connection to life. The key to an awakened purpose resides within our inner awakening and self-realisation.

Christopher J. Smith

# To be the Natural Self

The present moment and 'you' are both tightly connected, because the present moment gives us access to 'real life' and the only place we may be discovered is in this 'real life' which is within the present moment. Look around you, there is nothing else other than the 'now,' all life is happening inside of it. No purpose can be realised in the future, it can only be entered through 'you,' right now. In other words, you are the 'purpose,' the true you is the purpose in each and every moment. The purpose is to be yourself in the heart of the timeless moment, living consciously and totally within your current experience. Allowing yourself to express freely with whatever arises within the moment, whatever you feel, whatever you wish to say or however you wish to act without censoring yourself based on the fear of what other people or a society may think. Do not be too forceful or too expressive; also do not be suppressive, only express yourself as much as the true nature, no more and no less and natural expression will occur when you mature into your pure awakened nature.

Honour whatever you feel within the present moment, do not resist anything, allow it to be experienced and expressed naturally. As you continue with your pure meditation and deepening of awakening, you will find that your expression changes as the mind becomes less and you become more, then naturally your expression will be in perfect alignment with creation itself.

So your primary purpose is to come back to the true reality of self and life and observe how your unfolding makes your presence a gift to others...

*"I need no purpose, I am the purpose"*
*"I need no meaning, I am the meaning"*

# The Gift

I would suggest that at this stage of enlightenment one only need be themselves and anything they do will be a perfect expression of service to the world.

Then the smallest action may become a gift to those around you and as your natural state of joy radiates to all around you, an unseen energetic presence may be felt from you and everywhere you go, life will flourish. When our joyful and peaceful energy comes into contact with those around you, it will be felt, and people will warm to it. They may not know why they feel the way they do, but regardless, the positive effect will be there. We will become a beacon, a lighthouse of positivity and truth and strange, beautiful things may happen.

I remember an occasion where a friend who I had not seen for a while came to visit me. I invited him in to sit, I made us both a cup of green tea and we sat down. I was sat quietly not wishing to speak, and then my friend began to speak and a casual conversation began at a normal pace, whilst enjoying our teas. The room was very quiet with no music or other activity taking place and after around ten minutes or so, the conversation began to naturally peter out, until eventually we were sat quietly in silence.

We sat quietly and calmly for about fifty minutes, but initially I could feel some inner 'wrestling' inside the mind of my friend, which eventually calmed and then at this moment, there was no awkwardness or inner turbulence at all. Everything felt very right and natural.

My friend eventually said *"I feel so peaceful sat here with you, I'm not sure why but I do."* He also mentioned how the room had a particular peaceful atmosphere too, again he did not know why, but nonetheless, the effect was still felt and peace emerged within him.

Sometimes people can just sense our energy. As soon as they enter our vicinity it may be felt, and also be felt in the spaces that we occupy, like a particular home or room and the energy lingers, whether it be either light or dense. We all have the ability to sense this presence whether we are conscious of it or not. Occasions like these occur often, and so it is a testament to the power of our true presence that we need only be available to people and it will be felt far and wide in many different ways.

On many occasions I have seen how people will begin to open up about things very personal to them, and they will often mention how they do not usually speak about these things to anyone, but for some reason they feel the urge to 'let it all out' in my presence. Once they have spoken it is as if they have released and purged what needed to rise to the surface and be released. In just simply the act of conversation and listening it helps others to peel away the layers and expose their inner core.

Indeed, our presence is setting the foundation for others to enter into their own joyful and peaceful space within. When we become quiet we invite others to become quiet, when we are joyful we also invite others to become joyful and when we love we invite others to love. There is no more beautiful truth than this. Wherever we go, we are a potential positive influence to those around us, a walking invitation to truth and joy. This is the power of the awakened one, and whatever the awakened one does in the world is always of secondary importance to 'who they are.'

## The Secondary Purpose

The secondary purpose is anything that arises as a natural expression of your true self in the external world. Whatever you do in the world is always of a secondary importance to your awakened nature, as it is 'who you are' which determines the quality of what you do and are able to do in the world. It is the expansion of your awareness which enables you to maximise what you do and are able to give.

Take Mahatma Gandhi for example; there were millions of people all over India in the same position as him at that time, however Gandhi was able to affect more people through his words not necessarily because of what he did, but because of whom he was, his charisma, discipline, creative mind and presence. It was who he was that made the difference in what he did, and how what he did was received by others. One of our secondary purposes in life is to serve others in some kind of more pronounced service role and as stated before, our awakened state of being serves others without us even knowing, but to serve a larger amount of people knowingly, is certainly a great way to make a significant contribution to the world...

## Serving Others

*"The Path of Awakening is a path of service to the whole world"*

When we mention 'service' initially, we may think about someone engaging in a humanitarian role such as feeding a third world nation, or maybe participating in feeding the homeless or being part of a charity organisation, but service can appear in many, various forms.

Service is ultimately the act of contribution, a contribution of what people may need and want, what may help them evolve and what will help them discover more of life and themselves, or to just simply be free of suffering.

So in this regard, everything that brings the above to people is a type of service. One person's service may be to provide people with the best and most delicious food possible, whereas someone else may provide a great invention to the world. All the attributes described above, need, want, evolution and discovery, are just one type of service but another would be to act as a guide to Spiritual Awakening, happiness and inner discovery. But first and foremost, any service begins with ourselves, as it is not always what we serve, but more how we serve it. Do you serve from a genuine love and compassion for people, and with their best interests at heart, or do you serve because you feel obliged to, or because you are solely focussed on a pay cheque and only on what you can get out of it for yourself? The states of being that we hold, matter and 'who you are' matters even more.

When the personal self has been released, then there is a wonderful opportunity to be selfless in what we do, without any expectation of gain for 'ourselves,' but often we may do something purely for some personal reason, in other words, self-gain. Only when the personal self is removed from the equation, can we truly and completely be there for someone, otherwise the ego will always put its own agenda first, no matter how subtle.

Sometimes we may have the ability to temporarily relinquish the personal self in certain situations, and we are able to remove ourselves from the equation in order to help another. But an awakened being is always able to be selfless in all situations and in all that they do, and it is this factor that makes them a tremendous servant to the world.

## Provide Value

One of the greatest services we can provide to others is to give them something of value. There are so many ways we can provide value to people's lives but the first step of course is for us to discover our own innate value by discovering who we really are. Then whatever we may do or provide is more likely to be of value because what we are creating emanates from a heightened level of consciousness that signifies the quality of what we do. When we really provide something of value, we are supported by existence and by the people who are deeply touched by what you are, do and create. Providing value for people is one of the secrets to a bountiful life, because the more value we create for people the more that we are worth, and treasured in the eyes of others. The universal law of exchange will return to us as much as we give. The quality value we offer without expecting anything in return will be returned to us from support of life itself and the support of the lives we are affecting.

We can see how this principle works time and again, when we look around at many of the big companies in the world today. The reason that many of them stay around and are successful in the eyes of the world is that they provide good value. However, whether what they provide is good for mankind or not is of course, entirely another issue and is debatable, but this then invokes the question of whether or not it is better to give people what they *want,* or what they *need.*

We should never dictate what people should or should not have, only offer what *we* have by either recognising its need, through a certain level of consciousness, or that it is what people actually want. Our responsibility is to discern whether or not what certain people want is best for all concerned or whether it will only cause damage, but it is also the responsibility of all of us to be conscious in our choice-making ability. If we focus on providing good, ethical value that will make others happy, then that is a positive thing, but if we can also provide something of worth that makes others happy and at the same time is good for every one of us, then this is the ideal solution. The value we create and give to others is what we are worth in the eyes of the world, and by becoming a force of giving and not just receiving, many benefits will be given and provided to us, in return. When we are in alignment with who we are and in alignment with existence and we give, and be the value that we are, then we will be supported in whatever we do and will be endowed with plentiful resources and support.

# Responsibility

When we awaken to our true nature, it is not so that we can live a life of irresponsibility, only focussed upon our own success or on how we can be supported by the universe. We awaken in order to contribute to the very existence with which we are 'one.' We awaken the ability to respond to what is needed, we awaken 'response-ability.'

A Sufi story tells of a man who prayed continually for the awareness to succeed in life...

> *One night he dreamed of going into the forest to attain understanding. The next morning he went into the woods and wandered for several hours looking for some sign that would provide answers.*
>
> *When he finally stopped to rest, he saw a fox with no legs lying between two rocks in a cool place. Curious as to how a legless fox could survive, he waited until sunset when he observed a lion come and lay meat before the fox.*
>
> *"Ah, now I understand," the man thought. "The secret to success in life is to trust that God will take care of all my needs. I don't need to provide for myself. All I have to do is totally surrender to my all-sustaining God."*
>
> *Two weeks later, weakened and starving, the man had another dream. In it he heard a voice say, "Fool. Be like the lion, not like the fox."*

Responsibility means that we do what is needed, when it is needed without a second thought. We should help just as the lion helped, and be a hero of humanity. When we begin to see others as an extension of ourselves, and recognise the divinity that is within us, that is indeed within all sentient beings, then how could we *not* help, how can we *not* love others as ourselves? Once we awaken we cannot turn our back on those that need our help the most, because to do so would be like turning our back on ourselves.

So, be the lion that helped to relieve the suffering of the world with his very presence and action when it was most needed.

# Be an Example

*"Be what you wish to see in the world"*

The greatest service we can give to the world is not in what we do but in 'who we are,' because it is who we are that determines the quality of what we do, and how we do what we do.

Sometimes just being who we truly are is enough to act as an example to those around us. The way we act without saying a word can greatly affect those around us in a positive and beneficial way. If we are quiet and peaceful it can act as an invitation for others to become quiet and peaceful, if we are happy then others will become happy and if we are optimistic, others will also come to recognise positivity in many situations. Both fear and joy are infectious, have you noticed this?

When people panic around us, you may have noticed that it will spread, and conversely you may have noticed that when people are joyful this will also spread. We have all experienced the power and influence that one person can have over others. Have you ever been in a room when a person enters who seems to bring with them an unpleasant energy or attitude? This has the potential to bring the whole room down to the same level. Conversely, you may also have experienced a person at a party that is so happy and positive that they seem to bring the whole room and people up to their level. Both energies and states of being have influential power, this is the power we all have, and it does not matter so much what we do, but more from which quality of energy and consciousness it derives. We could be feeding the homeless with a bad attitude and only serve to bring others down and not help much at all, even do more damage than good, or conversely we may be stacking shelves in a supermarket but yet be such a joy to be around that we create more positive change than someone that works with a charity. It is more who we are and our state of being that makes the real difference and what we do is always secondary to who we are. This means that if we discover our true nature and allow our natural joy to shine through, then almost anything we do will be of great service to others.

> *"Your own Self-Realisation is the greatest service you can render the world"* Ramana Maharshi

It is only through the discovery of our true nature that we find the inner treasure and riches we are able to share with others. These treasures may be hidden talents, skills and wisdom, but most of all our greatest treasure is that of our 'Awakened Presence,' the energy of an Awakened being. All that we do in the world then becomes infused with that powerful and unmatched quality.

## Live this Life Joyfully

When people want to see in a darkened room, what is the obvious thing to do? Light it up! With so much suffering in the world, so much that goes untold and is happening in silence, that is taking place inside of people's minds, it is vitally important that we become the one without suffering. Otherwise if we are suffering and miserable, we are simply adding more to the sufferings of the world.

One of the greatest mistakes that people make, when it comes to trying to help those suffering, is to meet them at the same level by being in suffering ourselves, or by being dragged down into suffering. We should not 'go down' to try and bring someone up, we should 'stay up' and reach down to pull them up. In other words we should remain joyful and peaceful and do what we can, whenever we can, to help someone, or bring a smile to their face and to create a light, joyful energy and space for them to have the opportunity to become uplifted.

Do not *try* to be joyful, instead allow joy to come naturally as we move more and more deeply into our awakened natures. As the flower of your consciousness opens up, the natural result is the beautiful scent and aroma it gives forth.

Our joy is powerful, it has the potential to lift moods, bring smiles and change minds. When there is such darkness, even a tiny candle flame can make all the difference, and can lead many out of the blackness into light.

## Sharing

Sharing does not necessarily mean sharing objects or physical possessions with others, it can be the sharing of knowledge, insight or wisdom, but the most powerful sharing is the sharing of oneself, to be the presence and expression of our true selves in each moment and interaction.

When we give others the gift of 'us,' then we also give them the permission to be themselves fully, and in a world where people often think, act and become what society and other people expect of them, where being themselves is not the expected norm of society, the permission to step into their own true nature is much needed.

Just by simply sharing our time and presence is so powerful. To be with a person and listen silently, to acknowledge how they feel and allow them to share an issue or concern is of great importance. The strange thing is that as we stand in the timelessness of our heart, we find more 'time' and experience, more inner space where we can listen to others without being burdened by our own mind, and without thinking, 'I do not have time for this.' For one who has awakened there is so much space and extra time, because we stay empty and have the capacity to let others in and be with them completely and with a strong awareness of the present moment. Listen attentively to them and what they are saying without the distractions of a 'noisy' mind, without the worry, fear or restlessness that diverts your attention from being there fully with them.

The key to being there for others and selfless is that we have no personal sense of self, and by having no self we can be there for everyone, as often as needed. We will then become the space that is present for others to share and converse with, whether in speech or silence.

When there is no personal sense of self we are also free to be 'vulnerable.' But actually, for an awakened being this is just normality—it is a great source of strength and power, and is very inviting for others. To be vulnerable implies that there is something there that could be harmed or hurt, that there is a risk of some sort, and this is certainly true to the ego self. Because the personal ego self takes many things 'personally' and becomes offended, it often reacts defensively to try to maintain a certain mental position, belief or identity. Because the awakened being carries none of these things and has no personal identity, being 'vulnerable' does not mean anything significant to them. It may not appear so to others looking-in from outside, but for the awakened one it is just them simply being themselves, purely open and honest.

Because of this, a realised being is a friend to everyone, and someone that shares themselves completely, even to the world, if the world wants them.

## Passion

It has often been said that part of a being's purpose is to pursue their passion, to do what they feel passionate about and love above all else.

Passion is a powerful energy that comes from love, the love of someone, something or of life itself. It is a high vibrational state with high energy and if we can travel through life with this energy, we will serve ourselves and others very well, and all of our actions and pursuits will be more successful as passion will improve the quality of what we do, and infuse what we do with the energy for potential success in that area. When we do things that we dislike or even hate, the quality of what we do is often significantly diminished. This is because we do not pay it as much attention as we would something that we love. It also does not receive our undivided attention as part of our energy is resisting it and our mind is focussed on being elsewhere, whereas when we love something we give it all of our attention. Attention is energy; if we attempt to burn through ten leaves all at once with a laser beam, what are our chances of success compared to focusing all of its energy on one leaf at a time? Chances are that we will burn right through it much more quickly.

This is similar to our attention. When we love something we give it all our attention and this attention is quality attention, but when we dislike something we may only give it part of our focus, and this focus is of a poor and more negative quality. So our passion can lead to success in whatever field, and if we are passionate about contributing to the world in some way, to add something of value, then our passionate interest and attitudes will surely mean that we succeed.

Passion may be expressed in various ways. Sometimes it may manifest as a highly enthusiastic state, and yet at other times it may be as a very relaxed and peaceful state—either way, the energy of passion is like a fertiliser is to plants. Observe what happens to those things that you concentrate that type of energy upon.

## Passion to Serve

Many that serve in the world have become passionate about helping and contributing to others; they have often developed com-passion for others and wish to alleviate others of suffering. Many times we develop compassion through familiarity of a certain situation or issue, for example often people that volunteer to work with cancer patients have either experienced cancer themselves or have experienced having loved ones with cancer. When we have felt the suffering and pain that can come from certain experiences in life, we often develop a compassion for those who might be going through the same or similar things. This compassion can lead to a person being passionate about helping others, and with that type of passion and compassion together; they will serve people with an energy that will heighten the quality of that service.

As we awaken to our own trueness, we will see in others that which is in us, and through experience will recognise that the suffering in another is the same as we have experienced ourselves. When we notice this, how can we *not* help to serve and liberate another from physical, mental or emotional suffering? It just becomes natural in the same way that it is natural to attend to a graze on our knee, no special effort or encouragement is needed to attend to another part of us, and so in the same way we begin to see others as a greater aspect of ourselves. So what hurts another feels like a natural process, preventing or alleviating the suffering of another.

One of the greatest ways we can serve others and to shield them from this suffering, is by moving through this existence with pure joy, laughter and happiness. A huge mistake that is often made when it comes to serving others going through suffering and challenging times, is to bring ourselves down to the same suffering level to show a person empathy. However, this only serves to make things worse. The best thing that we can do is to show compassion, understanding, empathy and most of all joyfulness and if we are among many suffering people, then it is extremely important that we are the one who is happy and joyful, otherwise we will just add to the suffering of the world and will not have alleviated any of it at all. The world needs more joyful beings, awake to themselves, and they must infiltrate all aspects of society. Are you up to this task?

If you exist joyfully, you will help to remove suffering everywhere you go, it is always a win-win situation. And if you are joyful, you will feel good and others in your presence will feel good. If you stand in truth then wisdom will be yours and wisdom will be made available to others through your very existence. Serve from the heart, from one heart to another. This is *real* living on purpose...

## Passion for Work

For the majority of the population, passion and work are not two words that are often spoken together, but there is a minority of people who have committed themselves to a type of work that they love so much that they wake-up with passion for it every day. Whenever the world has transformed in a positive way, it has been due to these people. They are the inventors, entrepreneurs, creators and people of service in the world. There is one thing that each person who has been a success in their chosen field has in common... passion.

The late Steve Jobs once said that passion and love for what you do is important because when things become challenging and tough, it is your passion and love for what you are doing that will help you push through and persist in those times of hardship.

Persistence is often one of the keys to success, whether that be success on the spiritual path or on a business path or a path of service. When we continue along a path with love and passion, eventually reality will bend and wilt to our will, and success in our chosen pursuit will happen naturally. When we become awakened to our true nature, this path of passion, success and persistence becomes even more joyful and smooth, because when we merge into the ocean of life and live in a surrendered realisation of self, we are totally free to enjoy the whole journey without challenges being able to affect our hearts in any way. And so, in this respect we become a master creator, an effortless, joyful creator and what better way of living can there be than this? When this becomes translated into service to the world, there is no stopping us and great things will happen.

## Passion for Life

The most important passion we can have is for life itself, for the whole of life and existence, and passion for ourselves as the one life and creation. Ultimately it is our quality and experience of life in the here and now which really matters, as everything we do then becomes a quality extension of it. If we are passionate for life, then we will be enthusiastic and passionate for almost anything we do in the external world. Any pursuit in which we take part will be enjoyable and more than likely beneficial for others, purely because we are involved with it.

We need no future purpose or idea to be happy and contribute to the world. Life and life experience itself is more than enough to be excited about and when we truly appreciate the mystery and wonder of life, a natural zest for existing will persist. When we awake each day and truly know who we are and know that nothing can ever take that away, then we are completely free and free to play in the playground of existence. How we could we not enjoy that?

## Reaching our Potential

*"Just as a beautiful flower, you are here to blossom into your full potential"*

What does it mean to reach one's potential?

When we think of potential we may think of amazing feats of human accomplishment and ingenuity like building spaceships and computers, or pushing our bodies to great extremes. These are certainly outward extensions of our potential, but real potential is prior to any external movement, real potential begins within an inner movement.

What separates us from the rest of the animal kingdom is the ability to be introspective and to be Introspective requires a degree of awareness and stillness. The greater and more expansive our awareness is, the more easily it is to look within. Introspection is a very high level of intelligence, because introspection means intelligence beyond thought or instinct in which we move to a higher level from which we can see what works and what does not, what is in alignment and out of alignment. We may become aware of what is sparking all of our decisions, motivations and actions, and then change or adjust them accordingly if they are not working.

This is the real key to our potential in this human body and the experience we are having in it. On the bodily level if something is not working correctly we can introspectively change it. For example, often we unconsciously and automatically engage in activities that are damaging to the health of our bodies, consuming things with little or no awareness of what they contain which leads to excessive weight gain or an unhealthy body, but through introspection we can become aware of what thoughts, beliefs or tendencies may be harming us by proceeding with our behaviour and then discontinue that destructive behaviour.

If we could not introspect, we would just be at the mercy of our instincts and conditioned programming, and we would continue to act it out whilst never questioning it. Introspection gives us the ability to change our course towards better outcomes and towards maximising our human potential.

It is very safe to say that for all the amazing things that humans have done and achieved, we have only seen a fraction, a tip of the iceberg of what is possible. There is so much that we have left unexplored. As a species, we have engendered significant changes to the world, with great advances of technology, but we are yet to really fully explore the human body, mind and pure consciousness to its fullest potential.

Potential begins within us, not externally. In modern society we have often become so proud of our technology that we rely on it to do the things that we ourselves could achieve and have access to if we explored the inner world within us. It is said that today the fastest supercomputer is still no match for the human brain, with the human brain approximately thirty times faster, and I feel that we are still only scratching the surface of what is possible with the human brain's capacity. It has also often been said that we have access to all of our brain but yet only use around ten percent of it for regular function, so imagine the capability we would have if we knew how to connect with the other ninety percent of it. Many of the ancient and modern yogis achieved this, and we can too, but we must explore it, otherwise if we 'don't use it, we lose it.' What we ignore and neglect diminishes, and what we give our attention and care, increases. So give attention to the inner awareness, as it is awareness that is the foundation for all exploration.

Why is it that only a handful of us have access to these capacities? It is only down to the fact that we have not explored sufficiently how to access this ourselves? Instead of turning to computers and studying this through books, the most powerful exploration is what the great yogis have been doing for thousands of years, and that is to discover it for themselves by looking within and gaining familiarity with the body, mind and pure consciousness, by self-study. We do not have to be a master yogi to do this, but it certainly helps to have some good tried and tested techniques for this and the techniques and pointers supplied in this book will be more than enough for you to do so, if you have not begun to experiment with them already, because experiment is what you certainly must do. This is what it means to be an inner scientist and discover our own natures. Simply turn the attention within and look and feel the body, mind and pure consciousness. When the majority of the population begins to turn within and explore their own body and mind sufficiently, that is when we will see the greatest advancement of human potential, both internally and in the external world.

The basis for all potential and for what we can contribute to the world through that potential begins within. Within is the solid platform from which everything is born and springs forth, from where everything can be held up and supported. Awareness is the foundational intelligence of all creative potential and life. As we access our intelligence and potential, we will begin to evolve the body to higher levels, and as the body evolves to higher levels, we can contribute to helping others evolve.

## Help Evolve Life

*"Helping the human species to evolve is also helping life to further evolve, as the human species is life itself, it is a piece and aspect of the great existence"*

By reaching our potential through the access to the pure consciousness, we are helping to also evolve the body/mind organism. I have seen within my own experience and through the observation of those who have awakened to their true nature, how the body and mind can dramatically change as more of the pure consciousness is accessed, and how quickly this can happen. The bodily structure can change, the posture, voice and facial features, and the mind can also change, through the changing of perceptions and the thought process. It will be as if the whole body and mind has realigned itself.

Our DNA and the structure of the brain can literally change through inner awakening. This is supported by such fields of research as Epigenetics and Neuroplasticity. Epigenetics demonstrates how our DNA changes based on external and internal stimulus, like an environment, and inner environment of particular perceptions, thoughts and emotions, and possibly by etheric energies and pure consciousness itself. Neuroplasticity shows how the structure and wiring of the brain can change through meditation, affirmations, thoughts, beliefs and all life experiences, the brain literally rewires itself and makes new connections through our external experiences and our inner space of thoughts and beliefs. Evolution is not something that is necessarily a long and slow process, evolution or adaptation is happening all the time and access to greater levels of consciousness can awaken and change how the body and mind operates quite dramatically.

So as we access greater levels of consciousness and intelligence within ourselves, we bring the body and mind to new levels of evolution and capacity, and when we as pure consciousness become greater within this body, this demonstrates exactly what is possible for all beings on the planet. We may then also find that we have a positive influence on those around us and may inspire others to discover who they are and evolve themselves, thereby helping and assisting the whole human species to evolve to the next level of Intelligence and capability, even if it is only one person at a time.

## The New Era of Humanity

For thousands of years, spirituality was something that isolated most people from the rest of the world, and these early practisers of spirituality often lived a simple, material existence, as a monk, yogi or wanderer and their entire existence consisted of looking very deeply into their pure spiritual nature and exploring the inner dimensions of existence. This was greatly needed as these inner scientists were able to pass on tried and tested methods of exploring consciousness for us all. However, today we have the ability to expand and grow by both inner and outer technologies, and for us to help spread that to the rest of the world. We live in a new era where external life in most nations is completely different to that of the past, and this provides us with the ability to reach millions of people worldwide.

How can an awakened being merge the inner and outer worlds completely in harmony, excelling and pushing the boundaries of either aspect? Are we able to exist in the world with maximum intensity, having greater experiences and a heightened perception whilst also being able to share a message of what it means to be a complete human being with mind, body and spirit, using our maximum potential and capabilities? I am personally curious to understand what is possible, how far can a human being go when they are fully rooted in the unlimited consciousness, how much potential and greatness do they have, and how much can that be shared as an example to the whole human race, in order to 'raise the bar' of what is possible. How far can the body, mind and spirit all be expanded together? In other words, how can humanity really evolve on all levels of existence? I feel that a new generation and era must come about that will encompass spirituality and materialism together, to operate the world of business and this 'new era' will arise from a place of enlightened consciousness.

This new generation must be able to operate in the world of both form and the formless and their point of perception will be external to the physical, yet they will be able to both achieve their potential, and contribute to the furtherance of knowledge in the world. This new, modern being must be willing to push the limits of the status quo, go beyond all previous limits, and yet realise that 'how' it is done, is just as important as 'what' is done. The world must continue to change and evolve with time, and these new beings of the new era of humanity must lead the way and set the example, so that humanity as a whole, and its society, can move to a higher plane of existence and living.

## Rebellion against the Norm

We have a world and system in place that operates within certain 'norms,' of consciousness, and of certain beliefs, and norms of thinking and acting and ways of living, all of which exist within a purely materialist paradigm. These norms have arisen through our not really 'being ourselves,' and by our constant submission to social pressures and conditionings. Instead of being true to who we really are, we have in many ways become a clone of our society and are dictated-to by society's demands.

If we wish to break free from these norms and approach life with originality and uniqueness, then we must become rebels, a 'rebel without a cause,' in fact, because no cause is needed. 'We' are the cause and *must* be the cause. Our true nature is the cause, and our awakening is the rebellion.

By awakening and accepting who we really are, we break free from the norms and conditioning of society, and by doing so become the greatest rebels of all. Becoming this rebel will set us free from the prison of the conditioned mind. In fact we can spark a revolution, not a revolution of violence, but a revolution of internal sovereignty and freedom encouraging inner and outer freedom for all. This freedom is the freedom of the body and mind, not that of pure consciousness. Pure consciousness is always free and unbounded, and access to it is the beginning of freedom on the mind and body level.

A rebel is not afraid to question or go against the norms of society. When they see a better way, they are not afraid to speak out. They are mavericks and pioneers and are led by their own engines and energies and seek no approval or permission from society or other individuals. They are guided by their own innate intelligence and self-knowledge. At this time, more than ever before, humanity now needs these mavericks, as they are the pioneers that will lead us in new directions and to new ways of living that are positive and creative and outside the restrictive parameters of a fixed mind-set. Imagine the possibilities? A society's direction in modern times is led by a few that have convinced the masses that their way is the best, and even the 'only way,' but as new leaders emerge, leaders that will be the new heroes of humanity, and that really care for the wellbeing of all and not for their own bank accounts or agendas, then we will see real progress and a true evolution of the human species.

Too much money is continually being spent upon making already rich and influential people even more rich and influential at the expense of the rest of us. Far too much money is spent on war, weapons, conflict and exploitation, in order to benefit the interests of a select few. A new breed of human must arise, who will show us all a better, more caring and peaceful way, enabling us all to live together in peace and harmony, and in good health. We will experience a new world where everyone on the planet is cared-for equally and treated fairly, and according to his/her needs. When everyone in the world is able to benefit from the basics of food, water, shelter, health and education without exception, then we can say that humanity is finally in a position to really progress as a species, and as aspects of the pure consciousness itself.

## The Journey of the One is the Journey of the All

Living our realisation, is to be at peace within, it is also to end the war between the heart and the mind, and the conflict of the ego. When this war ends within, only then will all external wars cease. All the wars in the world occur ultimately because warring people have a warring mind, they have an internal battle within themselves, and so that translates and manifests itself into conflict. Conflict with neighbours and conflict with different races or religions because a mind in conflict always seeks more conflict, seeks more reason to be in conflict, and the remedy is always inner peace. Only when we are peaceful will our life become peaceful and the conflict in our world, end. It will end when we end the strife. It 'takes two to tango' as they say, and in other words, conflict can only happen when two people are engaging in it. When both sides are constantly reacting, it becomes a game of tennis... but if we refuse to hit the ball back, the game ends suddenly.

The more peaceful and in control of our own reactions we are, the less anyone can play that game with us, and so the conflict will immediately end. All it takes is a little wisdom and the willpower to refuse to take part in the game.

As we end the war within by connecting with our true awakened nature beyond the ego mind, we will become very peaceful, and that peace will spread through our lives and the lives of those around us. When enough of us are able to achieve this, we will bring that sense of peacefulness into worldly affairs and it will be the end of all wars and conflict, both on a family and community level and on a global level. So, be a true ambassador for world peace by first ending the war within your own Self, and then by aligning the heart and mind, not pulling them apart. This will all occur naturally and spontaneously when we discover the 'secret self' within.

## Love is the Key

Everything in the universe moves in cycles of change, life, death and rebirth. Preserving, deconstructing and transforming. We can see that this is the pattern through which everything on this planet moves, some things more quickly than others. We can observe this in our own bodies for example, cell tissue is constantly dying and being replaced, otherwise our bodies would soon die and the species would be unable to sustain itself.

In the field of thermodynamics, the breaking down of a system, energy or matter is referred to as 'entropy.' This is the process by which all matter and energy has a tendency to revert to its original basic state. This is indeed how the whole universe operates, as it is made up of energy and matter and pure energy at its most basic level. This may relate to an organism, galaxy or society, and occurs when those systems become unstable, and when chaos and randomness becomes more prevalent. We can also see how that may be the case in society with a civil war or in the human body with disease. And what is it that is very prevalent in creating this for a society or organisms? Fear often creates separation. It has been shown in wavelengths of frequency at the DNA level that fear creates long slow waves of vibration. These long slow waves create a stagnant or devolutionary effect, and the solution is to move away from entropy and into a more aligned, connective, and evolutionary system. Love, and more specifically unconditional love creates short, rapid wavelengths at the DNA level, and this is what brings people together, what brings cooperation and unity, to create a stable system that can continue to evolve to greater heights. It is worth mentioning though that this process of entropy and breaking down is also part of a natural life process. So it is not simply a case of good or bad, it is just a case of evolution or stagnation or completion or destruction, these are choices we need to make. Do we want to help build and contribute towards creating higher levels of evolution within this body and for the human species and a society or system, or do we want to choose a path of mediocrity or destruction of the body and the species?

Love, fear or remaining the same is the choice. As we discover our essential nature within, as the pure silent consciousness, we instigate a processing of our energies as the body, mind, emotion and action all come into alignment over a period of time. As they begin to complement each other in a harmonious flow and direction, our perception matches our thoughts, emotions and actions. As we go through this recalibration process, we may face some challenges both internally and externally, so please understand that if this happens we are not doing anything wrong, in fact we can be sure if that is happening from time to time that we are doing everything right. As the mind body and pure self, begin to align, we are given the opportunity to face a particular experience so that we can more quickly and strongly realign and integrate the experience, in the same way that a muscle under pressure breaks down its fibres only to be built-up to be stronger again.

The quicker that the aligning process or the true spiritual awakening process occurs, the more it is a joyful journey from that point onwards and the easier it becomes to navigate all further experiences. So the more in alignment those bodily energies become, the more intelligent, capable and evolved we become. In fact we become a walking reminder of what is possible for others and indeed for the whole of the human race. We set the bar of what is possible in a human lifetime whilst being connected to the immortal self within, fearless and completely free.

So if we want to speak of a purpose for the human species, then we must be the gift, and leave a positive impression on the world for a contribution towards its evolution. By being who we are in this moment and allowing all of the body's energies to align, we will then be choosing love, awareness and understanding, which can only help to bring joy and evolution to the world.

## Community Spirit

You may have heard people say something like, 'we have lost the old community spirit these days.' I know I have heard this said many times, but often when this is being said people are referring mostly to the physical side of community, people coming together physically, but for an awakened being, community spirit means so much more than just the ties of physicality.

# The Purpose of Gathering

The coming together of humanity has an evolutionary purpose and effect.

It is very true to say that all innovative ideas and inventions that have evolved society and moved human kind forwards have for the most part come from the individual genius mind. The initial idea and in inspiration comes usually from one individual, but the implementation of that idea or invention ultimately comes from teams of people and the larger aspect of humanity when it comes to making it a reality in society. The reason for this is that without the larger population behind an idea, it will never become a significant part of society and move society and Humankind forwards in a new direction, because if humanity decides they do not approve of something and are unwilling to use or purchase it, then it will not happen. This is why so much money (usually more money than is used to create the actual product) is used in advertisement campaigns, because the creators of the idea need to convince the population to back the idea or buy the product or service in order for it to be a success.

This demonstrates the power that we have as a majority collective. It sometimes may not seem to be the case in most societies, it may seem like the few have more control than the many. But this is only because collectively we have bought into the ideas that have been sold to us, whether they are ultimately beneficial or not, and what often stops us from changing the course of humanity ourselves as a collective, is the fact that we do not communicate with each other enough on deeper levels, and because of this we do not really express what we truly want. And so the ones who do express and are able to convince the mass of the people of their ideas and intentions are the ones who have control of where society and human evolution goes. We as a group must take charge ourselves by coming together and communing on a deeper level and then making collective intentions known, and then implementing those intentions. It would be a complete shift from minority 'direction-ing' to collective 'direction-ing' and for this to happen we must move to a deeper level of community spirit.

These are the three primary levels of community...

Christopher J. Smith

# Physically Together

The most common form of community we know is of the physical kind, where we literally come together in the flesh, using touch, the sharing of resources, food and equipment or that we congregate together for a good time, such as dancing or partying and generally having fun. This is beautiful, but even this level of communing can be missing something, and only reaches so deep in actual community spirit and human connection. In Western, modern society many people use alcohol for social interaction, and by doing this they bring their level of consciousness down to the most basic primal level. The brain literally downshifts into a lower and more instinctual level of consciousness, hence why there can be so much violence and conflict where alcohol is concerned. I have many years of experience witnessing this while I used to work on pub, club and nightclub doors as a doorman, and so to try and commune on the deepest levels possible through this primal state is not possible. Alcohol can certainly allow our inhibitions to drop and open-up more, but without a sober quality of consciousness from a deeper level, the interaction will be more primal, basic and superficial. So for us to come together in this way is not enough on its own if we wish to establish a deeper connection with people through the bond of body, mind and pure consciousness.

I feel that if the physical connection occurs in the right way, we will see actual physical contact with the larger community where possible, people coming together without having to necessarily drink alcohol. It is desirable to have more equal sharing of resources and a basic stable foundation of society where even the lowest in society have their basic needs taken care of, so that they may work towards education, life skills, societal contribution and personal development. We have many of these things already in modern western society, but there is of course still a lot more room for improvement and improvement will occur naturally the more we can generate a deeper sense of community, as on the two levels below.

## Mental Gathering

Due to the rise of the Internet and social media platforms, we have seen a greater form of mental gathering taking place. But still the majority of the population uses this platform for more basic, mundane and superficial things, posting 'selfies,' posting about what they hate or dislike, about why they are angry etc., but people also share inspiration, positivity and new expanding information, and this has seen an increase in the ability to share ideas and communicate with people from all over the world, which in turn has created a situation where we are now able to more easily set up events and gatherings and spread information. There are many positive outcomes of this mental gathering that is happening, but to take things to the next level we must go beyond the mental to the spiritual or nonphysical to allow that to influence both the mental and physical way we interact. The missing key to taking things to an even greater level is pure consciousness, because without that deeper connection, the intellectual mental level will just keep things on a 'sense of separation' level, on a personal level, and that means that we are communicating with someone who is separate from us, from who we are. This is where the spiritual comes into play.

## Spiritual Gathering

Spiritual gathering is something that happens very rarely, but those who have understood the importance of this type of gathering have made this a priority, as it is from this type of gathering that both the physical and mental gatherings are transformed and therefore human evolution is propelled forward.

Spiritual gathering begins within when we recognise the pure consciousness in others that is also within us. This happens when we truly awaken at the level of the heart.

## Awakening of the Heart

As we begin to understand the complexity, sufferings and misidentification of our own minds, we natural develop a compassion for all beings, as we see that the pains we have gone through are the pains that others have gone through also. The unconsciousness and misidentification we have experienced is the same as that that most are experiencing right now all over the world and throughout history. As we discover our own true nature as the pure consciousness within, we cannot help but see that this same pure consciousness is at play inside all beings, that it is present whether a being knows it or not, and so with that knowledge, a respect and honour is felt for all conscious life. How can we not come to love the very thing that we essentially are and that is behind the whole of existence and at the core of all sentient beings? It is only natural to do so.

As we recognise this and the mind begins to dissolve into the pure consciousness within, a sense of boundlessness is created, we move to a new level of experiencing, where the sense of separation and a personal self, collapses. Quite literally, we can begin to feel connected to all beings and all things, as if our consciousness is merged into all life and when this happens it is the beginning of true spiritual gathering.

The access to the 'Secret Self' that we are, is the community spirit at its deepest level. It is where the sense of boundlessness and oneness meet. This takes us to a whole different level of community, because now we begin to consider the whole of humanity instead of an individual personal sense of self called 'the ego.' When we make decisions based on what is best for all concerned instead of just the personal self, everything changes. Imagine a world where we always naturally do what is best for all concerned, instead of what is just best for one individual corporation, government or nation. When the whole human race is included in a collective decision for the wellbeing of us all, this would come naturally, especially when we recognise that on all levels we are one, one humanity, one mind and one pure consciousness having this experience as humanity. We should not just recognise it intellectually as an idea or scientific fact, but as an actual inner experiential reality, a daily living occurrence. When people talk about helping the world or people that are in need, it is often seen as an extraordinary thing for people to be humanitarian or a 'good Samaritan' and many often regard these people as heroes and super human, but in reality it should just be a normal human response. It should not be an effort to help and assist people, it should be as normal as attending to a cut on our finger. When we attend to a cut we do not have to motivate ourselves to do it, it just happens naturally because it is a part of us. In the very same way, when we regard all others as we do ourselves and know and have compassion for all, we will simply help and care for people without a second thought. I would suggest that we must begin to see beyond normal ideas about what family is, as we have mostly been taught to regard blood relationships as sacrosanct, but the bond of spirit is greater than the bond of blood, and so if we are to truly evolve and see humanity flourish, then we must change our sense of family from blood to humanity and from relations to spirit. This is the start of spiritual gathering.

So a true sense of oneness is where it all begins. This can occur in many ways, simple daily ways of connecting to those around you within your blood family and community—the simple inner acknowledgement and sense of feeling connected, meditation and contemplation of being connected with others. This is where the idea of an actual community building like a commune is extremely beneficial. Imagine a place where people come together to connect on a physical and spiritual level, where people can relax, share ideas and connect together in the soup of each other's energies through meditation and receptivity. Where collective decisions can be made on a community and collective level, where the Internet, social media and Skype can connect us altogether with intentions and decisions being made, or to just simply get a feel for another nation or community of people. It is happening on some levels, but there is a long way to go yet before the collective consciousness of humanity has these gatherings more frequently. But as always, it begins within us as an idea and a daily living experience.

# Divine Will

*"When ones consciousness has no thoughts in it, one can experience spirit and live in harmony with the universal forces"*

Divine will occurs as we become more connected to life in the moment, and in doing so move into alignment with the whole universal flow of existence. When the ice melts into the ocean, it becomes the ocean and gains all of its force. As the ego dissolves like a tablet in water, the entire existence with all its power, intelligence and wisdom becomes us, guiding us in the right direction with perfect timing and synchronicity and we become reacquainted with who we really are.

From this position we need not struggle anymore or feel as though we are alone in making personal decisions. Instead from the depths of the ocean, our decision has already been made.

This means that we can relax, accept and move in a 'surrendered action,' a kind of doing where we are not the doer, but simply a witness to what takes place within our experience. In this place of surrendered action, we move and go about our business peacefully, relaxed and totally satisfied, knowing that whatever comes is a perfect reflection and expression of who we are. Our Intuitive capacity will heighten and become more sensitive so we can navigate the flow of life, subtlety knowing when to turn left or when to turn right, feeling when one thing has come to an end and when another is ready to begin, the same way that the spider can feel the slightest touch of its web. What a beautiful way of being this is. People will sense this effortlessness in you, and it may bring them peace and effortlessness themselves if they allow it do so.

## Intention and Allowance

This beautiful surrendered flow does not negate the power of an intention; the difference here is that an intention will come from the deepest and truest depths of our being and heart, and not from a personal individual ego sense of self. At this stage of awakening, if the ego mind tries to 'muscle in' and fulfil its own desires and intentions, know that it's every attempt will be thwarted. The deeper we go within the heart of our being, the more natural and true intentions will make themselves known and they will come to manifest themselves with our participation. We will bear witness to the fact that we feel an urge to do something in particular to manifest the hearts true intention, which is the same intention as that of the universe itself. No longer are we operating separately, as an individual wave in the vastness of the ocean itself, what appeared as two becomes reacquainted as the 'One.' From this place the awakened purpose will come naturally and it will occur wholeheartedly. So quite simply, do what you can and leave the rest up to the hands of grace.

# Our Job is Simple

Whether we wish to call it a purpose or just simply being our true selves, our 'job' is actually very simple, because if it was complicated we would quickly fall back into the clutches of the ego identity.

Above all else, our 'job' is to simply relax and be our true selves, because it is from the place of the true, natural self that joy, clarity and all beautiful experiences arise and it is from the true self that the gift is given. What gift is this, you ask? Well, you, you are the gift, not necessarily what you are doing, but for sure what you are being, is the gift. Wherever you are at, within yourself right now, just be it and express it naturally as you feel, no more and no less, express no more than your true nature in each given moment.

As we move to deeper levels of awakening, self-realisation and a liberation of the mind, more and more of the natural self will emerge and be expressed.

Simply be yourself and live purposefully in the reality of the here and now. Be kind, compassionate and respectful, and do whatever feels right in your heart to do, and enjoy the unfolding mystery before you. If you live as yourself in this way, then you will be a walking gift to everyone with whom you come into contact.

Stay empty, because that is the only sure way to be full, full of life and love.

The monk's comments below expresses how we often feel the need to change the world...

> When I was a young man, I wanted to change the world.
>
> I found it was difficult to change the world, so I tried to change my nation.
>
> When I found I couldn't change the nation, I began to focus on my town. I couldn't change the town and so as an older man, I tried to change my family.
>
> Now, as an old man, I realise the only thing I can change is myself, and suddenly I realise that if long ago I had changed myself, I could have

## Christopher J. Smith

*made an impact on my family. My family and I could have made an impact on our town. Their impact could have changed the nation and I could indeed have changed the world.*

*Unknown Monk c. 1100 AD.*

Replace the word 'change' above with 'discovering who you already are.' It is not about changing anything, it is about discovering the beauty of what is already present within you and living from that natural being-ness, and as you move in the world in that state, your presence will be felt.

Do not try to change the world, just be yourself, and your contribution will come from that...

*"You ... are a gift to the world"*

# About the Author

Christopher J. Smith is a rising innovative Spiritual and Meditation Teacher, Mystic, Inspirational speaker, Health Coach, Personal Trainer, Author and Video Maker for the new era of spirituality, actualization and human wellbeing.

He lives in Greasbrough, a village in northern England where he pursues his passion of writing, making videos and teaching Spirituality, Meditation, Empowerment and Human Wellbeing practices. He travels around the world speaking and giving workshops and retreats based upon his teachings.

To learn more about Christopher J. Smith and to keep up to date with his teachings, services and events, visit...

- www.silenttruth.co.uk
- Silent Truth on Youtube
- Silent Truth on Facebook
- silenttruthstore@gmail.com

www.ingramcontent.com/pod-product-compliance
Lightning Source LLC
Chambersburg PA
CBHW031132160426
43193CB00008B/110